Courts, Panchayats and Nagarpalikas

K.C. SIVARAMAKRISHNAN

After joining the Indian Administrative Service (IAS) in 1958 and holding various assignments in West Bengal, K.C. Sivaramakrishnan moved to Delhi in 1985 where he served as the first Project Director of the Central Ganga Authority, Secretary in the Ministry of Urban Development, and Secretary (Supply) till his retirement in 1992.

He also served in the World Bank as Senior Advisor, Urban Management. Since his return to the country in 1996, Sivaramakrishnan has been with the Centre for Policy Research as Professor. Presently, he is Chairman of the CPR Board. He is also associated with the Institute of Social Sciences, Delhi, as Senior Fellow.

In the academic sphere, Sivaramakrishnan was a Parvin Fellow at Woodrow Wilson School, Princeton University (1965), Visiting Professor and Homi Bhabha Fellow at the Indian Institute of Management, Calcutta (1977), and Senior Lecturer at the Economic Development Institute of the World Bank (1978-1982).

Trained in economics, political science and law, he has authored several books and papers on urban management, decentralisation, electoral reforms and environment. He is also enrolled as a member of the Supreme Court Bar.

Courts, Panchayats and Nagarpalikas

Background and Review of the Case Law

K.C. Sivaramakrishnan

ACADEMIC FOUNDATION
NEW DELHI

First published in 2009
by

ACADEMIC FOUNDATION
4772-73 / 23 Bharat Ram Road, (23 Ansari Road),
Darya Ganj, New Delhi - 110 002 (India).
Phones : 23245001 / 02 / 03 / 04.
Fax : +91-11-23245005.
E-mail : academic@vsnl.com
www. academicfoundation.com

Cataloging in Publication Data--DK
Courtesy: D.K. Agencies (P) Ltd. <docinfo@dkagencies.com>

Sivaramakrishnan, K. C. (Kallidaikurichi Chidambarakrishnan), 1935-
Courts, panchayats, nagarpalikas : background and review of the case law / K.C. Sivaramakrishnan.
p. cm.
In Indian context.
Includes bibliographical references (p.).
Includes index.
ISBN 13: 9788171886883
ISBN 10: 8171886884

1. Election law--India. 2. Local government--Law and legislation--India. 3. Panchayat--India. 4. Municipal government--India. I. Title.

DDC 342.540 7 22

Typeset by Italics India, New Delhi.
Printed and bound in India.

Contents

Foreword

I am happy to be invited to subscribe this Foreword to Prof. Sivaramakrishnan's excellent compilation and analysis of the case-law on *panchayats* and *nagar palikas*. As a senior member of the Indian Administrative Service, Prof. Sivaramakrishnan held many high positions of great responsibility. He is presently Research Professor at the Centre for Policy Research and has turned his brilliant and deep-ploughing mind to the urgent issues of contemporary relevance of the Constitutional and legal frame work of the units of local self government. He has authored and published several works of distinction. His abiding interest in and commitment to the working of institutions of local self government has enriched the current discourse on the topic.

The present work "Courts, Panchayats and Nagarpalikas" is a study of special importance. The clear mandate of the Constitutional 73rd and 74th Amendments is that the State Legislature will, by law, devolve various functions and tasks upon the *panchayats* and municipalities in such a manner that "the exercise of the executive, legislative and financial tasks in this regard are harmonised with the domain of the State." These amendments are rightly regarded as the Constitutional underpinnings for widening and deepening the roots of Indian Democracy. But the sad part is that despite the passage of one and a half decades, the process of decentralisation and devolution of power envisaged by the Constitution has been tardy.

The wielders of political power and the bureaucracy have failed to bestow a decorous deference towards this constitutional mandate.

Constitution is not a self executing instrument. As pointed out by Sir Alladi Krishnaswami Iyer that the "proper functioning of the constitution will to a large extent depend upon ancillary or organic laws passed to implement the constitution; and judicial decisions interpreting the constitution, the Supreme Court, being the final arbiter. Above all it is the law abiding spirit of the average citizen in India that I regard as the greatest asset in the proper working of the constitution."

In one of his writings the author says "For most citizens urbanisation is a series of irritants and deficiencies. Lack of basic services, crumbling infrastructure, congestion, pollution, slums, crimes—the list is endless. In any city, big or small, if the question is asked, 'who is in-charge of this city', the answer is painfully simple—'No one'."

The problems of urbanisation and urban governance are yet to be resolved to eliminate parallel and mutually conflicting systems—both legal and administrative—that quite often work at cross purposes and 'mutual in-effectuation'. The author says: "In this medley of confusion the courts have come to our aid once again by stirring up memories of what planning signified."

Courts had understood the idea and concept of urban planning in a rather restrictive sense. However the author sees a refreshing fresh breeze in the proper understanding of the idea of "planning" in a recent opinion of the Bombay High Court which said: "Planning has both social and economic aims. A proper spatial relationship between the communities in the region and the constituent parts of a town, compactness of development and an efficient arrangement of communication routes all wastefully and thus increases wealth...socially successful planning tends to make people's lives happier because it results in a physical environment conducive to health, which allows convenient passage from place to place which facilities social inter course." According to the author, Judicial statesmanship in expounding this important Constitutional provision will hold the key for the future of democracy.

This book analyses the various strands in the judicial approach to the problems of decentralised planning and governance. The great potential and significance of this constitutional development—*Panchayati Raj*—is yet to unfold itself in a full measure. These constitutional reforms in self-government constitute, in a non-trivial sense, the second birth of democracy in India. They are not to be seen as attempts at mere decentralisation as some choose to think. They have a greater dimension of the potential for a 'Three Tier Federalism' in India, an experiment which could have a deeper message. It is not merely some 'administrative federalism' as some scholars consider them. They are not mere 'expressions of decentralisation' as the idea of decentralisation implies and presupposes the existence of a higher legal authority. These are, perhaps, legalistic approaches that tend to ignore the great thrust towards demands for innovative and qualitative changes in the political institutions of the Indian State, which is emerging as a pattern towards multi-level federalism or, not in the distant future, towards the idea of 'a federation of federations'. It is important that judges do realise the importance of the Constitutional mandate in interpreting the adequacy of legislations to translate the Constitutional phrase into reality and that in the background of this constitutional mandate the areas of legislative inadequacy become justiciable. In this background one of the strong strands of sustaining democracy is the need to provide a vigorous refreshment to the movement of noncentralisation of power envisioned by the 73rd and 74th Constitutional Amendments.

This flexibility in the concept of federalism holds out new opportunities of purposeful innovations. Great global thrust towards democracy, international human rights regime, increasing pattern of internationalisation of domestic issues, global economic interdependence, emergence of supra national institutions as in the European Union, have substantially changed the global scenario. Traditional high walls of domestic sovereignty are crumbling. One of the fundamental concepts underlying the international human rights norms is the architecture of an inclusive, pluralist societies as essential for the support for human rights. Some recent pronouncements of the European Court of Human Rights have addressed the fundamental links between substantive foundations of democracy and polity.

The stunning technological innovations coupled with political movements for self-government have the inevitable influence on the patterns of political organisations. New innovative ideas that enhance the capacity of exiting institutions to manage the forces of change are necessary. No political institution, including federalism, can remain static and be frozen in time. The political upheavals resulting from assertions of the human spirit for a place in the sun can be handled only by imaginative political innovations.

Prof. Sivaramakrishnan has undertaken a task of painstaking research and insight. The editorial policy of this enduring contribution is innovative in that it seeks to combine and fuse the constitutional principles with policies of governance in this important area. With his characteristic modesty in one of his letters to me he wrote: "I am not competent to write a book on the subject exclusively for the legal fraternity." But the truth is that the legal community will vastly benefit from his work and approach.

The survival and strengthening of democracy is the most urgent task. Herman Finer said:

> Democracy has its defects: the overcoming of hereditary privileges and the winning of equality takes time and strains the patience while the pain and stress of injustice continue to prevail. Collective action that promises vast benefits is retarded by special interests that hold strategic controls. Special ability and insights may be subordinated to the grosser claims of the mass of average men.
>
> However, the political, social and economic gifts of democracy endow mankind with vast riches. We are so accustomed to the exercise of our civil rights that we have ceased to realise that they are as vital to our moral life as breathing is to physical, and we take this miracle for granted.

Prof. Sivaramakrishnan's work will furnish enduring support to the strengthening of the very roots of democracy in India. The book deserves and is entitled to wide reception.

—M.N.Venkatachaliah

Former Chief Justice of India

Preface and Acknowledgements

The idea of this book started at an "adda", the Bengali word for a free flowing but intense conversation, in the Kolkata residence of Debu Bandhopadhyay, veteran civil servant and an undaunted crusader of land reforms, rural development and decentralisation.

One of the items discussed was the so-called third tier of government sought to be established by the 73rd and the 74th Amendments to the Constitution and why it has come under severe attack. Litigations relating to elections were numerous but that did not seem to be the main reason. Deliberate circumvention of the constitutional spirit, if not the letter, appeared to be the favoured instrument. The 'adda' concluded that an analysis of the legal process used to dilute decentralisation was necessary.

Obviously a venture of this kind required considerable resources for collection and analysis of numerous High Court and Supreme Court judgements. Dr. George Mathew of the Institute of Social Sciences was strongly attracted by the idea. In keeping with his sturdy optimism and readiness to take up new initiatives without worrying about funds, he urged me to commence the work. Fortunately his enthusiasm found concrete support from the Ministry of Panchayati Raj which wanted a study of this kind to be undertaken. It was Shri Mani Shanker Aiyar, the Minister who has been an ardent and consistent champion of decentralisation who gave the study the rather respectable title "Panchayati Raj

Jurisprudence". Shri Avdhesh Kaushal the indefatigable fighter from Dehradun, whose voice in support of Van Gujjars, human rights and decentralisation has been heard far and wide, took up a similar study covering the northern and western states which served as a useful reference point. Both studies went apace and in due course of time, the reports were submitted to the Ministry of Panchayati Raj.

I did not want to stop there. Contentions and legal disputes are not confined to *panchayats* alone. The Municipalities and Corporations have had their share as well. I was keen to present together, in a single volume the legal issues and their adjudication, common to both the *panchayat* and the *nagarpalika* domains. Unlike the Panchayati Raj Ministry which had Shri Mani Shanker Aiyar, there was no source of ideological, much less financial support on the urban side. Here again, the ISS agreed to enlarge the venture and continue its support.

Several people have helped in this large and complex task which has taken more than two years to complete. In the compilation of the case law, Advocates Amber Qumaruddin, Bishwajit Singh, Sunita Rao, Bapu Hedurshetti, Vallinayagam and Jamshed Bey, were of great help. Budhadeb Ghosh and Jayaraman, former civil servants who have successfully transformed themselves into serious scholars were most helpful in the analytical work involved. Without the assistance of these persons, it would not have been possible to compile the basic material needed for this book.

Several leading members of the legal fraternity have given me both inspiration and valuable guidance. First and foremost I should express my gratitude to Justice M.N. Venkatachaliah, former Chief Justice of the Supreme Court of India for writing a Foreword to this book and his advice from time to time about the treatment and approach of this book. Shri Madhava Menon, one of India's foremost legal scholars very kindly spent time to go through the manuscript at different stages. My colleague in the CPR, Shri Subhash Kashyap reviewed with diligence and care the manuscript and made several valuable suggestions which I have tried to incorporate to the best of my ability. Shri P.P. Rao, Shri Prashant Bhushan, Shri Rajeev

Dhavan, Shri Sanjay Parikh and Kumar Shankardass, all luminaries of the Supreme Court Bar have provided me the opportunity to hear them in the Court and also in seminars and discussions elsewhere which reinforced my belief that 'power to the people' through elected representative institutions is a worthwhile cause. I am grateful to Gerald Frug of Harvard Law School for his valuable comments on the manuscript. I gratefully acknowledge the range of advice and assistance received from all these jurists. If my endeavours have fallen short of their expectations, the responsibility is mine and not theirs.

Dr. Pai Panandiker, former President, CPR was one of the first persons to encourage me to pursue serious studies in the field of decentralisation. My earlier book under the title "Power to the People" published by the CPR was largely a result of this endeavour. Dr. Pratap Bhanu Mehta, current President and several of my faculty colleagues in the CPR have also strongly supported my belief that an account about the jurisprudence of the *Panchayat* and *Nagarpalikas* is eminently worthwhile and will be a useful addition to the material on the subject.

A special word of thanks is due to my long time colleague Shri M.M. Arora. From the inception to the completion of this study, he pursued and kept track of the large volume of case law material from different states and helped me to sift through and organise them subject wise.

I am thankful to C.B. Vinod for preparing the index of cases and Sarala Gopinathan for the sizeable secretarial work in getting the manuscript ready.

I must also record my thankful appreciation to Rituraj and Sanu Kapila of the Academic Foundation for bringing out this publication within a reasonable time.

K.C. Sivaramakrishnan

Introduction

The 73rd and 74th Amendments became law more than a decade ago but the implementation of these amendments in the different states has been uneven to say the least. The course of implementation has also been marked by several controversies and disputes mostly political but significantly, legal as well. A large number of cases have been adjudicated in the different High Courts and also the Supreme Court. It is estimated there are more than 500 cases which have been adjudicated in this period.

Historical Background

Decentralisation in India has had a long history. Historians and social science researchers have analysed and written much about *panchayats* in India, their evolution as self-governing bodies and their role as a platform of interface between the villages and the higher authorities. During the Medieval and Islamic periods of Indian history the characteristics of the village *panchayats* remained more or less unaltered. In British India both *panchayats* and municipalities had to work mainly under government control. The British government sought to meet the demand for autonomy by offering concessions at the lower levels of administration by giving powers of limited self-government to distrtict boards in rural areas and municipalities in urban areas.

That these local bodies had the essence of self-government was recognised by the British Colonial administration. In the words of

Charles Metcalfe, the Governor General of India in 1835, these village communities were referred to as "little republics". There was an additional recognition that these village and town committees should mobilise the funds needed for their upkeep rather than draw upon the Imperial Government's resources. In 1870, Lord Mayo, the Viceroy, secured the passage of a resolution for decentralisation of power aimed at meeting the demands of the people but primarily designed to augment imperial finances. The Famine Commission of 1880 pointed to the absence of local bodies as a major impediment in delivering relief supplies to famine-striken people and underlined the need to expand the self-government to the villages as well. However, most of the village *panchayats* and municipalities set up during this period comprised nominated members with very little or no elective element at all.

The Ripon Resolution of 1882 providing for rural local boards with two-thirds of membership to be composed of elected, non-official persons and presided over by a non-official Chairman could be said to be the Magna Carta of local government in British India. However, Lord Ripon's enthusiasm was not shared by the other echelons of British Indian government. The report of the Royal Commission on decentralisation released in 1909 lamented the slow progress and underlined the importance of self-government through *panchayats*.

In 1919, Edwin Montagu the Secretary of State for India and Lord Chelmsford the Viceroy forged a partnership in authoring what is known as the Montagu-Chelmsford Reforms of 1919 which made local self-government under the proposed scheme of Dyarchy, a transferred subject. This brought self-government under the domain of Indian Ministers in the provinces. To make local self-government both fully representative and responsible, the reforms suggested that popular control in local bodies and maximum possible independence from outside control, should be the objective.

The years following the Montague-Chelmsford report were the 'time of waiting' in local government and in national affairs. Indian political opinion was moving strongly towards Independence. The British Government's declaration promising responsible government to India through 'gradual development of self-governance in local institutions' was resented as a poor second best. For a brief period from 1920 to 1924 when the moderates in the Congress party held power at the provincial level under the dyarchy system, some progress was made in the structure and performance of both rural and urban governments. Surendra Nath Banerjee was regarded as creating a 'veritable *swaraj* in the government of the second largest city in the Empire, Calcutta'. Four-fifths of the members of the Corporation were elected, while the Mayor and the Chief Executive Officer were in turn elected by the members. In other provinces like U.P. and Bombay similar initiatives were taken but more in regard to district boards. However, the 1923 elections brought great changes under the influence of Motilal Nehru and C.R. Das. The Congress policy towards dyarchy was reversed. *Poorna Swaraj* or full Independence was the goal to be achieved. Communal representation in local bodies also assumed more importance than before. In Calcutta itself an overwhelming Congress majority assumed control with C.R. Das becoming the Mayor and Subhash Chandra Bose, the Chief Executive Officer. The Swarajists, as they were called, ran the municipality on rigid party lines and all policy decisions were made by the party caucus.

In the decades which followed, the energy of the leaders at all levels was concentrated on the attainment of national Independence. Inevitably, the progress of local government suffered. Instead of serving as the school of political education, it became a mere annexe to the national political arena where the struggle for Independence was moving towards its climax. This relegation of local government to a secondary position has persisted well after Independence and is the key to a proper understanding of the problems of local self-government to this day. Though the Government of India Act, 1935 placed local government as a subject under Entry 12 of the provincial legislative list, neither the enactment of legislation nor its implementation were adequate in achieving the objective of local self-government. Matters had to wait till the country's Independence.

The Constitutional Position

Gandhiji's desire to make village *panchayats* the very foundation of democracy in Independent India, by providing for direct elections, only at the local level and thereafter for the *panchayats* and municipalities to choose representatives for provincial Assemblies and Parliament was not accepted by most of the leaders of post-Independent India. The first draft of India's Constitution circulated after Mahatma's martyrdom did not include any provision for the *panchayats*. In May 1948, a letter from the President of the Constituent Assembly, Dr. Rajendra Prasad, initiated a discussion in the Constituent Assembly. Dr. B.R. Ambedkar widely recognised as the principal author of the Constitution was himself not in favour of making any constitutional provision for the *panchayats*. His description of the *panchayat* as "dens of ignorance and localism" is well known. As a compromise, in November 1948 Shri K. Santhanam formulated an amendment, which was eventually included in the non-mandatory chapter containing the Directive Principles of State Policy. Article 40 of this chapter reads as follows:

> The state shall take steps to organise village *panchayats* and endow them with such power and authority as may be necessary to enable them to function as units of self-government.

While these words would be cited as the underlying rationale for the 73rd and the 74th Constitutional Amendments, at the time of the drafting of the Constitution they were considered more as a concession to Gandhian sentiments rather than an organising principle of the structure of governance.

Further more it should also be noted that in Schedule 7 of the Constitution comprising the Union, State and Concurrent Lists, which was substantially a repetition of the 1935 Government of India Act, local government was considered essentially as a creation of the provincial governments with the powers and responsibilities of these 'creatures' to be determined principally by the State governments. Entry 5 of the State List reads as follows:

> Local government that is to say the constitution and powers of municipal corporations, improvements trusts, district boards, mining settlement authorities and other local authorities for the purpose of local self-government or village administration.

In Mohammad Maqbal and Mohammad Kaja *versus* State of Maharashtra (AIR 1982 BOM 312), it has been held that this entry is very wide and empowers the State Legislature to legislate with respect to any subject relating to local government including the constitution of such authorities. In Municipal Corporation, Delhi *versus* Children's Book Trust AIR 1952 SC 1456, it has also been held that though a representative body, a local authority is a subordinate authority created by statute. It cannot therefore claim the power of taxation which belongs to the State Legislature. It can exercise taxing power only if such power is conferred by the law creating it and such exercise will also be limited to the extent provided for in the law. It should also be noted that the word '*panchayats*' does not occur anywhere else in the State List under Schedule 7.

In the case of cantonment areas Entry 3 of the Union List reads as follows:

> Delimitation of cantonment areas, local self-government in such areas, the constitution and powers within such areas of cantonment authorities and the regulation of house accommodation including the control of rents in such areas.

The use of the word local self-government is thus common to Entry 3 in the Union List and Entry 5 in the State List. There was an understandable expectation that the States would enact suitable legislation in this regard reflecting the self goverment aspect.

Community Development and *Panchayats*

In the first decade after Independence, community development blocks were established as part of a nation wide programme. The lessons drawn from experimental projects in Nilokheri, Shantiniketan, Etawah and Baroda to mobilise participation of the people at the village level towards undertaking various projects like roads, drinking water, sanitation etc. provided the necessary inspiration. Despite the commitment and zeal of Shri S.K. Dey who was the driving force behind the community development programme, in the absence of effective institutions for people's participation the programme did not progress. The Balwantrai Mehta Committee, appointed in 1957 to study the community development programme observed as follows:

> Admittedly one of the least successful aspects of community development and social extension service work was its attempt to evoke popular initiative. So long as we do not cover or create a representative and democratic institution which will cite local interest, supervision and care necessary to ensure that expenditure of money upon local objects conforms with the needs and visions of the locality, entrusted with adequate power and assign to it appropriate finances, we will never be able to evoke local interest and local initiative in the field of development. The committee, therefore, recommend the establishment of a three-tier system with village *panchayats*, a *panchayat samiti* co-terminus with the community development block and a district level *panchayat*. The *panchayat samiti* is to be a crucial part of the system

The National Development Council accepted the recommendations of the study team and urged the State governments to devise *panchayat* systems appropriate to the State needs. By mid 60s about 60,000 village *panchayats*, 7500 *panchayat samitis* and 330 *zilla parishads* had been set up across the country. Some of the States like Maharashtra, Karnataka, Tamil Nadu and West Bengal did undertake elaborate exercises for this purpose. In Tamil Nadu, for example, the Government placed a White Paper in 1957 on the reform of local administration, which was discussed at length in the State Legislature. Eventually the Madras Panchayats Act, 1958 and Madras District Development Council Act, 1958 were enacted. These two enactments resulted in the creation of panchayat unions co-terminus with development blocks, entrustment of developmental and social welfare functions to the *panchayat* Unions and Village Panchayats, abolition of District Boards and the creation of District Development Council as an advisory body. In effect this was a two-tier system, which operated on democratic lines for well over two decades.

In Maharashtra, the Bombay Village Panchayats Act, 1958 and the Maharashtra Zilla Parishads and Panchayat Samitis Act, 1961 created a three-tier system. In Kerala the decentralisation process had a chequered history. In 1958 itself, a committee headed by the Chief Minister E.M.S. Namboodiripad recommended a three-tier structure of village *panchayats*, block *panchayats* and *taluk panchayats*. In 1960, the Kerala Panchayat Act was passed with amendments in 1965, 1967 and 1971. Though these laws envisaged an impressive list of duties and functions, various problems in actual implementation were encountered partly because of frequent political changes in the State.

Parallel Bodies Emerge

It will thus be seen that while *panchayats* as entities were established across the country in different states, the main objective was to use them as agencies for implementing development schemes under the community development programme. Once political and financial support to that programme itself weakened, the driving force behind the *panchayat* system also diminished. Parallel programmes were launched by the Government on a large scale such as the Intensive Agricultural District Programme, Small Farmers Development Agency, Intensive Tribal Development Programme etc., bypassing the *panchayats*. By 1967, the Ministry of Community Development itself was reduced to the status of a department and brought under the Ministry of Food and Agriculture. In 1971, the title community development was dropped. This should not be regarded as just a cosmetic change. While creation of the *panchayat* structure was prompted by the community development programme, the end of the community development programme also marked the decline of *panchayats* as agents of change and agencies of development. The design and implementation of development schemes became once again the preserve of the officialdom.

The next important stage in the development of the *panchayat* system came about with the change of government at the national level in 1979. A committee under the Chairmanship of Ashok Mehta was asked to take a fresh look. The Committee laid strong emphasise on the *panchayats* functioning not merely as agencies of development but becoming genuine representative institutions at various levels below the State. The Ashok Mehta Committee recommendations were followed up with some enthusiasm in West Bengal, Karnataka and Andhra Pradesh among others. The second-generation *panchayats* received more powers. Their orientation was significantly political which did result in an increased measure of public enthusiasm evident particularly in West Bengal and Karnataka.

The Municipal Scenario

Municipal administration had a rather feeble start in British India. The East India Company granted a charter as early as 1687 for setting up a corporation in Madras which consisted of the Mayor, 12 Aldermen and 60 or more Burgesses. But this body was concerned more with regulation of public order and some modest sanitation services. In 1842, a formal measure of municipal organisation was applied in the Bengal presidency. In 1850, a more comprehensive act followed which included powers of taxation. By 1881, there were about 700 municipalities in British India but in as many as 550 of them the members were all nominated while the rest were partly elected.

It was Lord Ripon's Resolution of 1882, which initiated a major change in local government. The main rationale behind Lord Ripon's reforms was that "if local government is to have any vitality then it should evolve out of local circumstances. If it has to be created artificially, at least it should be planned in detail by local administration and not be imposed ready-made by the state government." But in the British India of 1882, the Viceroy was almost alone in his liberalism. Nevertheless, by 1884 the presidency towns of Madras, Bombay and Calcutta had corporations with a fairly wide range of regulatory and taxing powers and executive responsibility for rendering basic services of water supply, sanitation and public health.

Unfortunately, in the years after Independence there was a noticeable reversal. Most of the urban local bodies across the country came under supercession irrespective of the political party, which was in power at the Centre or the States. Indeed the phenomenon of supercession began soon after Independence itself with the axing of the elected body of the Calcutta Corporation which was in the vanguard of the movement for Independence. The Madras Corporation was superceded in 1973 which lasted for 24 years. Several other corporations and municipalities were also under supercession and run by administrators. Such supercession clearly signified the relegation of municipal government to a secondary position. This, despite the fact that the Indian sub-continent had shared a common tradition of municipal bodies serving as cradles of democracy, which had nursed many provincial and national leaders such as Jawaharlal Nehru, Vallabhai Patel, B.C. Roy, Rajagopalachari, Nurul Amin or Shurawardhy to mention a few. Local government became a lesser government. The situation in urban areas was in rather sharp contrast to the significant initiatives undertaken in some states towards rural self government. Recognising the possible political outcome of the process, the Government of India set up a committee in June 1986 headed by the noted Jurist Dr. L.M. Singhvi to prepare a concept paper on the revitalisation of the *panchayats* in particular and local government in general. The committee recommended that local self-government should be constitutionally recognised, protected and preserved by the inclusion of a new chapter in the Constitution.

Amending the Constitution

Accepting the recommendations of the Singhvi Committee, the Rajiv Gandhi government initiated the exercise to amend the Constitution. On 15th May 1989, the 64th Constitution Amendment Bill was introduced. The statement of objects and reasons mentioned "having regard to the inadequacies in the existing system and keeping in view the directive principles of state policy enshrined in Article 40 of the Constitution which aims at endowing *panchayats* with such powers and authority as are necessary to enable them to function as units of self-government, it is proposed to add a new section to the Constitution relating to the *Panchayats*." About three months later, on 8th of August, the 65th Amendment Bill was introduced with similar objectives to provide a constitutional mandate to *Nagarpalikas*. Between May and October 1989, the debates proceeded in the Lok Sabha and Rajya Sabha. Both bills were passed by the Lok Sabha but defeated in the Rajya Sabha as the votes fell short of the two-third majority required, by a margin of three.

However, an important effect of the Amendment initiative was that it had elevated decentralisation from a mere administrative exercise to an important element of the political agenda not confined to Rajiv Gandhi's party only. The Janata Dal, a major opposition party of the time led by V.P. Singh appointed a committee under the Chairmanship of S.R. Bommai, former Chief Minister of Karnataka. The essence of Bommai report was picked up when the V.P. Singh government took office a few months later. After introducing a composite bill for constitutional recognition of rural and urban local bodies, the government itself went out of office. Eventually the successor government of Narasimha Rao revived the earlier versions of the Amendment Bills. These were substantially modified by a Joint Parliament Committee and the amendments were passed in December 1992. After Presidential assent and ratification by the requisite number of states, the amendments came into force in mid-1993.

An Overview of the 73rd and the 74th Amendments

Though the 73rd and the 74th Amendments as they presently stand are considered as companion pieces, they are substantially a duplication of each other. Part IX entitled *Panchayats* and Part IXA entitled Municipalities have a total of 16 and 18 Articles respectively. Out of these as many as 9 relating to elections, reservations, disqualifications, duration of the local bodies, state finance commissions, bar to jurisdiction of courts, continuance of existing laws and applications to union territories are either identical or nearly identical. Article 243ZD on District Planning Committees is applicable to both *panchayats* and municipalities. So is Article 243ZE on Metropolitan Planning Committees where the metropolitan areas include *panchayats*. The question may then be asked why instead of two separate amendments one composite amendment was not considered.

The circumstances under which the precursors of these amendments namely the 64th Constitutional Amendment Bill introduced in May 1989 and the 65th Constitutional Amendment Bill introduced in August 1989 have been described in other publications. It has been brought out that the amendment relating to *Nagarpalikas* was an afterthought. After defeat of the 64th and 65th Amendment Bills, the successor government of V.P. Singh introduced a composite bill but as mentioned before the Government itself went out of office and the Bill lapsed. When the Narasimha Rao government revived the initiative, the Panchayat and Nagarpalika Amendment Bills were pursued by the Rural Development and Urban Development Ministries separately, in keeping with the administrative more as a matter of division of responsibilities. Convenience and rules of business prevailed rather than any conscious application of mind about the substantive similarities and differences in the proposed legislations.

It will be useful at this stage to present a brief overview of the salient features of the 73rd and the 74th Amendments.

Definitions

Article 243 provides the definitions of a district, *gram sabha*, intermediate level *panchayat*, *panchayat* area, population and village. Under clause (b) *Gram Sabha* is defined as a body consisting of persons registered in the electoral rolls relating to village comprised within the area of a *panchayat* at the village level. This is a very important provision because it gives a constitutional recognition to all the registered voters within a village as members of the *Gram Sabha*. It should also be noted that such a definition was not provided in the 64th Constitution Amendment Bill. The concept of all the registered voters forming the *Gram Sabha* was introduced in the composite amendment bill introduced by the V.P. Singh government. This provision was incorporated in the Amendment Bill introduced by the Narasimha Rao government.

Article 243P contains the definitions in regard to municipalities such as a municipal area, a *nagar panchayat*, a municipal council, a municipal corporation and a metropolitan area. Since three levels or types of municipalities are envisaged, the 65th Amendment Bill had stipulated population criteria for each, such as 20,000 to 3 lakhs for a municipal council, 3 lakhs or more for a municipal corporation, and a *nagar panchayat* for an area in transition from rural to an urban area. However, this quantitative criteria has been omitted in the 74th Amendment, though a reference to population, density, revenue and economic factors have been mentioned.

Constitution and Composition

Article 243B and Article 243Q related to the Constitution of Panchayats and Municipalities. An important aspect of Article 243Q is that under the proviso it is open to the Governor of a State not to constitute a municipality for an area specified as an industrial township. This proviso permits an exclusion of some areas from the application of the constitutional provisions. The implications of this are discussed in a subsequent chapter.

Composition

Article 243C mandates that all seats in a *panchayat* shall be filled through direct elections from territorial constituencies of the relevant *panchayat* area. Article 243C further provides that the Chairpersons of the *Panchayats* at the intermediate or district level shall be elected by and from amongst the elected members thereof but it is open to a State Legislature to provide for direct election for the Chairperson of a village level *panchayat*.

Article 243R provides likewise for the composition of municipalities to be filled by persons chosen by direct election from the territorial constituencies in the relevant municipal area. However, the manner of election of the Chairperson of a municipality is left to be decided by the State Legislature. Both Articles 243C and 243R provide for representation to members of the Lok Sabha, Rajya Sabha, Legislative Assembly and Legislative Council where they exist except that in the case of village *panchayats* such representation has not been envisaged.

Reservations

Article 243D in regard to *panchayats* and Article 243T in regard to municipalities similarly provide for reservation of seats for women to the extent of one-third of the total number, reservation for SC/ ST in proportion to their population and similar reservation in the case of Chairperson as well. Both Articles also enable the State Legislatures to provide for reservation in favour of backward classes.

Elections

Article 243E in regard to *panchayats* and 243U in regard to municipalities stipulate that the duration of each *panchayat* or municipality shall be for five years and no longer and requires that fresh elections be completed before the expiry of the duration. Both Articles do envisage dissolution of a *panchayat* or a municipality but Article 243U requires a municipality to be given a reasonable opportunity of being heard before its dissolution. The absence of such a provision in regard to *panchayat* should not be construed as an unfettered power to dissolve because it is a well established norm that an opportunity to be heard is part of the process of natural justice.

Disqualifications

The provisions regarding disqualification in Articles 243F and 243V are identical.

Powers, Authority and Responsibilities

Article 243G in respect of *panchayats* and 243W in respect of municipalities are also couched in similar language. It is important to note that both articles envisage, that the main objective is to enable the *panchayats* and municipalities to function as institutions of self-government. The interpretation of these two articles is most important in determining the functional domain of the *panchayats* and municipalities which is discussed at length in the relevant chapter.

Power to Impose Taxes

Article 243H and 243X are also formulated in identical language. The position is the same in regard to the Finance Commission. While the Constitution of the Commission is described in Article 243I, the principles governing the review of finances are similar in Articles 243I and 243Y. The provisions regarding audit of accounts, elections by an independent State Election Commission, application to Union

Territories and non-application to certain areas contained in Articles 243J, 243K, 243L, 243M, 243Z, 243ZA, 243ZB and 243ZC are also similar in content and language. Similarly Articles 243O and 243Z barring interference by courts in electoral matters are also identical provisions.

Conformity to State Laws

The continuance of existing laws in regard to *panchayats* and municipalities are an important stipulation under Articles 243N and 243ZF. The Parliament did envisage that several aspects in the establishment and functioning of *panchayats* and municipalities would be dealt with in numerous existing state laws. Harmonising these laws so as to bring them into conformity with the provisions of the Constitution as amended through the 73rd and the 74th Amendments, was envisaged as a specific exercise to be undertaken by the States. A time period of one year was stipulated for this purpose. Unfortunately this Constitutional provision, which is as much a signal for action and a signpost for compliance was not observed by most of the States. In many cases the so-called conformity legislation was limited only to the composition and constitution of the *panchayats* and municipalities and even this minimal legislation was enacted only in the last minute.

Brief Overview of State Laws

An overview of the laws enacted by the different states in regard to *panchayats* and municipalities in the wake of the 73rd and the 74th Amendments merits a separate exercise. In regard to *panchayats* such studies have been undertaken by other institutions and also as part of reports commissioned by different ministries. However, in regard to municipalities such studies are not available. Even compilation of the municipal laws are limited to a few of States.

Given the fact that in almost all the States, legislation regarding *panchayats* and municipalities existed before, it is to be expected that there will be significant variation in their provisions. Since local self-government is a state subject, uniformity of laws and regulations was not sought by Constitutional Amendments. What the amendments did provide was an organisational design and structure relating to the composition and constitution of these bodies as well as the parameters within which their powers and responsibilities would be determined and exercised. Most of the State laws, whether they relate to the *panchayats* or municipalities repeat the language of the Constitutional Amendments in matters of elections, composition, reservations etc. Though the amendments provided an opportunity for the States to redefine the structure of the *panchayat* and the municipal system as well as the substance of their functions very few states utilised the opportunity to do so. Atleast for the initial 2 or 3 years the focus of the effort has been on compliance to the Constitutional provisions to the minimum extent rather than on elaborations or rationalisation. New enactments to replace existing ones were undertaken only in a few states in subsequent years. In the case of *panchayats* many of the States found it necessary to either enact new legislation or comprehensively amend the existing laws because the three-tier structure of village, intermediate level and district *panchayats* was a new prescription in the Constitution itself. In the case of municipalities many of the States had a common Act for municipal councils and separate Acts for each corporation or groups of corporations. Tamil Nadu and Kerala are the two states where a comprehensive legislation was enacted for urban local bodies after an extensive review of the requirements as also consideration in detail by the State Legislature.

The internal structure of the *panchayats* and municipal bodies has been left untouched in most state laws. Though Constitutional provisions allow flexibility to the State Legislatures to deal with matters like manner of elected chairpersons and internal structure, in regard to urban local bodies many of the States have left the previously existing system of indirectly elected Mayors and Municipal Chairpersons as well as the exercise of powers mainly by the Standing Committees to continue. However, in West Bengal, an innovative arrangement of Mayor-in-Council providing for a cabinet type system was introduced for the Calcutta Corporation. This was done even before the Constitutional Amendments had come into force. The system of Mayor-in-Council or President-in-

Council in the case of municipalities has been adopted in Madhya Pradesh. Maharashtra introduced the same system for Mumbai but in less than two years gave it up. In most of the States mayors and municipal chairpersons continue to be ceremonial figures with a tenure of office ranging from 1 to 1 ½ years rather than the term of five years provided in the Constitution itself for the Municipalities or the Corporation. Direct elections of the Mayor or Chairpersons of municipalities has been provided only in Tamil Nadu, Madhya Pradesh, Uttar Pradesh and Uttarakhand. In other states, the chairpersons are elected by and from amongst members of the Municipal Council or the Corporation as the case may be.

In keeping with the Constitutional prescription all states have established State Election Commissions to conduct elections to *panchayats* and municipalities. But the range of responsibilities to be exercised by these Commissions varies from one state to another. In Maharashtra, Gujarat and Kerala, the responsibilities cover a wide gamut from the preparation of electoral rolls to delimitation, reservations and conduct of elections. In other states these responsibilities are divided between the State Election Commission and the State government departments. The implications of such division and the litigations, which have ensued, are discussed separately in the Chapter on the case law relating to elections.

Similarly, the State Finance Commissions are also a uniform prescription under the Constitution. While all the States have set up such Commissions and in many these Commissions have been established atleast twice in regard to the actions taken on their recommendations, the progress across the States is highly uneven. This uneven and largely unsatisfactory implementation of the SFC recommendations has been the subject of several comparative studies by specialised organisations.

Why this Book

Early in 2004, the Ministry of Panchayati Raj commissioned the Institute of Social Sciences, to undertake a study on *Panchayati Raj* Jurisprudence. The study comprised three broad elements. One was an analysis of the Case Law emerging from various litigations adjudicated in the High Courts and the Supreme Court. The second was a review of the *panchayati raj* laws enacted by various state governments. The third part contained a review of the various central and state laws on different subjects impinging on the functional domain of the *panchayats*. The study undertaken by the Institute of Social Sciences covered Maharashtra, the southern and the eastern states. The Rural Litigation and Entitlement Kendra (RLEK), Dehra Dun was commissioned to undertake a similar study in regard to the other states. These reports have since been submitted to the Ministry of Panchayati Raj.

Though these studies, though focused on *panchayats*, they revealed that on several issues like elections, reservation, functional domain etc., the legal problems were common to the *panchayats* and the municipalities. Since the 73rd and 74th Constitutional Amendments are companion pieces. There are more than 4500 corporations, municipalities and *nagar panchayats* in the country. *Panchayats* are far more numerous with about 2.4 lakhs *panchayat* bodies at different levels. Cases relating to both *panchayats* and municipalities are equally relevant and critical in determining what can be regarded as settled law on decentralisation.

A separate study focussing on case law, but not limited to *panchayats* and which would bring out the jurisprudential points common for both rural and urban local bodies has therefore been felt necessary. Such a study would be of much relevance and use to policy makers, scholars and researchers interested in decentralisation as well as the legal fraternity. This book seeks to fulfill this important need. While the number of cases involved is very large, the more important cases considered in the High Courts and the Apex Court numbering about 250 have been analysed for the purposes of this publication. Some cases though not pertaining directly to *panchayats* and *nagarpalikas* have also been taken note because of their importance in the evolution of settled law.

The Book consists of eight main chapters. Each of the chapters begins with a brief description about the items considered and then proceeds to analyse the various cases, which have been arranged state-wise in an alphabetical order. The cases adjudicated in the

Supreme Court are presented thereafter. Some of the judgements have gone into a careful analysis of the state laws and their constitutional vires. It is important that the rationale of these judgements is properly understood. To help this, extracts from the judgements from some important cases have been reproduced.

At the end a list of the cases analysed has been presented chapter wise.

A postscripts chapter has also been added as an overall update of the legal scenario in regard to the *panchayats* and *nagarpalikas*.

1

Elections

It has often been claimed that a major success of the 73rd and the 74th Constitutional Amendments is the holding of two and more rounds of elections to rural and urban bodies in most of the States. The constitutionally mandated State Election Commissioners have, without doubt, contributed to this success. It has also been mentioned, frequently, that the more than three million persons elected from the *panchayats* and *nagarpalikas* are "probably the largest number of representatives elected through adult franchise anywhere in the world." It is to be expected that such a large scale effort will inevitably give rise to numerous disputes relating to the elections. Cases adjudicated may be considered in regard to in the following categories:

(i) The system for conducting *panchayat* and municipal elections; the role and responsibilities of the State Election Commissions.

(ii) The bar to interference by Courts under Article 243O and 243ZG; the extent of application.

(iii) Cases relating to electoral rolls.

(iv) Cases relating to delimitation of constituencies, whether it is an executive or legislative function of the state and if the latter what is the opportunity to the public to be heard.

The law and procedure regarding elections to *panchayats* and municipalities, as envisaged in the 73rd and 74th Constitutional

Amendments, generally follow the pattern well established in the country for Assembly and Parliament elections. When the pre-cursors of the 73rd and 74th Amendments i.e. the 64th and the 65th Constitution Amendment Bills were considered by the Parliament, it was provided that the Election Commission of India would be responsible for conducting elections to the *panchayats* and municipalities. However, due to the disinclination of the Election Commission of India to take up this work and other factors, it was decided that separate State Election Commissions would be set up and provisions were made in the Bills for the 73rd and the 74th Amendments. Nevertheless the language in these provisions are identical to Article 324 under which "the superintendence, direction and control of the preparation of the electoral rolls for, and the conduct of all elections to the Parliament and to the Legislature of every State shall be vested in the Election Commission". It will be useful to take note of the range of responsibilities of the Election Commission of India to understand better what differences if any, exist in regard to the role of the State Election Commissioners.

Article 327 enables the Parliament to enact laws with respect to the elections to the Parliament and State Assemblies. The Representation of People's Act 1951, the Delimitation Act 1972, the Delimitation Act 2002 and the various rules such as Conduct of Election Rules, 1961 are all examples of such laws and regulations made thereunder. Under this regime, delimitation is the only major responsibility entrusted to a separate Delimitation Commission which as presently constituted, comprises a former Judge of the Supreme Court (Justice Kuldip Singh as Chairman), one Election Commissioner of India and the State Election Commissioner appointed under Article 243K for the State concerned. The Commission has since completed its work in regard to Delimitation of Parliament and Assembly Constituencies on the basis of the 2001 Census. The Report has been released in May 2008.

The range of responsibilities of the Election Commission of India itself came up for judicial consideration in the Association for Democratic Reforms and People's Union for Civil Liberties *versus* Union of India in Civil Appeal No.7178 of 2001 as also Mohinder

Singh Gill *versus* Chief Election Commissioner, (1978) 1 SCC 405). The Apex Court held that under Article 324, "the phrase 'conduct of elections' is held to be of wide amplitude which would include power to make all necessary provisions for conducting free and fair elections." The Court further held that the power of the Election Commission of India under Article 324 of the Constitution which is plenary in character can encompass all such provisions. The question is to what extent this interpretation can be or has been applied with regard to the State Election Commissions.

The State Election Commissions: Role and Responsibilities

The language of Article 243K and 243ZA are identical to Article 324 and therefore envisage a composite set of responsibilities. However, under clause 4 of 243K as also clause 2 of 243ZA, the Constitution provides "subject to the provisions of this Constitution, the Legislature of a State may, by law, make provision with respect to all matters relating to, or in connection with elections to the *panchayats* or to the municipalities as the case may be." As enabling provisions, these are nearly identical to Article 327 of the Constitution which enables the Parliament to make provisions with respect to elections to the Parliament and Legislatures. However, the laws passed in different states and the rules thereunder, do vary from state to state and accordingly the range of responsibilities entrusted to the State Election Commissions also differs.

So far as the SECs are concerned, since their role and responsibilities are also couched in language identical to Article 324, the interpretation of the Supreme Court regarding the powers of the Election Commission of India can be taken as a guide for the SECs as well, in regard to elections to local bodies. The language of Articles 243K and 243ZA envisage a composite set of responsibilities for the SEC which cannot be artificially split. However, such an artificial split has happened in some of the states with the result that the state executive has interposed itself in this composite scheme of responsibilities which in turn has affected the stream and sequence of actions necessary to organise elections and resulted in delays. Delimitation, identification and rotation of reserved constituencies and notification for elections are some of the activities which have been taken over by the executive in some states, while in some others they are vested in the SEC such as West Bengal, Kerala, Bihar, Gujarat and Maharashtra. In the case of Karnataka, these powers were initially with the State Election Commission but later on taken over by the state government. In Channigappa *versus* Karnataka (2000(6) KLJ 163 decided on 14.7.2000), the action of the state government in taking away the responsibilities of reservation of constituencies and rotation from the Karnataka SEC and entrusting the same to the Deputy Commissioner was challenged, as going against Article 243(K). The court held that "delimitation and adjustment of constituencies was an act of precedence, in the matter of conduct of elections and not a part of the electoral process." It was held therefore that the state government's action did not infringe Article 243K.

As a result of this varying division of responsibilities in regard to the organisational regime for holding *panchayat* and municipal elections certain consequences have ensued. One is the delay in the preparation of electoral rolls as also delimitation of *panchayats* and municipal constituencies. The second relates to the identification and rotation of constituencies reserved for women, SC/ST and backward classes in some states. The third is the delay in holding the elections in time. Matters relating to reservation are discussed in a subsequent chapter. Litigation pertaining to electoral rolls, and delimitation and the outcome of the case law in this regard are discussed in this chapter. But before doing so we may consider to what extent disputes regarding elections are subject to judicial examination.

Bar to Interference by Courts: Extent of Application

Article 243-O and 243ZG stipulating a bar to interference by the courts in electoral matters is similar in letter and substance to Article 329 which provides for a similar exclusion in regard to elections to the Parliament and the State Legislatures. There have been a number of cases agitated and adjudicated about the scope and effect of Article 329 *viz.* Ponnusami *versus* Returning Officer, Namakkal 1952 SCR 218 (AIR 1952 SC 64) and Meghraj Kothari *versus* Delimitation Commission (1967 SC 669 (V54 C144). Similarly there have been several cases relating to local body elections and the extent of application of Articles 243-O and 243ZG. The general intent of these Articles is that disputes about the delimitation of constituencies or the outcome of elections should be settled by a special arrangement or procedure such as election tribunals or other alternative mechanism for dispute resolution rather than taking recourse to the High Courts. In reality, this has not happened.

The High Courts have generally held that once the notification is issued calling for elections, the process should continue without interruption and end with the declaration of results and the courts should not therefore interfere in the process. However, in some cases, courts have also held that decisions taken by election authorities, even after the issue of an election notification can be examined by the court if any miscarriage of justice or denial of judicial remedy is likely. In other words the courts have not accepted any blanket ban or ouster of their writ jurisdiction though it has been generally recognised that writ powers should be exercised cautiously.

The scope of Article 243-O in barring the courts, among other matters, came up specifically for adjudication in Kunhadullah (2000(3) KLT 45) decided on 3.8.2000. This case related to delimitation procedures which are dealt with in greater detail later in this chapter. For the present, it may be noted, the High Court came to the conclusion that the delimitation procedures followed by the State Election Commission, Kerala were not constitutionally valid. The Court held that the bar under Article 243-O necessarily presupposes the existence of a constitutionally valid law and if that is not the case, such a law cannot claim immunity from judicial review. Later, this judgement came up on appeal to the Supreme Court. At that hearing both the Kerala State Election Commission and the respondents agreed that they would accept the judgement of the High Court provided the terms of various *gram panchayats* for which elections have already been held, were not disturbed. The Supreme Court in its judgement of November 5, 2003 endorsed this agreement. In the context of this, the protection available under Article 243-O may be taken as settled, provided the law itself is *intra vires* of the Constitution.

Cases Relating to Electoral Rolls

We may now consider cases relating to local bodies in categories such as electoral rolls, delimitation, nomination of candidates, election results and the timely conduct of elections. Since nominations are related to qualification/disqualification, these are considered in a separate chapter. Disputes regarding elections and challenges to the decisions of election tribunals or similar authorities are also considered separately.

Andhra Pradesh

In Medisetty Chennakesavalu (2002 (1) ALT 94 decided on 3.10.2001), three writ petitions were filed challenging the electoral notification for elections in the Nerusupalle *Gram Panchayat* in Cuddapah district of Andhra Pradesh alleging that names of 86 voters were wrongly deleted from the electoral rolls and 81 names were wrongly included. The notification for elections was dated 16.8.2001 and elections were held on 17.8.2001. The electoral rolls were published on 30.7.2001 but the AP Panchayat rules provided for objections and changes thereafter until before the elections. The court held that wrongful deletion or inclusion in the electoral rolls could be a ground for challenging the election through an election petition before the Election Tribunal. The court further held that since remedy by this route was available to the petitioners it would not be appropriate for the High Court to stop the elections for which the notification had already been issued. The petitions were accordingly dismissed.

However, in a subsequent case Kotiswara Rao and Others *versus* the State Election Commissioner, AP (WP 16530 of 2002, decided on 25.9.2002), the AP High Court admitted a petition challenging exclusion of names and directed that the election authorities should prepare the final electoral roll following the procedure stipulated in the registration of electors roll. In this case a notification for an election had not been issued.

Bihar

In Chand Prasad and Others *versus* State of Bihar in a batch of Writ Petitions 2242, 2276, 2280 etc. of 2001, the exclusion of several voters, location of polling booths and reconstitution of some *panchayat* constituencies were all agitated. Though the notification for the elections had issued, the learned single judge directed the District Electoral officer concerned to prepare a supplementary voters list. This decision, dated 5.3.2001, was appealed against by the State Election Commissioner in LPA Nos. 257, 282, 283 etc. The orders of the learned single judge were set aside by the Division Bench on 6.4.2001, holding "once the election process has started it should be concluded as early as possible and there should be no undue interference by the court. Such interference by the court under Article 226 of the Constitution, on the ground of non-compliance of the provisions of the act or rules will interrupt or delay the elections." Accordingly the order passed by the learned single judge was set aside.

Karnataka

In Basanagowda and Another *versus* State of Karnataka and Others (2000(6) Kar.L.J 526 decided on 21.2.2000), 11 writ petitions were filed challenging wrongful inclusion of voters and other defects in the electoral roll. The petitioners had not filed similar objections when the preparation of the electoral rolls or their revision were actually taking place. The High Court also noted that "none of the voters, who have, according to the petitioners, been improperly included or excluded from the electoral rolls of the constituencies have been added as party respondents to these proceedings. No finding can therefore be recorded in regard to the validity of their inclusion or exclusion. The challenge to the electoral rolls and consequential relief in the circumstances is unsustainable." The Court however added that in the event these objections are raised in any election petition subsequently the authorities concerned are expected and indeed duty bound to look into the objections and determine the same in accordance with law.

Kerala

In a case before the Kerala High Court (State Election Commission *versus* Krishnan WA 2067 of 2000 decided on 26.9.2000), the State Election Commission filed an appeal against the orders of the single Judge of the High Court in directing the inclusion of certain persons in the electoral roll of a particular *gram panchayat* even though a notification for the election had issued and the last date for filing nominations had also passed. The court set aside the order of the single judge and allowed the appeal.

Punjab

In the Punjab and Haryana High Court in the case of Bagichi Singh *versus* Punjab State Election Commission (CWP No.7324 of 1999, decided on 13.2.2001), the High Court quashed an order of the SEC regarding the inclusion and deletion of certain names in the voters list. Here a notification for election had not been issued.

Tripura

In Ratanlal Nath and others *versus* State of Tripura (1997 (III) GLT (SC) 8 in Civil appeal No. 1640-1641 of 1997 decided on 25.2.1997), the validity of the rules under the Tripura Panchayats (Delimitation of Constituencies) Rules, 1993 came up for consideration before the Apex Court. The Apex Court held that the only source on which the electoral rolls are to be based is the population as ascertained at the last preceding census of which the relevant figures have been published. It is only where the census figures are not available, other sources can be used. The Apex Court held that the Tripura rules were consistent with the provisions of the Tripura Panchayats Act.

Supreme Court

The cases adjudicated as above indicate that the High Courts, generally, have avoided interference once the election process has started even though some of the actions in that process might be flawed. Where a High Court's decision has been a departure from such practice of non-interference, even after notification has been issued, the Supreme Court has reversed such decision. In Bodula Krishnaiah *versus* SEC (1996 (3) SCC 416 decided on 20.3.1996), the Apex Court set aside the orders of the AP High Court directing a fresh poll because the names of some persons were not included in the electoral roll. The case related to elections to a *gram panchayat* in the Nalgonda District of AP for which the electoral rolls were to be finalised 30 days prior to the poll. Elections were to be held on 27.6.1995 but by an order dated 26.6.1995 the High Court directed that 94 persons be allowed to participate in the election. However, on the date of the poll itself they could not exercise their franchise due to various other reasons. Subsequently the High Court gave a direction not to declare the result of the election followed by another order directing the Revenue Divisional Officer, Nalgonda to scrutinise the claims of the persons seeking to be voters. Eventually on 2/12/1995 the RDO found that only 20 of the persons concerned fulfilled requirements of residence and qualified to be voters. Thereafter, the High Court directed that a fresh poll be conducted for these persons.

In the appeal against these orders of the High Court, the Apex Court held that once the notification for the election was issued, the High Court would not be justified in issuing directions to stall the election process. In its judgement, the Apex Court also referred to the judgement of the Constitution Bench of the Court in Ponnuswamy's case (1952 SCR 218/AIR 1952 SC 64), wherein the court had held that elections should be concluded as early as possible according to time schedule and all controversial matters and disputes arising out of elections should be postponed till after the elections are over so that the election proceedings may not be unduly retarded or protracted. The judgement also emphasised that this principle of non-interference was also laid down in Lakshmi Charan Singh's case (1985-4 SEC 689) where again a Division Bench had held "though the High Court did not lack the jurisdiction to entertain the writ petition, no High Court in the exercise of its power under Article 226 of the Constitution should pass any orders interim or otherwise which has the tendency or effect of postponing an election. The High Courts must observe a self imposed limitation on their power to act under Article 226... that limitation has to be observed irrespective of the fact whether the preparation and publication of electoral rolls are a part of the process of the election within the meaning of Article 329 (b) of the Constitution." It can thus be taken that so far as challenges to the electoral rolls are concerned—though

High Courts may entertain the same—they cannot pass a direction to delay the election process once a notification for the elections has been issued.

Cases on Delimitation

Article 243C on the composition of *panchayats* provides the basic principles of delimitation. Clause 2 of this Articles states that "all the seats in a *panchayat* shall be filled by persons chosen by direct election from territorial constituencies in the *panchayat* area and for this purpose each *panchayat* area shall be divided into territorial constituencies in such manner that the ratio between the population of each constituency and the number of seats allotted to it shall as far as practicable be the same throughout the *panchayat* area." In other words the population-seat ratio has to have parity within the *panchayat*. Additionally the proviso to clause 1 of Article 243C also stipulates that the population-seat ratio in a *panchayat* as far as practicable be the same throughout the state. It is interesting to note that this principle of parity is not stated specifically so far as municipalities are concerned, though it has been generally followed. Article 243R in this regard states that all the seats in a municipality shall be filled by persons chosen by direct election from the territorial constituencies in the municipal area and for this purpose each municipal area shall be divided into territorial constituencies to be known as wards.

It is appropriate to mention that the language of Articles 243C and 243R are a substantial repetition of Clause 2 (a) and (b) of Article 81 of the Constitution in regard to the composition of the House of the People and clause (2) of Article 170 on the composition of Legislative Assemblies. The provisions relating to delimitation of territorial constituencies in the *panchayats* and municipalities are contained in the respective laws of the states concerned. As observed earlier these provisions do vary from one state to another. Litigation before the courts relates mainly to the provisions in the state laws and actual adherence to the same.

Some aspects of the delimitation exercise and the extent of judicial challenge came up for consideration in State of UP and Others *versus* Pradhan Sangh Kshettra Samiti and others (1995 Supp (2) SCC 305) decided on 24.3.1995. The judgement contains several decisions but those pertaining to delimitation are indicated below:

(a) Delimitation of *panchayat* area, constituencies in such areas and allotment of seats to the constituencies are matters to be decided by the State government and not open to judicial scrutiny, more so after notification for holding the election has issued *"It is for the government to decide in what manner the panchayat areas and the constituencies in each panchayat area will delimited. It is not for the Court to dictate the manner in which the same would be done"* (emphasis supplied). So long as the *panchayat* areas and the constituencies are delimited in conformity with the constitutional provisions or without committing a breach thereof, the courts cannot interfere with the same.

(b) Action of including more villages than one under one *gram panchayat* results in civil consequences. In such cases people of the areas concerned should have an opportunity of being heard but if in view of urgency such an opportunity is given after the decision that would be sufficient in compliance with the principle of natural justice *viz., Audi Alteram Partem* (No one should be condemned unheard).

In this case, the judgement delivered on 2.12.1994 by the Allahabad High Court was impugned. The High Court had held that the definitions of "village", "*gram panchayat*" and "*panchayat* area" in the UP Panchayat Act were ultra vires of the respective definitions given in Article 243D, G and E read with Article 243C. The High Court had further held that:

(i) The village has to be a habitat according to the anthropological concept.

(ii) For the purposes of constituting *panchayats*, the village can be specified only in accordance with wishes of the inhabitants.

(iii) The Governor has to act independently of the State government in the matter of such specification.

In deciding on the appeal against this judgement, the Apex Court relied on Meghraj Kothari *versus* Delimitation Commission (1967-1 SCR 400/ AIR 1967 SC 669) whereby the court had held that a notification of the delimitation of the constituencies or allotment of seats to such constituencies are to be regarded as laws not subject to the scrutiny of any court. Article 243-O of the Constitution has enacted a similar bar on the interference by the courts in electoral matters particularly after the notification for the election has been issued. In the instant case, the Apex Court found that the High Court had not only entertained a challenge to such a notification but has also gone into the merits of the alleged grievances, though the challenge was made after the notification was issued on 21.8.1994. Accordingly the orders of the High Court were set aside.

Prima facie this particular decision of the Apex Court of March 1995 should be regarded as having settled the law so far as interference by Courts is concerned in matters of delimitation. However, in some of the subsequent cases before the High Courts some related points continued to be agitated and adjudicated.

Andhra Pradesh

In Raghunath Rao *versus* Government of AP (1999 (1) ALT39, decided on 20.11.1998), the decision of the District Collector acting on behalf of the Panchayati Raj department and bifurcating Sitarampuram *gram panchayat* and constituting Marribandham as a separate *gram panchayat* was challenged. The bifurcation was made on the basis of distance and other factors. A Division bench of the High Court held that jurisdiction under Article 226 was maintainable in this case and that bifurcation on the grounds of distance alone was not justifiable

In a subsequent case before the Andhra High Court (Maineni Prabhakar Rao 2002 (3) ALT 114 decided on 4.2.2002), the issue of bifurcation of a *gram panchayat* came up again for adjudication. Members of Kolluru *Gram Panchayat*, Guntur, had challenged the validity of the notification excluding certain hamlets from the Revenue Village of Kolluru and forming them into a separate *Gram Panchayat*. The court held that the collector having issued a show-cause notice seeking the views of the *Gram Panchayat* as to why the bifurcation did not wait for the minimum period of 10-days for receiving the response. Since this reasonable opportunity was not afforded, the impugned notification of the Collector was quashed and directed to consider the entire matter afresh.

In another case before the AP High Court, D Suryanarayan and others *versus* Government of AP (2000 (2) ALT 787 decided on 24.3.2000), a Division Bench held that before a *nagar panchayat* could be constituted as provided for in Article 243Q for a transitional area, the six *gram panchayats* covered in the proposed area should have been first declared as a "transitional area". Article 243 Q reads as follows: "1. There shall be constituted in every state (a) a *Nagar Panchayat* (by whatever name called) for a transitional area, that is to say, an area in transition from a rural area to an urban area".

Kerala

In the Kerala High Court, the extent of the bar to interference by Courts under Article 243-O in delimitation matters came up specifically for adjudication in Kunhabdullah (2000(3) KLT 45 decided on 3.8.2000). Section 10 of the Kerala Panchayati Raj Act, 1994 (Act 13 of 1994) provides for the division of *panchayats* into constituencies by the State Election Commission or an officer authorised by them in this behalf. Sub-section (2) lays down the procedure by which objections and suggestions from the public with respect to the proposals for delimitation should be considered and decided. Sub-section (3) states that an order made by the State Election Commission or the officer authorised by it shall not be called in question in any court of law. The district collector was authorised by the State Election Commission to undertake delimitation of constituencies in a *panchayat*. By an Amendment Act (Act 13 of 2000), a new Sub-section 10A was introduced whereby the State Election Commission was empowered to review the delimitation orders issued by the District Collector.

The delimitation of wards ordered by the District Collector acting as a delegate of the Election Commission was reviewed by the Commission and a *de novo* delimitation was done. It was contended by the Commission that this *de novo* delimitation was not subject to judicial review as stipulated under section 10(3) of the Panchayat Act and Article 243-O. The High Court held that this bar would not be attracted when sweeping changes are made by the Election Commission to the delimitation orders duly passed by the District Collector earlier after hearing objections. The State Election Commission acting under the guise of the power to review could not make sweeping changes of the Collector's orders.

The High Court after considering the procedure adopted by the State Election Commission in reviewing the orders of the District Collector held that the newly introduced Section 10A of the PR Act read with the previously existing Section 10(3) excluding consideration by a court of law had resulted in an inconsistency and anomaly. The court held that an order of delimitation passed by the District Collector was made after a lengthy exercise and after following due procedure for hearing and disposal of objections from the public if any, and thus reached finality. Such an order therefore enjoyed immunity from being called in question in any court of law vide Section 10(3). Such an order of the District Collector could be reviewed by the State Election Commission only for the purpose of correcting errors apparent on the face of the record as provided for in Section 11 of the Kerala Panchayat Act. This power to review did not entitle the State Election Commission to make sweeping changes, which in effect amounted to a *de novo* delimitation. The High Court rejected the contention of the State Election Commission that this *de novo* delimitation could not be questioned in a court of law under Section 10 (3) of the Panchayat Act as well as Article 243-O of the Constitution. The High Court held that the SEC in reviewing the delimitation orders passed by the District Collector whether *suo motu* or on an application for review could not pass orders as it deemed fit, without going through a process of public hearing and objection in much the same manner as the District Collector had to do. Without such a procedure of natural justice, the High Court held that the powers conferred on the State Election Commission under the amended Section 10A amounted to conferring arbitrary power which cannot be justified by "guidelines" devised by the repository of the power himself. In the absence of statutory guidelines the vesting of such unguided, unbridled power cannot be held to be valid merely because it is exercised by a high official.

The Court further stated that "the bar under Article 243-O necessarily presupposes the existence of a valid law and if that law is vulnerable to attack under the Constitution being offensive to Article 14, such a law cannot claim immunity from judicial review." Accordingly Section 10A was held *ultra vires* and the SECs orders were quashed.

The decision of the Kerala High Court was challenged in the Supreme Court in Civil Appeal No.4702 of 2000 with other petitions. In declaring Section 10A of the Act as unconstitutional and therefore null and void, the High Court had said that all orders passed by the Election Commission by virtue of the powers under this section were "*non est*" in the eye of law. While entertaining the appeal, the Supreme Court stayed operation of this part of the High Courts judgement. Thereafter, elections to the *gram panchayats* were held and the *gram panchayats* constituted for a period of five years. While hearing the case subsequently, both the appellant i.e. the Kerala State Election Commission and the respondents agreed that they would accept the judgement passed by the High Court provided the terms of various *gram panchayats* were not disturbed. In view of this, the Supreme Court disposed off the appeal in terms of its interim order with the direction that the elections held in pursuance of its order dated 20.10.2000 shall stand and the *panchayats* allowed to complete the term of five years.

In K.P. Raveendran and Another *versus* State of Kerala (AIR 2005 KER 319) decided on 5.8.2005, an interesting issue emerged. The question was whether a rural area which at one point of time had been notified as "smaller urban area" or a "larger urban area" in terms of Article 243Q of the Constitution could become once again a rural area. In the instant case, in November 1999 the Government notified certain areas as "smaller urban area" and "larger urban areas" with effect from 1.10.2000. Some of these areas were included in some municipalities and some others were included in a corporation. In a subsequent reorganisation of some municipal areas, the government decided to exclude some of these areas from the respective municipal jurisdictions and make them once again as village *panchayats*. This action was impugned in the case.

It was held that various criteria have been provided in the Constitution itself for establishing a *nagar panchayat* as a transitional area as also for setting up the two types of urban areas namely "smaller urban areas" and "larger urban areas". The Court held that once such areas have been thus constituted, it is not permissible to take part or whole of any of these areas and reconstitute them as village *panchayats*. In other words an area falling within Part IX A of the Constitution cannot be retransmitted into an area falling within Part IX of the Constitution. The Court noted that prior to the 73rd and the 74th Amendments, the Kerala Municipalities Act, 1960 did contain a provision for the abolition of municipalities. But in the Kerala Municipality Act, 1994 such a provision did not exist because it would be contrary to constitutional provisions in Part IXA.

In sum, the court held that a rural area after its transition to be an urban area, thereby becoming a "smaller urban area" or a "larger urban area" in terms of Article 243Q of the Constitution cannot be converted again to become a rural area. Hence, the impugned "de-linking" of certain urban areas in the municipalities for being treated as rural areas was declared unconstitutional and void.

Public Consultation in Matters of Delimitation

While the state laws and regulations usually prescribe a procedure of publishing draft notification and hearing of objections, in cases of redefining or modifying *panchayat* and municipal boundaries or wards the extent of consultation required has not been clear. As a result there have been some litigations of significance.

Maharashtra

In Ganpatrao Bhosale *versus* State of Maharashtra (1997 (3) MLJ) the extent of consultation required in delimiting village *panchayats* came up for consideration. Under the Bombay Village Panchayat Act, one *panchayat* for each village is envisaged but it authorises the government to form a *panchayat* for a group of revenue villages as well, after consulting the *panchayat* concerned and the Standing

Committee of the *Zilla Parishad*, However, consultation or an exchange of views with each individual concerned is not necessary. The court also held that the power given to the government to include, exclude or otherwise modify the limits of a village for forming a *panchayat* is constitutionally valid and what is required is that the statutory procedure envisaged for the purpose should be complied with.

In Gram Sudhar Samiti, Mahadulla (2004 (4) MLJ 309, WP No.1823 of 1989 decided on 11.6.2004), the Bombay High Court held that in the process of 'declaring' a village for purposes of constituting a village *panchayat*, consultation with the village or villages concerned is necessary when some areas are taken from one village and added to another.

The above decision was referred to and reinforced in a subsequent case before the Bombay High Court. In Ashok Ganpath Jadhav *versus* State Election Commission (2000-4 MLJ 150, WP No.2597 of 2000 decided on 29.6.2000), it was held that under the provisions of the Bombay Village Panchayats Act, it is mandatory that prior to passing a delimitation order for delimiting a village *panchayat* or separating a group *gram panchayat* into two village *panchayats* an opportunity of hearing to the village residents is afforded. This opportunity of hearing may be by way of displaying notice and it is not necessary to give individual notice. Where such an opportunity is not afforded the order of delimitation is not valid and liable to set aside by the Court invoking Article 226 notwithstanding Article 243-O.

In Kamaljeet Singh *versus* State of Punjab (CWP No.337 of 2002 decided on 7.3.2002), the extent of consultation required in matters of delimitation as well as constitution of *panchayat* or municipal bodies came up for detailed consideration. In this case, the petitioners some of whom being ex-councillors of the Nagar Panchayat Badhni Kalan in the District Moga, filed a petition for quashing a notification of the Punjab Government, de-notifying the *nagar panchayat*. The question before the court was whether the rules of natural justice were required to be observed by the state government and opportunity of hearing had to be given to the residents of the particular local area, before notifying that area as a *nagar panchayat* or a municipality or de-notifying an existing *nagar panchayat* or including or excluding that area in an existing or proposed *nagar panchayat* or municipality. The Punjab and Haryana High Court referred to the judgement of the Supreme Court in Baldev Singh and others *versus* State of Himachal Pradesh (AIR 1987 SC 1239) wherein the Supreme Court interpreted Section 256 of Himachal Pradesh Municipal Act, 1968 and held as under:

> *Citizens of India have a right to decide, what should be the nature of their society in which they live-agrarian, semi-urban or urban. Admittedly, the way of life varies, depending upon where one lives. Inclusion of an area covered by a Gram Panchayat within a notified area would certainly involve civil consequences. In such circumstances, it is necessary that people who will be affected by the change should be given an opportunity of being heard,* otherwise they would be visited with serious consequences like loss of office in *gram panchayats,* an imposition of a way of life, higher incidence of tax and like (emphasis supplied).
>
> It is true that Section 256 of the HPM Act does not in clear terms provide a right of hearing but the settled position of law is that where exercise of a power results in civil consequences to citizens, unless the statute specifically rules out the application of natural justice, the rules of natural justice would apply. Therefore, before the notified area is constituted in terms of Section 256, the people of the locality should be afforded an opportunity of being heard and the administrative decision by the State Government should be taken after considering the views of the residents. Denial of such opportunity is not in consonance with the scheme of the Rule of Law governing our society. However, the hearing contemplated need not be oral and can be by inviting objections and disposing them off in a fair way.

The High Court also referred its own judgement by a Division Bench in Veekay Oils Pvt. Ltd. *versus* State of Punjab (1994-2107 PLR 234) wherein it was held that inclusion of a village in the municipal limits of Ahmedgarh was liable to be quashed on the ground that the affected parties were not given an opportunity of hearing.

Accordingly relying on both these cases the High Court held that the decision to de-notify the *nagar panchayat,* Badhni Kalan is violative of the rules of natural justice and therefore set aside the same.

Andhra Pradesh

In a case decided very recently the matter came to be reviewed in detail.

In P.V.V. Prasad and Others *versus* Government of AP and others, the processes followed in setting up the Greater Vishakhapatnam Municipal Corporation were challenged (2006(2) ALD 797 WP Nos. 25147, 25771 and 25772 of 2005 decided on 16.2.2006). In this case the AP Government proposed to include the Gajuwaka Municipality and 32 *gram panchayats* in the limits of Greater Vishakhapatnam Municipal Corporation. In July 2005, the government asked the District Collector to obtain and furnish views of the 32 *gram panchayats*. Of these, 23 opposed the inclusion and passed a resolution accordingly. The government after considering the report of the District Collector asked the 23 GPs to show cause as to why the resolutions passed by them opposing their inclusion into the limits of the Vishakhapatnam Municipal Corporation should not be cancelled. After examining the objections raised again the government decided to cancel the said resolutions. In November 2005, the government also issued an order constituting the Greater Visakhapatnam Municipal Corporation including Gajuwaka Municipality and 32 *gram panchayats.* The petitioners thereafter challenged this order in the High Court. It was argued that a *panchayat* constituted under Article 243 has a right to continue for five years from the date appointed for its first meeting unless sooner dissolved and abolishing it was not permissible under the Constitution. In such a case fresh elections will have to be conducted. The petitioners further contended that they themselves or the representatives of the affected *gram panchayats* were not given an opportunity of being heard and the process of the Collector obtaining their views was not the same as a hearing.

On behalf of the Government of AP it was argued as follows:

> The function of the Government in establishing a Corporation under the Act is neither executive nor administrative. It is a legislative process. No judicial duty is laid on the Government in discharge of statutory duties. The only question to be examined is whether statutory provisions have been complied with. If they are complied with, then

> the Court could say no more. In the present case the Government did publish the proposal by draft notification and also considered the representations received. It was only thereafter a decision was taken to abolish the *gram panchayats* and include their areas in Greater Visakhapatnam Municipal Corporation. The court cannot sit in judgement over such decision. It cannot lay down norms for the exercise of that power. It cannot substitute even its juster will for theirs.
>
> The government in exercise of these powers is not subject to the rules of natural justice any more than the legislature itself. The rules of natural justice are not applicable to the legislative action plenary or subordinate. The procedural requirement of hearing is not implied in exercise of power unless the hearing was expressly prescribed.

Without specifically ruling on the position taken by the state government, the court referred to the Apex Court's observations in some landmark judgement as in Maneka Gandhi (SC/0133/1978) and Tulsiram Patel (SC/0373/1985) that principles of natural justice are a part of the guarantee of equality contained in Article 14 of the Constitution. In the present case, however, the High Court in considering the need for harmony between social interest and individual right noted that while 23 of the 32 *gram panchayats* had opposed their inclusion in the Visakhapatnam Municipal Corporation, the government had indeed considered the objections and cancelled the resolutions by invoking powers under Section 246(1) of the Andhra Pradesh Panchayat Raj Act, 1994 and issued G.O.Ms. No.379 dated 21.22.2005. The reasons for cancellation of the resolutions passed by the petitioner/*gram panchayats* have been detailed in G.O.Ms. No.379 dated 21.11.2005

The court also took note of the observations of the Apex Court in Baldev Singh's case and came to the conclusion that in the instant case the views of the *panchayats* were also considered by the government. The court rejected the contention that a *panchayat* as an institution cannot be abolished. The court also observed that the objections of the petitioners—*gram panchayats* regarding their inclusion in the Visakhapatnam Municipal Corporation have indeed been considered by the government but the government decided to constitute the Greater Visakhapatnam Municipal Corporation in the larger public interest. Accordingly the petitions were dismissed.

Some Recent Cases on Delimitation

Before concluding the Section on Delimitation we may also refer to some recent judgements of the Allahabad and Karnataka High Courts. The facts regarding these cases with a rather complicated history are as follows:

(i) Election to 11 Municipal Corporations in UP were held last in the year 2000. Under Article 243U "every municipality (which term includes a corporation) unless sooner dissolved under any law for the time being in force, shall continue for five years from the date appointed for its first meeting and no longer." It is clear that the words 'no longer' are mandatory. The constitutional intent is that elections must be so organised that one elected corporation is succeeded by another at the end of its term without any hiatus.

(ii) The UP Corporations Act, 1959 requires that elections to municipal corporations are held after dividing the municipal areas into 'wards' on the basis of the last preceding census.

(iii) The State Election Commission had commenced preparations for a fresh delimitation of municipal constituencies based on the 2001 Census.

(iv) However, another delimitation exercise by the Delimitation Commission of India dealing with the Parliament and assembly constituencies was in progress. This Commission asked the State Election Commissioner of UP not to alter the boundaries of municipal and *panchayat* wards till the delimitation of the Assembly and Parliamentary constituencies was over.

(v) Accordingly the State Election Commission abandoned its work of fresh delimitation. This meant that the Corporation wards would have remained as they were in 2004.

In May 2005, one Kamlesh Singh and another Shiv Sewak Singh filed on 2.9.2005 a writ petition (Civil Misc. WP No.59093 of 2005) seeking a direction to the UP State Election Commission and other authorities concerned not to hold elections until the delimitation of municipal wards on the basis of the 2001 Census was done as required under the UP Municipal Corporations Act. The Court noted that as on the date of filing the writ petition there was no notification for holding the election. The Court further noted that so long as the case subsisted the matter was sub judice and the state of UP could not oust the Court jurisdiction by resorting to issue of notification for holding election. Besides, if elections have to be held on the basis of the 1991 Census when the published figures for the 2001 Census were available that would be a violation of the statute. In the High Court's view, the Delimitation Commission's and the State Election Commission's exercises were in two separate fields and taking up of work on one could not be held to stop the work on the other. On 28.10.2005, the Court directed the UP State Election Commission to proceed expeditiously with the delimitation exercise since the 2001 figures were already available and asked the SEC to file an affidavit indicating the time schedule for this work and also take steps to complete the exercise within the shortest possible time. On 14.11.2005, the state government filed an affidavit in response indicating that the final publication of delimitation could be completed earliest by 30th May 2006.

Apprehending delay in completing the work of delimitation, the state legislature stepped in to amend the UP Urban Local Self-Government Laws providing for the appointment of an administrator to take over the functioning of the municipalities till such time the elections are held. This Amendment Act received the assent of the Governor on 26.11.2005. Orders were also issued by the state government asking district magistrates to take over as administrators of the corporations.

On 27.11.2005, another writ petition was filed by Anugrah Narain Singh challenging this amendment. The petition was heard regularly till 13.12.2005. The court held that in the circumstances of the case a hiatus in the succession of previously elected mayors and corporators by freshly elected ones was inevitable. While the amendment was within the legislative competence of the state, the decision to appoint administrators went against the substance of Article 243U stipulating that elections be held within six months in the case of dissolution of a municipality. The court quashed the order of the State government dated 28.11.2005 appointing administrators and directed them to handover the charge of the mayor and elected representatives to the erstwhile mayors and corporators so long any un-expired period of their tenure was available. The court also directed the U.P. State Election Commission to expeditiously complete the delimitation process so that fresh elections could be held to all the corporations within a period of six months from the date on which the tenure of the previously elected corporations would end.

The decision of the Division Bench of the Allahabad High Court was challenged in an appeal before the SC in January 2006 but was disposed off in November that year since elections to the corporation were held by then.

In a very recent case decided by the Karnataka High Court on 21.6.2006, a similar issue as to whether municipal elections can be held without undertaking a fresh delimitation of constituencies on the basis of the latest census has been raised. In Bharamraj S. Parmaj *versus* State of Karnataka and others Writ Petition No.8003 of 2006 was considered along with Writ Petition No.8004 of 2006. The Petitioners were ex-corporators of the Belgaum Municipal Corporation. The Petitioners contended that the State Election Commission and other parties were seeking to hold elections to the Belgaum Municipal Corporation without fresh delimitation on the basis of 2001 Census and were proceeding to hold elections by keeping the existing 58 wards in Belgaum and 55 wards in Gulbarga without delimiting them. It was further contended by the petitioners that this would affect the parity of voters to a constituency between the different wards. The state authorities argued that elections had to be held by end of June 2006 in keeping with the constitutional mandate to hold elections in time so upon completion of the tenure, a freshly elected body could succeed without any hiatus of time.

In considering the case, the court referred to the judgement of the Division Bench of Karnataka in the case of Prof. B.K. Chandrashekhar *versus* State of Karnataka WP 3679 of 1999 decided on 17.3.1999. In that case the Division Bench held as under:

> During the course of arguments we had asked Mr. Acharya, learned Counsel appearing for State Election Commission as to within how much time the Election Commission would be able to hold election, if the ordinance is given effect to. According to him, it will take in all atleast seven months to hold the elections as fresh notifications under Section 5(1)(2) and (5) have to be issued. On the expiry of the period of five years, the present elected bodies would become *functus officio.* The *gram panchayats* will not be having any elected body which would result in break down of the democratic set up envisaged by the Constitution. In order to prevent such a situation and would be necessary to direct the respondents to hold elections to the *gram panchayats* in the State of Karnataka immediately. *We are not holding that the State Legislature does not have the competence to amend Sections 4 and 5 of the Panchayati Raj Act. If it has the power to enact it has necessarily the power to amend those provisions as well* (emphasis supplied). But as the amendment results in nullifying the Mandate of the Constitution of India especially when the process of election had begun, the same is held to be not applicable to the present elections to *gram panchayats* due to be held in the month of March/April 1999. *If there is conflict between the mandatory provisions of the Constitution and the right of the State Legislature to enact laws which falls within its legislative competence and which results in nullifying the mandate of the Constitution then in such a case provision of the Constitution would take precedence* (emphasis supplied). If such a view is not taken then the mandate of the Constitution can be flouted with impunity by the state legislature on one pretext or the other. The Constitution is Supreme and the laws by the legislature have to be enacted subject to the provisions of the Constitution of India and therefore subservient to it. Press note annexure 'B' issued by the Election Commission attached in W.P. 3826/99 is quashed.

After referring to Chandrasekhar's case, the court held that the duration of five years as prescribed for municipalities and the holding of elections are mandatory and if these are flouted there would be a breakdown in the democratic set up. The court considered in some detail whether in the instant case there was element of public interest involved in the petitions. The court came to the conclusion that even if the chances of the petitioners getting elected are affected to a certain extent on account of the population ratio, not being maintained with reference to each ward, this by itself will not be a ground to delay the holding of elections. *While holding the elections according to the de facto situation with the existing wards would be contrary to the state laws on delimitation, postponing the elections for this purpose to fulfill a statutory requirement would result in disobedience of the Constitutional mandate,* which was not permissible (emphasis supplied). The court came to the conclusion that violation of the statutory duty would not affect the interest of the public though it might affect the interest of the candidates contesting the elections. But this was no ground to entertain the writ petition under the clock of public interest litigation. Accordingly the petitions were dismissed.

Industrial Townships

This decision of the Karnataka High Court delivered by a two Judge Bench is subsequent to the decision of the Allahabad High Court referred to earlier and as such no reference could be made to it in Allahabad. Hopefully when the appeal from the Allahabad High Court's decision is considered by the Apex Court, the judgement in Bharamraj as well as other relevant cases would be cited and argued in the context of the constitutional stipulation.

An unique situation exists in regard to industrial townships where it is open to a state government to declare a particular area as an 'Industrial Township' under the proviso to Article 243-Q, in lieu of a municipality. The proviso reads as follows:

> Provided that a municipality under this clause may not be constituted in such urban area or part thereof as the Governor may, having regard to the size of the area and the municipal services being provided or proposed to be provided by an industrial establishment in that area and such other factors as he may deem fit, by public notification, specify to be an industrial township.

For several years Jamshedpur has been run by a Notified Area Committee since 1922. The Tata Zamindari Company owned most of the land in the industrial area and residential townships of Tata Steel and other factories. In 1984, the land vested with State of Bihar as a consequence of the Bihar Land Reform Act, but the Jamshedpur lands were leased to Tata Steel. The Notified Area Committee arrangement continued by which Tata Steel has been providing various municipal services such as water supply, sanitation etc. After the 74th Amendment came into existence, the setting up of an elected municipality in keeping with the democratic regime of local governments has been proposed. In a recent case Jawaharlal Sharma *versus* State of Jharkhand and others, the subject came up for consideration. In view of the special and complex situation obtaining in Jamshedpur extracts of the Judgement in WP 4388 of 2003 considered along with WP No.517 and 872 of 2006 and WP (PIL) No. 364 of 2006 decided on 23.6.2006 are presented as Annexure A-1.1 at the end of this chapter. However, the Judgement is under appeal before the Supreme Court which has stayed further action by the Jharkhand government in setting up a Municipal corporation. Some moot points arise.

The judgement of the Jharkhand High Court emphasises the need for a conscious application of mind by the state government and the various steps needed to be gone through before deciding whether a given area is to be constituted into a municipality or municipal corporation or into an industrial township under the proviso to Article 243-Q. In the context of the judgement, it may be worth examining to what extent the constitutional and other legal requirements have been fulfilled in declaring or treating some of the existing areas as Industrial Township. It is open to question whether a development authority such as NOIDA can be regarded as an industry *per se* and the area acquired and developed by it can come under the purview of the proviso to Article 243-Q. The judgement also assumes special significance in the present context of SEZ townships being developed under the provision of the Special Economic Zone Act, 2005.

Conclusions

In this chapter, we have considered organisational and related arrangements for holding of elections to *panchayats* and municipalities, the role and responsibilities of the State Election Commissions and the divergence in the arrangements between different states. We have also considered some important cases in the different High Courts as also the Supreme Court in regard to electoral rolls and delimitation of constituencies and the exclusion available under the provisions in Article 243-Q.

The following conclusions can be drawn in summary:

(a) Articles 243-O of the Constitution couched in identical terms to Article 329 does not appear to be a complete and effective bar to interference by the courts. However, the High Courts as well as the Apex Court have held that when a notification for elections have been issued, the court should observe a self-imposed limitation of not interfering with the process of elections so as to delay their conclusion.

(b) The jurisdiction of the High Courts under Article 226 is inherent and cannot be ousted.

(c) Challenges to the inclusion and exclusion of names in the electoral rolls have to be determined by the appropriate authorities assigned with this task or authorised to hear appeals therefrom and these have to be determined in accordance with the state laws.

(d) The substance and process of delimitation and procedure for the same are essentially, matters to be decided by the State governments. However, these have to be consistent with the state laws and also satisfy the norms of natural justice.

(e) So far as delimitation is concerned the constitutional intent and provisions are clear that such delimitation has to be based on the published figures of the Census prior to the election and therefore a periodicity in delimitation in keeping with the periodicity of the Census is enjoined.

(f) However, the law on delay in holding the periodical delimitation and consequential delay in holding of the elections does not appear to be fully settled as yet. Nevertheless, holding of elections within the time stipulated by the Constitution has been emphasised by the Supreme Court in Kishansingh Tomar's case (see chapter 5).

(g) The line of distinction between delimitation and including or excluding any particular area while constituting, enlarging, abridging or amalgamating any *panchayat* or municipality appears to be thin. While the initial process of delimiting territorial wards or constituencies seems to enjoy a measure of immunity from judicial interference because of Article 243-O and 243ZG, the immunity is dependent on whether the relevant state law is itself constitutionally valid.

(h) The extent of applicability of the proviso to Article 243-Q under which industrial townships may not be constituted into municipalities is unclear and may require further judicial interpretation.

Annexure A-1.1

Extracts from the Judgement in Jawaharlal Sharma versus State of Jharkhand and others

W.P.(PIL) 4388 of 2003 along with W.P.(C) 517 and 872 of 2006 and W.P. (PIL) 364 of 2006 decided on 23.6.2006

As all these four writ petitions relate to the constitution of the municipal corporation at Jamshedpur and in three of them the notification inviting objection for constitution of such Municipal Corporation at Jamshedpur is under challenge and common question of law being involved, they were heard together and are being disposed of by this common judgement.

Out of these four analogous writ petitions, two, namely, W.P. (PIL) No.4388 of 2003 and W.P. (PIL) No.364 of 2006 have been preferred as public interest litigation. In W.P. (PIL) No.4388 of 2003 prayer has been made to direct the state to replace Jamshedpur Notified Area Committee by duly elected Municipal Body (Corporation) in accordance with the provisions, contained in part-IXA of the Constitution of India.

In W.P. (PIL) No.364 of 2006 prayer has been made to declare the Notification dated 6th December 2005 as illegal and unconstitutional and to command the respondents to declare Jamshedpur Township as an "Industrial Township" as per Article 243Q of the Constitution of India.

One Shalkhan Murmoo in WP(C) No.872 of 2006 has also challenged the same notification dated 6th December, 2005 on the ground that the same is violative of the Constitution of India and the provisions of "Panchayat (Extension of Scheduled Areas) Act, 1996" (hereinafter to be referred as PESA, 1996) as well as the provisions of "Jharkhand Panchayat Raj Act, 2001".

Fourth writ petition i.e. WP(C) No.517 of 2006 has been preferred by the Tata Steel Ltd. (earlier known as Tata Iron & Steel company) for a declaration that Section 2(1) of the Bihar Municipal Corporation Act, 1978 (Bihar Act 12 of 1978) ultra vires of Article 243Q read with Article 243ZF of the Constitution of India, as the same is not in consonance with the aforesaid constitutional provisions. It has also challenged the notification dated 6th December, 2005, published by the Government of Jharkhand in the official Gazette dated 8th December, 2005, whereby and whereunder, a draft proposal has been published for declaration and formation of Jamshedpur Municipal Corporation over the areas, falling under Jamshedpur and Mango Notified Area Committees and Jugsalai Municipality and for that purpose the state of Jharkhand has invited objections and suggestions from the persons, to be affected by the said notification. Prayer has also been made for a direction on the respondent state to issue an appropriate notification under Sub-section (4) of Section 4 of the Bihar and Orissa Municipal Act, 1922 and to declare Jamshedpur Township as an "Industrial Township", as envisaged under Section 3(11A) of the said Act and to appoint a Committee to carry out the aims and object of the said Act and to carry out the purpose of the Act in the "Industrial Township".

III. WP (C) No.517 of 2006: The petitioner Tata Steel Ltd., is a company, registered under the Companies Act, 1956. Its steel plant at Jamshedpur was established in the year 1907 by Sir Jamshed Ji N Tata..........................

III.4 According to the petitioner, the municipal facilities in the township of Jamshedpur were and are being provided by the petitioner company, the Head of the Town Division of the petitioner Company used to be nominated as the Chairman of the Jamshedpur Notified Area Committee. The majority of the members nominated in the Committee were representatives of the petitioner Company. The Heads of the Public Health Department and Town Planning and Engineering Department of the petitioner's Company, besides others, were nominated members of the Jamshedpur Notified Area Committee and functioned as Health Officer and Engineer respectively. The Jamshedpur Notified Area Committee had limited functions, such as registration of vehicles, registration of births and deaths, approval of the building plans, enforcing public health measures and to provide licence to hazardous trades. Along with the plant of Tata Steel other major industries also came up in Jamshedpur, such as, Tata Motors Ltd, Tata Pigments Ltd., Tinplate Company of India Ltd, Lafarge India Ltd, Timken India Ltd, Indian Steel and Wire Products etc. Besides, other industries and small scale industries, ancillary to these major industries, are located in and around the town of Jamshedpur. The employees of the industries, developed around the town of Jamshedpur, also reside in Jamshedpur and avail the municipal facilities, provided by the petitioner company.

III.5 According to the petitioner, various services are being provided by the Tata Steel since its inception for the last nine decades with the help of structured departments and skilled manpower...

III.6 On behalf of the petitioner it was also submitted that in a meeting held on 10th August, 1999 in the Chamber of the Chief Secretary to the Government of Bihar between the State authorities and the company, it was decided that Jamshedpur and Bokaro will be declared to be Industrial Townships. Such decision was also communicated by letter No.2811 dated 2nd August 2000. Inspite of such decision taken by the erstwhile State of Bihar, in a recent meeting held on 8th October, 2005 under the Chairmanship of the Hon'ble Minister, Incharge of Urban Development Department, Jharkhand, Ranchi, a different decision was taken ignoring the earlier decision of the state.

III.7 Learned Counsel for the petitioner company further submitted that in the recent agreement by which the state government has renewed the lease in favour of the company for further 30 years, it has been mentioned that the petitioner company is to provide municipal services to the people, residing in the area and, in fact, providing such facilities of water and waste management; planning, engineering and construction; power services; public health and horticulture services etc., as detailed above.

III.8 It appears that a writ petition being Writ Petition (Civil) No.154 of 1988 was filed by one Jawaharlal Sharma (Petitioner in analogous WP (PIL)

No.4388 of 2003) before the Supreme Court for converting the Jamshedpur Notified Area Committee into a Municipality. The State of Bihar, in the said writ petition, filed a counter affidavit and took the plea that as per the lease agreement of 1984 the petitioner company is to render municipal services and without powers, privilege and right the company could not have the requisite control over the town of Jamshedpur, which is necessary to carry out its function. The Supreme Court by order dated 21st August, 1989 directed the State of Bihar to issue a notification under Section 390A of the Municipal Act, declaring its function to convert Jamshedpur Notified Area Committee into a Municipality and to invite objections. Pursuant thereto, Notification No.4806 dated 23rd November, 1990 was issued in this regard against which a writ petition being C.W.J.C No.156 of 1991 was preferred before the Patna High Court. The case was admitted and interim order was passed on 11th January, 1991 against which S.L.P. (C) No.14677 of 1993 was preferred before the Supreme Court. During pendency of S.L.P.(C) No.14677 of 1999, C.W.J.C. No.156 of 1991 was finally disposed of and the Patna High Court by order dated 25th November, 1992 directed the State of Bihar to consider and dispose of all the objections.

III.9 In the meantime, with effect from 1st June 1993 the "Constitution (Seventy-fourth Amendment) Act, 1992 came into effect, as a result of which Part-IX(A) was added in the Constitution, which deals with constitution of municipalities. Article 243P while defines municipal areas, municipality etc...

11. In regard to the Municipalities, three sets of law were continuing in the erstwhile State of Bihar, namely (i) Bihar and Orissa Municipal Corporation Act, 1922 (B&O Act 7 of 1922); (ii) Patna Municipal Corporation Act, 1951 (Bihar Act 13 of 1952), and (iii) The Bihar Municipal Corporation Act, 1978 (Bihar Act 12 of 1978). After "Constitution (74th Amendment) Act, 1922", the State of Bihar made certain amendments in Bihar and Orissa Municipal Corporation Act, 1922 vide Act 2 of 1995, Sub-section (11A): "Industrial Township" (meaning) was inserted in Section 3 of the Act, 1922, which reads as follows:

"Section 3. Definitions: In this Act, unless there be something repugnant in the subject or context.

[(11A) "Industrial Township" means such urban area or part thereof as the state government may, having regard to the size of the area and the municipal services being provided or proposed to be provided by an industrial establishment in that area and such other factors as the state government may deem fit, by public notification, specify to be an industrial township.]"...

III. 14 Though the aforesaid amendment was made in two of the Acts, namely Bihar and Orissa Municipal Corporation Act, 1922 and Patna Municipal Corporation Act, 1951, making provisions for "Industrial Township" no such amendment was made in Bihar Municipal Corporation Act, 1978. Section 2(1) of the Bihar Municipal Corporation Act, 1978 enables the state government to constitute a Municipal Corporation in an area for providing better organised and coordinated civil facilities. The state government may by notification in the official gazette declare any area, including the area of any other Municipality and/or the Notified Area Committee with such other contiguous area, to be a Municipal Corporation. This provision is consistent with Part IXA of the Constitution, including Article 243Q. If by amendment no similar provision is introduced in Section 2 like proviso to Article 243Q(1)(c), that will not render Section 2 ultra vires of Article 243Q. Part IXA of the Constitution, as introduced by the "Constitution (74th Amendment) Act, 1992" including Article 243Q is a mandate of the Constitution and all States are bound to give effect to it by constituting a municipality for a transitional area, smaller urban area and larger urban area, except villages/rural areas, where *panchayats* are to be constituted. Therefore, the submission made by the petitioner company that Section 2(1) of the Bihar Municipal Corporation Act, 1978 *ultra vires* the Constitution cannot be accepted and as such, is rejected.

If both the aforesaid provisions i.e. Article 243Q of the Constitution of India and Section 2 of the Bihar Municipal Corporation Act, 1978 are read together then it will be evident that the State/Governor/Competent authority for constitution of a municipality is required to take the following steps, one after another;

(i) The Governor having regard to the population of the area, density of the population therein, revenue generated for local administration, percentage of the employment in non-agricultural activities, the economic importance or such other factors, as he may deem fit, will first determine and specify whether the area will be treated to be a transitional area or smaller urban area or a larger urban area, in terms of Clause (2) of Article 243Q;

(ii) After such decision is taken by the Governor under Clause (2) of Article 243Q but before publication of final notification under Article 243Q(2), the state government will publish a draft of the proposed notification under Article 243Q(2) of the Constitution in the official Gazette for the information of all persons, likely to be affected therefrom, inviting objections and suggestions in terms of Section 2(3) of the Bihar Municipal Corporation Act, 1978;

(iii) On expiry of a period of six weeks and after considering objection or suggestion, of any, as may be received by the State Government within the said period, if so necessary, the Governor may issue public notification, specifying that area to be an "Industrial Township", in terms of proviso to clause 1(C) of Article 243Q of the Constitution of India;

(iv) If the Governor having regard to the size of the area and taking into consideration the municipal services as being provided or proposed to be provided by an industrial establishment in that area and such other factors, as he may deem fit, is of the opinion that no notification under "Industrial Township" is required to be issued, in such case after taking into consideration the objections, as may be received, and if so required, after making such amendment in the draft, final notification under Sub-section (2) to Article 243Q read with Section 2(3) (b) of the Bihar Municipal Corporation Act, 1978 is to be issued;

(v) Once it is decided and public notification is issued, specifying the area to be an "Industrial Township", in such case there shall be no municipality in the said area. The concerned industrial establishment of that area will provide the municipal services to all persons, living in that area;

(vi) If no public notification declaring such area as "Industrial Township" is issued, the State Government will take steps for constitution of municipalities in terms of Clause (1) of Article 243Q of the Constitution read with Section (1) of the Bihar Municipal Corporation Act, 1978.

III. 28 In the present case no decision has been taken by the Governor of the State, taking into consideration the population of the area, the density of the population therein, revenue generated for the local administration, the percentage of employment in non-agricultural activities, the economic importance and other facts, as to whether the area in question will be declared to be a transitional area or a small urban area or a larger urban area, as required under Clause (2) of Article 243Q of the Constitution of India. Without such decision of the Governor, the state government has issued the proposed draft notification dated 6th December, 2005 under Sub-section (1) and (2) of Section 2 of the Bihar Municipal Corporation Act, 1978. There is nothing on record to suggest that the matter was placed before the State Government (Cabinet) to take decision for the purposes of advising the Governor of the State. It appears that a meeting was held on 8th October, 2005 under the Chairmanship of the Hon'ble Minister, Urban Development Department of the state, in which some of the officers and heads of the Industries took part. In the said meeting a decision was taken for constitution of Municipal Corporation in the area, which was circulated by the Urban Development Department, Government of Jharkhand, Ranchi vide letter No.2598 dated 12th November, 2005 (Annexure 17 to the writ petition). On the basis of such decision taken under the Chairmanship of the Hon'ble Minister of Urban Development Department of the State of Jharkhand and without any advice or decision of the Governor of the State, the impugned notification was issued on 6th December, 2005 and published in the official gazette on 8th December, 2005.

III.29 In the preceding paragraphs, we have discussed as to how steps to be taken in terms Article 243Qread with Section 2 of the Bihar Municipal Corporation Act, 1978. The aforesaid procedure has not been followed in the present case, while notification dated 6th December, 2005 was issued. In this background, the notification, in question, cannot be upheld.

IV.1 W.P.(C) No.872/06 Petitioner Shalkhan Murmoo has also challenged the impugned notification dated 6th December, 2005, published in the Jharkhand Gazette on 8th December, 2005. The said petitioner has specifically pleaded that the villages, as shown between serial no.4 to 21of the notification dated 6th December, 2005 are rural areas (villages). It was argued that those villages are neither transitional areas nor smaller or larger urban areas. The villages shown between serial nos. 4 to 21 of the notification dated 6th December, 2005 have been declared as scheduled areas and are guided by Part IX of the Constitution of India read with the Panchayat (Extension to Scheduled Areas) Act, 1996. It has been specifically pleaded that the aforesaid villages and several other small villages, such as, Kancha having a population of 446, Baragovindpur having a population of 1476, Manpota having a population of 1415, Nutandip having a population of 386, Lupangdih having a population of 454, are rural areas and also scheduled areas. In respect of these areas, already steps have been taken for the *panchayat* election and, thus, according to the petitioner, Shalkhan Murmoo, such areas cannot be included in the Jamshedpur Municipal Corporation.

IV.2 The respondent state has not disputed the aforesaid fact by filing any affidavit. On the other hand, learned Advocate General submitted that the aforesaid mistake with regard to serial nos.4 to 21 have been detected and though a decision has been taken in the file to delete those villages from the final notification, but in view of pendency of these cases, no final notification has been issued. From the aforesaid facts, it will be evident that even the respondents while issuing the impugned notification dated 6th December, 2005 in exercise of power, conferred under Sub-section (1) and (2) of Section 2 of the Bihar Municipal Corporation Act, 1978 had not applied their mind nor have taken care of Article 243Q(2) of the Constitution of India.

V. W.P (PIL) No.364/06: In this Public Interest Litigation, the petitioner firm has also challenged the aforesaid notification dated 6th December, 2005. In view of the findings, as given above, no further decision is required to be given in this case.

VI. In view of the discussions, made above, while this Court is of the opinion that Section 2 of the Bihar Municipal Corporation Act, 1978 is *intra vires* to the Constitution, not being in conflict with any of the provisions of the Constitution, hold that the notification dated 6th December, 2005, issued by the respondents and published in Jharkhand Gazette on 8th December, 2005 is illegal and without jurisdiction. The said notification dated 6th December, 2005 published in the official gazette on 8th December, 2005 is accordingly set aside. The case is remitted to the state government to act in terms of Article 243Q of the Constitution of India and the relevant provisions of law, relating to constitution of Municipality/Industrial Township, as the case may be. They should follow the procedure in accordance with law and in the manner, as discussed at paragraph 3(XXVII) of this judgement. As the Governor of the state, in accordance with law is required to act on the advice of the state government, it is made clear that the State authorities will place the matter before the State i.e. the Cabinet for its recommendation and decision, in accordance with law. It is expected that the respondents will act accordingly and will take a decision at an early date, preferably within three months from the date of receipt/production of a copy of this order.

2

Disqualifications

In this chapter, we will consider the following items:

(i) Background to the regime of disqualification in contesting elections to *panchayat* and *nagarpalikas*.

(ii) Nature and types of disqualification.

Examples:

- the two child norm
- caste affiliations
- financial interest
- office of profit
- criminal convictions

(iii) Information to be disclosed by candidates contesting elections.

Background

For elections to state legislatures and the Parliament, the law on disqualification is contained in the Representation of the People's Act, 1950 as amended by the Representation of the People Second Amendment Act, 2002 as well as the Representation of the People Act, 1951, as amended in 1959 and twice in 2002. In the case of elections to *panchayats* and municipalities, the basic premise is if a person is disqualified for contesting elections to the state legislature, he will be disqualified to contest elections to *panchayats* and municipalities as well. Additionally, it is open to the state legislature under enabling provisions as contained in Articles 243F and 243V of the Constitution to stipulate other disqualifications. The case law in regard to the application of the RP Acts has been extensively dealt with in a large number of cases in the High Courts as well as the Apex Court so far as elections to the Parliament and the state assemblies are concerned. In less than a decade the number of cases relating to disqualifications for contesting *panchayat* and municipal elections have also been numerous. A review of these cases indicates that a wide variety of issues have been agitated. Apart from the stipulations in the RP Acts, the two-child norm and caste affiliations required for contesting reserved seats, have been important issues. Financial interest as well as holding an office of profit, have also been cited as grounds in the cases. In some respects the legal regime is not very different to what has prevailed for long in regard to Parliament and assembly elections.

In some respects like the two child norm, some states have attempted to strike new ground in the hope electoral reforms and selection of suitable candidates may also be initiated from local body level rather than being derived only from national legislation. The interpretation of the stipulations regarding office of profit and financial interest also indicate some variance between Parliament and Assembly elections on the one hand and *panchayat* and municipal elections on the other. Discussion of the case law will help in understanding better the legal regime of electoral disqualifications which is yet to evolve fully in the country. Societal norms and considerations have had their influence in this process of evolution. For instance family planning has been high on the agenda of the national and state governments for several years. The measures taken have ranged widely from awareness programmes about planned parenthood to financial incentives for sterilisation. During the days of the emergency early in the 70s, several governments it was alleged, used coercive methods to promote sterilisation. That political leaders and persons seeking elective offices should set an example by limiting the size of their own family has been a frequently expressed view. Additionally, unauthorised occupation of land belonging to a *panchayat* or a municipality, non-payment of local taxes or non-performance of statutory duties specified in *panchayat* or municipal laws have also been cited as grounds for disqualification.

Types of Disqualification

Some of the states like Andhra, Karnataka, Haryana, Rajasthan, Orissa etc., have stipulated norms in their state laws about the number of children a candidate can have. The application of these laws in disqualifying candidates have given rise to some litigation.

Andhra Pradesh

The relevant provisions of the AP Panchayati Raj Act in section 19(3) reads as follows:

> A person having more than two children shall be disqualified for election or for continuing as member;
>
> Provided that the birth within one year from the date of commencement of the Andhra Pradesh Panchayati Raj Act, 1994 hereinafter in this section referred to as the date of such commencement, of an additional child, shall not be taken into consideration for the purposes of this section;
>
> Provided further that a person having more than two children (excluding the child if any born within one year from the date of such commencement) shall not be disqualified under this section for so long as the number of the children he had on the date of such commencement does not increase;
>
> Provided also that the government may direct that the disqualification in this section shall not apply in respect of a person for reasons to be recorded in writing;

It will be apparent that the actual application of these provisions would require clear evidence of facts, often unlikely to be available.

B.K. Parthasarathi [AIR (2000) A.P. 156] decided on 14.9.1999

The appellant who was chairman of Anantapur *Zilla Parishad* challenged the orders of the AP government seeking to remove him from the post. He was initially elected as Member of Rodam territorial constituency of Anantapur district and subsequently was also elected as Chairman of the *Zilla Parishad* on 20.3.1995. At the time, he contested the election to the office of *Zilla Parishad*, Member, he had four children. However, after being elected as Chairman, *Zila Parishad*, Anantapur, a female child was born to him on 28.4.1997. Birth of an additional child beyond permissible level during the holding of the office under the A.P. Panchayat Act would disqualify a person to hold such office. The petitioner was therefore issued proceedings dated 3.8.1997 intimating about the disqualification. Shri Parthasarathi challenged this order, citing among other grounds, infringement of privacy offending Articles 19 and 21 of the Constitution. A Division Bench held that the right to contest election is a statutory right subject to statutory stipulations. It therefore, upheld the two-child norm stipulated in the Andhra Panchayati Raj Act. It is appropriate to reproduce an extract from the judgement as below:

> We have given our consideration to the genesis of the problem *vis-à-vis* the legislative intention which is brought under Section 19(3) of the A.P. Panchayati Raj Act, 1994. As is evident from the various decisions which are discussed by us, the privacy of a person to lead a life according to his desire has been well recognised by courts. However, there is no reason for us to hold that through the impugned legislation, the privacy of an individual is attacked or sought to be taken away. The legislature, through the impugned legislation, prescribed certain disqualifications for a person either to hold or contest the elected office under the Act if he procreates more children than the prescribed limit. *At the cost of repetition, we must say that choosing to contest an elected office is not a fundamental right but only a right arising out of a statute* (emphasis supplied). That being so, no grievances could be made out on the ground that the right to liberty and right to privacy of an individual are deprived by the impugned legislation. The legislature however, has visualised a contingency arising out of birth of an additional child, during holding of an elected office, which disqualifies a person from holding such office, by empowering the government to hold that such disqualification may not apply in respect of a person, by recording reasons in writing. Therefore, notwithstanding the birth of an additional child beyond the prescribed limit, the government is still empowered to permit such persons to continue in office, by recording reasons in writing. When the legislature has provided this remedy, it cannot be said that the impugned provision is a draconian act of the legislature whereby the right to privacy of a person is deprived and such deprivation offends articles 19 and 21 of the Constitution of India.

> For the foregoing reasons, we find no merit in these writ petitions and we accordingly dismiss the same holding that the rigour of the provision as brought out under Section 19(3) of the Andhra Pradesh Panchayati Raj Act, 1994 is not violative of any fundamental rights or it is in the nature of depriving the privacy of an individual.

In a subsequent case Ragiboyina Bhulakshmi (2002(3) ACT 549) of 2001, decided on 2.4.2002, the case related to the petitioner's election as *sarpanch* of Tatarlapalli *gram panchayat* in Guntur district defeating second respondent in the *gram panchayat* election held on 20.8.2001. She had assumed charge and was discharging her functions as *sarpanch* from the said time onwards. The 2nd respondent filed an election petition before the Election Tribunal headed by the District Munsif. The election petition was filed on the ground that the petitioner was disqualified since prior to getting elected as *sarpanch* she had three children, which is a disqualification under Section 19(3) of the Act. The writ petition was filed questioning the election petition on the ground of discrimination and also on the ground of the remedy being more harsh than provided under Section 22 of the Act. It was also stated that under Section 22 of the Act any voter can give an intimation that a particular member of the *gram panchayat* was disqualified but only a member or executive authority, on the direction of the *gram panchayat* alone, will be entitled to file a petition to declare such member as disqualified under sections 17, 18, 19 and 20 of the Act. The order of the District Munsif were upheld and the petition was dismissed.

Punjab and Haryana

Fazru and Anr. *versus* State of Haryana (CWP No. 11439 of 1997) (1998) IPLR222 decided on 4.11.1997

In this civil writ petition the petitioner challenged the Constitutional Validity of Section 175 (1)(q) of the Haryana Panchayati Raj Act, 1994 stipulating the two-child norm as impinging upon one's private life and liberty and also violating Article 14 of the Constitution of India. It was held that the two-child norm is not a violation of Article 14 of the Constitution of India and right to fight election is merely a statutory right.

In Jagat Singh *versus* State of Haryana, CWP No. 533 of 2001 decided on 4.2.2002 the question arose as to whether a person having more than two children could avoid disqualification under Section 175(I) by giving one child in adoption. The Court held that the arrangement was devoid of any merit for the simple reason that the expression "having more than two children" would include children given in adoption. Had the legislature intended otherwise a separate provision would have been added.

Rajasthan

A number of cases were adjudicated in the Rajasthan High Court relating to the two-child norm.

In Mukesh Kumar Ajmera *versus* State of Rajasthan CWP No.2340 of 1997 decided on 4.4.1997, it was held that a person would be disqualified if the number of his children became more than two even after his election. In other words, exceeding the two-child norm would render a *sarpanch* ineligible to continue to hold the office in the event that the number of his children exceeds two.

This stand of the High Court was reiterated in Ansi Devi Vs. State of Rajasthan and others, CWP No. 1730 of 2001 decided on 7.11.2001. In this case the petitioner had been disqualified because she had more than two children at the time of her election. The High Court held the relevant provisions in the Rajasthan Act stipulating the two-child norm as valid and not infringing the Constitution.

In Bhadar Ram *versus* Sant Ram and Anr. C.W.P. No. 963 of 2002 decided on 19.3.2002. The petitioner was elected as *sarpanch* of *gram panchayat* 29 DWD on 31.1.2000. An objection was taken before the Returning Officer that in view of provisions of Section 19(1) (iv) of Rajasthan Panchayati Raj Act, 1994, the petitioner was not qualified to be a candidate at election because he was father of five children and two of them were born after 27.11.1995, a date after which any offspring in addition to two children has been construed to be a disqualification for being candidate at election. The returning officer did not react to the objection and accepted the nomination papers of the petitioner. After the election of the petitioner as *sarpanch* an election petition was filed challenging the election of the petitioner by the respondent No.1, Sant Ram. The Election Tribunal came to the conclusion that two offsprings of the petitioner were indeed born after 27.11.1995 and therefore, the petitioner was disqualified from being elected as *sarpanch*. In the writ petition the Hon'ble High Court did not find any infirmity in the order of the Election Tribunal and held the same to be correct.

The Supreme Court

The two-child norm stipulated in various state laws and its constitutional validity eventually came up before the Apex Court through numerous writ petitions in Javed's case (2003(8) SCC 369, decided on 30.7.2003). Some of these were on special leave to appeal and some arose from the High Court decisions. The *vires* of the Haryana Panchayati Raj Act, 1994 Sections 175 and 177 in the context of Articles 14, 21, 25, 38, 47, 51A, 243F, 243G and 246 were extensively argued. A three Judge Bench of the Supreme Court consisting of R.C. Lahoti, Ashok Bhan and Arun Kumar J.J. upheld the validity of the Act. Apart from the reasonableness of the differentiation, which the impugned act sought to make between those having more than two children and others, the issue of religious belief and practices was also agitated. The Apex Court upheld the validity of the relevant state laws. The Court held that the "classification was founded on an intelligible differentia and that the object of the law was to create a disincentive in keeping with the family welfare programme and policy through a disqualification for a *panchayat* office, which at any rate was only a statutory right." The disqualification based on the two-child norm and the right to contest an election, the court held, did not contravene any fundamental right. In view of the important implications as well as significant interpretations of the law and the relevant constitutional provisions, extracts of the Supreme Court judgement (2003(8) SCC 369) are reproduced in the Annexure A-2.1.

It is however important to mention that while the matter has become settled law, the policy itself is now being questioned in the Central as well as some of the state governments. It is being argued that the two-child norm is insensitive to gender issues and of dubious value in population planning. While the law on the matter is settled, the policy continues to be in debate. The Ministry of Panchayati Raj itself has expressed the view in various papers and seminars that it considers the two-child norm as regressive. However, so long as the law remains on the statute books of some of the states, its constitutional validity is settled as per the Apex Court's decision in Javed's case.

Financial Interest

The nature and extent of financial interest perceived to be held by a candidate at the time of contesting elections or thereafter and how this can amount to a disqualification have been dealt with in several cases adjudicated before the different High Courts.

Andhra

In Chava Rosaiah *versus* Chintala Venkateswarlu and another (2004(1) (ALT 327) D.B, decided on 21.11.2003), the High Court held that whether a particular type of financial interest acted as a disqualification has to be decided in the first instance by the district court and only thereafter disqualification and removal can take place. The judgement relates to the procedure for determining disqualifications.

Maharashtra

In Indumati Laxman Bhakare *versus* State of Maharashtra (2004(3) MHLJ decided on 17.3.2004), the question arose whether the spouse of a councillor who was executing various contracts on behalf of the Municipal Council could be considered disqualified. In this case Indumati contested the election to the post of the President of the Municipal Council of Sambola, which was held on 2nd December 2001 and was declared elected to the post, which was reserved for women. It transpired, the husband of the elected candidate had been awarded by the Sambole Municipal Council various contracts for maintenance of roads, sewerage etc. A total of 19 different categories of work had been awarded to him at a cost of over Rs. 10 lakhs. On 9th November 2001, which was the date on which the contractor's wife Indumati filed her nomination, her spouse, the contractor wrote to the Chief Executive Officer of the Municipal Council that as his wife intended to contest as a candidate either to the post of a member of the Municipal Council or to the post of the President, he was not in a position to complete the work, which had been awarded to him previously under the contracts. The contractor further undertook that he would be responsible to the Municipal Council to reimburse any loss that may be incurred on account of termination of the contracts. In response to this letter the Chief Executive Officer of the municipality by a letter of the same date stated that all the contracts stood terminated. However, on 25th January, 2002 i.e. about two months after Smt. Indumati was declared elected as President of the Municipal Council, the Council sanctioned the payment of all the bills of the contractor in respect of the work which had been completed upto 9th November. The Council further resolved fresh tenders would be invited for the work which remained to be completed and any financial loss caused to the Municipal Council would be recovered from the contractor in accordance with what had been agreed upon by him.

An election petition was filed challenging the election of Smt. Indumati on the ground that though her spouse had terminated his contracts with the Municipal Council before Indumati's nomination, the financial interest subsisted in so far as payments were still due to the contractor and the resolution of the Council dated 25th January, 2002 to which Smt. Indumati was a party in her capacity as President of the Council amounted to a conflict of interest and duty. The petition accordingly sought her disqualification in view of the provisions of section 16(I)(i) of the Maharashtra Municipal Councils, Nagar Panchayats and Industrial Townships Act, 1965.

The Additional District Judge who heard the election petition held that there was indeed a conflict of interest. The contracts awarded to Smt. Indumati's spouse though terminated prior to her contesting the elections subsisted as a financial interest, since payments were not made. As such the Additional District Judge held Smt. Indumati incurred a disqualification. The appeal challenging this decision was dismissed by the Maharashtra High Court. This case illustrates how a financial interest can subsist unless fully and completely extinguished or else it would generate a conflict of interest and therefore a disqualification to contest the election.

In Rajan Ramnath Patil *versus* State of Maharashtra, 2001(3) MHLJ, the High Court considering Section 16(3) (b) of the Maharashtra Municipal Councils, Nagar Panchayats and Industrial Townships Act gave an important interpretation of another kind of financial interest. This provision of the state law reads as follows:

> 16(3) a person shall not be deemed to have incurred disqualification under clause (i) of sub-section (1) by reason of having any share or interest in any company or cooperative society which contracts with the Council or be employed by on behalf of the Council.

The petitioner who was an elected councillor of the Municipal Council was also elected as Chairman of the Education Committee constituted under Section 63 of the Maharashtra Municipal Councils, Nagar Panchayats and Industrial Townships Act. He was also Chairman of the Kalasgiri Nagari Co-operative Credit Society. As chairman of the Education Committee the petitioner decided that Rs. Five lakhs of the Primary Education Fund be placed as a fixed deposit in the Kalasgiri Nagari Co-operative Credit Society. The petitioner was called upon to show cause as to why action under Section 44(I)(b) of the Maharashtra Municipal Councils, Nagar Panchayats and Industrial Townships act should not be taken against him. Eventually, the Collector disqualified the petitioner under Section 44(I)(b) read with Section 16(3)(b) of the said Act. Order of the Collector was challenged in the writ petition.

The High Court held that the co-operative credit society in which the primary education fund had made the fixed deposit did not contract with or was employed by or on behalf of the Municipal Council. There was no conflict of financial interest between the Municipal Council and the Credit Society. Therefore, the Collector was not justified in taking action against the Petitioner under Section 44(I)(b) read with Section 16(3)(b) of the Act. The impugned order disqualifying the petitioner as councillor was accordingly quashed and set aside.

Tamil Nadu

R. Kannimuthu *versus* Rajendran and Two Others (2001(4) CTC 366 decided on 14.9.2001)

In this case, the question came up whether contracts awarded to the elected chairperson's son who was dependent on him amounted to a disqualification. Evidence showed that the son was living with his father as a dependent. As such the Court held this would be a disqualification. Similarly in K.V. Muthurama Lingam (2003 (1) MLJ 700), the Madras High Court held that a person is disqualified from contesting elections, if he has a subsisting contract with the *gram panchayat* at the time of election as specified under Section 37 of the relevant state act.

Office of Profit

Holding an "Office of Profit" as a disqualification for contesting elections has been a vexed issue for several years in regard to elections to the Parliament and the state legislatures. The definition of such an office and the various factors which would render holding such an office a disqualification, have been the subject of several election petitions and adjudication in different High Courts. It is open to the Parliament to declare some such offices as not disqualifying. The list of such offices was expanded significantly to contain 55 items by the Parliament (Prevention of Disqualification) Amendment Act, 2006. Legislatures have found it more convenient to specify various offices and excluding them from being an electoral disqualification rather than devise and apply objective criteria to identify such offices. However, the principles in this regard have been laid down in Supreme Court judgement in the well known Inamdar's case.

As in the case of elections to the Parliament and the state legislatures the holding of an "Office of Profit" as a ground for disqualification has affected the *panchayat* and municipal elections as well. However, a review of the cases and judgements in the different High Courts presents a highly varied picture. The cases reviewed are from Bihar, Kerala, Karnataka, Maharashtra and UP.

Bihar

Janakdhari Prasad *Versus* the State Election Commission
AIR 2004 PAT 133 decided on 4.8.2004

In this case while the petitioner was Assistant Government Pleader, he contested the election for membership of *Panchayat Samiti*, Nagarnousa in the district of Nalanda and got elected. Later an election petition was filed before the State Election Commission on the ground that the petitioner was disqualified because of his holding, on the relevant date, the position of Assistant Government Pleader which should be regarded as an office of profit under the government.

Section 139(1) (c) of the Bihar Panchayati Raj Act states that a person shall be disqualified before election or after election for holding the post as member of the *Panchayati Samiti* etc., if he is "in the service of the central or state government or any local authority." Accordingly, the State Election Commission held him as disqualified. A writ petition No. (WJC 4322 of 2004) was filed in the High Court of Patna challenging this order. After careful examination of the terms and conditions attached to the engagement and work of Assistant Government Pleader, the High Court held that the Assistant Government Pleader is appointed to assist the Government Pleader and for the professional work rendered, he is paid remuneration but not paid any retainer fee. He is basically an advocate like any other in the roll of the State Bar Council and besides giving professional advice to other litigants, he also advises and represents the state governments in courts of law. The engagement of an advocate as an Assistant Government Pleader is a professional engagement and the relationship between the state and the Assistant Government Pleader is that of a 'lawyer and client' and not 'master and servant.' There is no age limit, salary or time scale and no conduct or disciplinary rules other than the code of conduct.

The High Court held that these factors show that the Assistant Government Pleader cannot be said to be 'in the service of the state government' so as to bring him within the mischief of Section 139(1)(c) of the Act. The High Court further observed that a person may hold an "office of profit" under the state but at the same time cannot be said to be 'in service of the state.' Accordingly the High Court allowed the application and set aside the impugned order. It may be mentioned in this connection that five years before this judgement, a similar issue had come to the attention of the Supreme Court.

In Rabindra Nayak *versus* Collector, Mayurbanj (AIR, 1999 SC 1120/1999(1) SCALE 564) the Apex court laid stress more on the person holding the appointment of Assistant Public Prosecutor on the relevant date rather than the duration or other aspects of the appointment. The orders in the Janakdhari Prasad's case do not show that any reference was made to the Apex Court's judgement though it had come five years earlier. It is a moot point whether this would have affected the decision.

Kerala

Marykutty Mathew (2002(3) KLT 773 Decided on 8.11.2002

An employee of a co-operative society registered under the provision of the Kerala Co-operative Societies Act, 1969 was elected as a member of the *panchayat*. It was alleged that while retaining employment she continued to hold office as a member of the *panchayat*. The question was whether the State Election Commission could determine whether this was a disqualification under Section 36 of the Kerala Panchayati Raj Act?

Chapter VII of the Kerala Panchayati Raj Act comprising Sections 29 to 38 deals with qualifications and disqualifications of candidates and members. S.30 provides as follows:

> 30. Disqualification of officers and employees of government, local authorities, etc., (1) No officer or employee in a state or central government or of a local authority or a corporation controlled by the state or central government or of a local authority or any company in which the state or central government or a local authority (not less than fifty one per cent share) or of a statutory Board or of any

University in the state shall be qualified for election or for holding office as a member of a *panchayat* at any level.

Explanation: For the purpose of this section, company means a Government company as defined in S.617 of the Companies Act, 1956 (Central Act 1 of 1956) and includes a co-operative Society registered or deemed to be registered under the Kerala Co-operative Societies Act, 1969 (21 of 1969).

S.36. Determination of subsequent disqualification of a member (1) Wherever a question arises as to whether a member has become disqualified under S.30 or S.35 except clause (n) thereof after having been elected as a member, any member of the *panchayat* concerned or any other person entitled to vote at the election in which the member was elected, may file a petition before the State Election Commission, for decision.

The High Court held that in view of clause (b) of Article 243-O of the Constitution an election to the *panchayat* can be disputed only by an election petition as provided under the Kerala Panchayati Raj Act, 1994. The court noted that Section 36 provided for "Determination of subsequent disqualification of a member" and it is only those questions regarding disqualification under Section 30 or Section 35, after having been elected as a member, are referable to the State Election Commission. In other words, once a candidate is elected as a member, even assuming he had at the time of election, incurred disqualifications under Section 30 or Section 35 of the Kerala Panchayati Raj Act, it is not for the State Election Commission to embark upon an enquiry regarding such disqualification after the election. The jurisdiction of the State Election Commission is confined to disqualification incurred after having been elected as a member. In case, a member accepts employment in a Co-operative Society subsequent to the elections, it is a matter for the Commission to consider whether this amounted to a post election disqualification. The State Election Commission has no jurisdiction to entertain a petition with regard to a disqualification already incurred by a member under Section 30 or 35 of the Act prior to the election.

Mercy John (2002 (3) KLT decided on 22.5.2003)

The important question that arose for consideration in this case was whether a teacher of an aided school managed by the *Panchayat* was disqualified under Section 30(a) of the Kerala Panchayati Raj Act from contesting the election for being chosen to fill a seat in the *panchayat*. The Kerala Panchayats (Spread of Education) Rules, 1964 read as follows:

> *Panchayat* may establish and maintain schools subject to the provisions of the Kerala Education Act.
>
> (1) A *panchayat* may, subject to the provisions of the Kerala Education Act, 1958 (6 of 1959) and the rules made thereunder establish and maintain schools providing facilities for the spread of education within the *panchayat* area.
>
> (2) For the purposes of the Kerala Education Act, 1958 and the rules made thereunder, such schools shall be considered as aided schools. The *panchayat* shall be the educational agency, and the Executive Officer of the *panchayat* shall be the manager, in respect of such schools.
>
> (3) Every appointment to a school established and maintained by a *panchayat* shall be made by the manager with the approval of the educational agency in accordance with the provisions of the Kerala Education Act, 1958 and the rules made thereunder.

Section 34(g) reads as follows:

> 34. Disqualification of candidates. (1) A person shall be disqualified for being chosen as and for being a member of a *panchayat* at any level if he:
>
> (g) is interested in a subsisting contract made with or any work being done for the government or the *panchayat* concerned except as a shareholder (other than a Director) in a company or except as permitted by rules made under this Act.

It was held that teachers of an aided school managed by the *panchayat* is not disqualified under Section 30(1) of the Act from contesting the election for seats in the *panchayat* since they are not employees of the *panchayat*. It was further held that an elected candidate working as an Implementation Officer of People's Planning Scheme of a Panchayat cannot be treated as a contractor or doing any work for the "concerned *panchayat*." The above disqualification would apply for contesting to the 'concerned *panchayat*' only and not to the district *panchayat*. The High Court also opined that the law does not permit duplication or repetitive decisions on the same issue by different statutory authorities at different stages. Further probe is possible only in appeal, revision or other forms by higher authorities.

Karnataka

M. Kumar *versus* Bharat Earth Movers Ltd and Others (AIR 1999 KAR LJ 193 (FB) decided on 22nd January 1999

This is an important case, which went up to the full bench of the Karnataka High Court addressing the question whether a company like Bharat Earth Movers Ltd where the government is a majority share holder should be regarded as 'other authorities' under Article 12 of the Constitution and therefore the employees of such companies are disqualified to become councillors of municipal corporations. Briefly stated the facts are the petitioner M. Kumar was a workman in the Bharat Earth Movers Ltd. Two other persons, one Chandramma and one Muni Raju were working as office staff in the Indian Telephone Industries. All the petitioners sought permission from their respective company managements to contest the Bangalore City Corporation Elections. This permission was refused. A writ petition was then moved. A Single Judge of the Karnataka High Court referred the matter to a Division Bench for adjudication of the constitutional validity of Section 26(1)(c) of the Karnataka Municipal Corporation Act. This Section reads as follows:

> 26. General disqualification for becoming a Councillor
>
> (1) A person shall be disqualified for being chosen as and for being a Councillor:
>
> If he holds any office of profit under the Government of India or the government of any state specified in the First Schedule to the Constitution of India, or under any local or other authority subject to the control of any of the said governments other than such offices as are declared by rules made under this Act not to disqualify the holder.

Article 12 of the Constitution reads as follows:

> 12. Definition: In this part, unless the context otherwise requires, 'the State' includes the Government and Parliament of India and the government and the legislature of each of the States and all local or

other authorities within the territory of India or under the control of the Government of India.

The Division Bench referred the matter to a full bench for adjudication to consider (a) whether the employees of the respondent company are eligible to contest elections in the Municipal Corporation in view of the provisions of Section 26(1)(c) of the KMC Act, 1976 and (b) whether 'other authority' referred to in Article 12 of the Constitution of India is only with reference to exercise of fundamental rights in respect of the matters enumerated in Parts III and IV of the Constitution of India and not for the purpose of Chapter XIV of the Constitution and thereby Section 26(1)(c) of the KMC Act does not disqualify the employees of the Government Company or other public sectors.

There were elaborate arguments during the case before a Full Bench comprising three judges, Acting Chief Justice Bhaskara Rao, N S Veerabhadraiah J and Ravindran J. The CJ and Veerabhadraiah J held that these companies where the government was a majority shareholder do come within the meaning of the words "other authority." Holding an office in these companies therefore amounts to holding an office of profit in terms of Section 26(1)(c) of the KMC Act. As such the employees of Bharat Earth Movers Ltd and Indian Telephone Industries are disqualified to contest the elections of the Municipal Corporation. Shri Raveendran J in his dissenting judgement examined the intent of an electoral law excluding persons holding an office of profit from contesting elections. Referring to the Supreme Court's decision in Madhukar G.E. Pankakar Vs. Jaswant Chobbildas Rajani (AIR 1976 SC2283) as also the observations of the Constitution Bench of the Apex court in Kirpal Singh Vs. Uttam Singh and another (AIR 1986 SC 300), Justice Raveendran held that there was no logic in excluding the employees of public sector undertakings from municipal elections. It is relevant and useful to note some of the observations which the Apex Court had made in both these cases as quoted in Justice Ravindran's dissenting judgement.

(From Madhukar's Case)

After all, all laws are a means to an end. What is the legislative end here in disqualifying holders of offices of profit under the Government? Obviously to avoid a conflict between duty and interest, to cut out the misuse of official position, to advance private benefit and to avert the likelihood of influencing government to promote personal advantage. So this is the mischief to be suppressed. At the same time we have to bear in mind that our Constitution mandates the state to undertake multiform public welfare and socio-economic activities involving technical persons, welfare workers and lay people on a massive scale so that participatory government may prove a progressive reality. In such an expanding situation, can we keep out from elective posts at various levels many doctors, lawyers, engineers and scientists, not to speak of an army of other non-officials who are wanted in various fields, not as full time government servants but as part-time participants in people's projects sponsored by the government?. For instance, if a National Legal Service Authority funded largely by the state comes into being, a large segment of the legal profession may be employed part-time in the ennobling occupation of legal aid to the poor. Doctors, lawyers, engineers, scientists and other experts may have to be invited into local bodies, legislatures and like political and administrative organs based on election if these vital limbs of representative government are not to be the monopoly of populist politicians or lay members but sprinkled with technicians in an age which belongs to technology. *So, an interpretation of 'office of profit' to cast the net so wide that all our citizens with specialties and know-how are inhibited from entering elected organs of public administration and offering semi-voluntary services in para-official, statutory or like projects run or directed by government or Corporation controlled by the state may be detrimental to democracy itself* (emphasis supplied). Even athletes may hesitate to come into sports councils if some fee for services is paid and that proves their funeral if elected to a *panchayat*. A balanced view even if it involves 'judicious irreverence' to vintage precedents, is the wiser desideratum.

The clear and undoubted object of Article 191(1)(a) to (e) and the provisions of the Representation of the People Act (including Section 10) is the preservation of the purity and integrity of the election process by preventing government or state employees from taking part in the elections. But, Section 10 appears to confine the disqualification in so far as it relates to the employees of government companies to the 'top-brass' only if such an uncouth expression may be allowed to creep into the judgement of a court. Nowadays the

> activities of the state are so manifold and prolific that the state has been forced in the interests of better management and administration and in order to further the Directive Principles of State Policy, to set up various corporations which are but mere instrumentalities of the state. Is the principle of Article 191(1)(a) then to be extended to employees of state corporations also by enacting appropriate laws under Article 191(1)(e)? Or are employees of public corporations to be treated differently from employees of the government. Are not some of them in a better position to exert undesirable pressure than government employees? On the other hand, are a tremendously large number of employees of public corporations to be denied the opportunity to being chosen as representatives of the people? Do all the considerations applicable to government employees equally apply to employees of public sector undertakings? Is there no distinguishing feature? Are a large mass of highly or moderately literate people to be denied the right to speak for the public? Is the right to be elected, to be confined, without meaning any disrespect to anyone but the professional politicians only? These are some of the vital questions posed and which require to be answered. The answer should be best given by the elected representatives of the people themselves. We are not shirking the decision on these questions but our decision can only be confined to interpretation. That is why, we recommend to the government to have the matter examined by the Law commission very early. When a suitable occasion arises in the future, we will of course, deal with the matter, probably helped by new legislation.

Justice Raveendran made a reference to the situation in Bangalore and nearby areas such as Kolar Gold Fields or Dooravaninagar, which are virtually made up of employees of ITI and their families. The learned judge pointed out that there is no reason why they should be prevented from having a say in the local self-government. They, as a category are interested in the welfare of the area, where they reside and if they are elected there will be no conflict between their duties and functions as councillors and their duties and functions as employees of public sector undertakings. Therefore, they should not be excluded from participation in the running of the local authority unless the statute specifically bars or excludes them. According to the dissenting judgement Section 26(1)(c) of the KMC Act is not intended to exclude the employees of government companies and therefore there is no legal bar for the employees of the Bharat Earth Movers Ltd and Indian Telephone Industries to contest the elections. The points contained in the dissenting judgement merit careful consideration. However, the majority judgement prevailed which does not appear to have been challenged in the Apex Court subsequently.

Shashikala *versus* State of Karnataka (ILR 2005 KIR 1.4.2005) decided 1.8.2005

The extent to which the application or non-application of mind can occur in determining whether a particular position is an office of profit is illustrated in this case. Here the petitioner was working as a cook under food for work programme called "Bisy Oota" scheme and earning Rs. 650/- per month. The nomination of the petitioner for contesting the *gram panchayat* election was rejected on the ground that she was holding an office of profit. In deciding the writ petition filed to challenge this decision, the court held non-disclosure of the employment under the *Bisy Oota* scheme is not fatal to contest the election. The court also held that the clarification issued by the State Election Commission that staff working under the *Bisy Oota* scheme are disqualified to contest was not constitutionally valid. The court held that every resident of the *gram panchayat* area whose name is enlisted in the voters list has got a statutory right to contest the elections of a *gram panchayat*. Such right cannot be taken away by the executive orders passed by the State government. The writ petition was accordingly allowed and the respondent Returning Officer was directed to accept the nomination of the petitioner.

Maharashtra

M.P. Deulkar *versus* Commissioner Nagpur Division (W.P. No. 325 of 2003 decided on 26.2.2003)

The petitioner, an employee with Western Coal Fields, a subsidiary of Coal India Ltd was elected as Councilor of *Zila Parishad* Chandrapura. The petitioner was working as Pump *Khalasi* of Western India Coal Field Ltd. Proceedings under section 40 of the

Maharashtra Zila Parishad and Panchayat Samiti Act 1961 seeking to disqualify the petitioner was initiated as it was claimed he was holding an 'office of profit under the government.' Eventually, he was disqualified under the provision of Section 16(1)(h) of the said Act by the order of the Commissioner, Nagpur Division which was challenged in this writ petition by Deulkar.

It was specifically urged before the Commissioner that in a similar case decided by the Apex Court in Pradyut Bordolai Vs. Swapan Roy, 2001(2) SCC 19, it was held that holding a post in the North East India Coal Fields, another subsidiary of Coal India was not an 'office of profit under the government' and as such the petitioner was not to be disqualified in functioning as a member of the legislative assembly. Nevertheless the Commissioner did not take into consideration this decision. The High Court, in allowing the writ petition, clarified the various characteristics of an 'office of profit under the government' and set aside the order of the Commissioner, Nagpur, and held Deulkar the petitioner, was entitled to function as Councillor of the Chandrapura *Zilla Parishad*.

Anil Tatya Rao Solanki 2001 (1) MLJ 457 decided on 8.10.1999

The petitioner was elected as a councilor of the Beed Municipal Council in December 1996. At that time the petitioner was not employed anywhere. In November 1997, the petitioner was appointed as daily wage contractor by Maharashtra State Road Transport Corporation, Beed. A petition was moved before the Collector for disqualification. The Collector after making the necessary enquiry disqualified him on 15.12.1998 under Section 19 (1)(g) under the Maharashtra Nagar Panchayat, Municipal Council and Industrial Townships Act. This was challenged in a writ petition. The High Court held that the Maharashtra State Road Transport Corporation is a separate statutory body even though there may be government support to such a body. The post of a daily wage contractor, which the petitioner was holding, was not an office of profit under the government or any Local Body. Accordingly the order was quashed.

Uttar Pradesh

Meghraj Singh *versus* State of U.P. and Others,
C.W.P. No. 15482 of 2001 (3) AWC 1880, decided on 26.4.2004

Meghraj Singh, the petitioner who was working as a conductor in the U.P. State Road Transport Corporation successfully contested for the office of *Pradhan* of Hazratpur *panchayat* in Bulandshar district on 14.6.2004. Later his election was challenged in an election petition on the ground that as an employee of the UPSRTC under the state government, he stood disqualified. The District *Panchayat* officer acting as the Prescribed Authority, after hearing the petition held Meghraj Singh was disqualified and directed him to hand over charge to the *Up-pradhan* by his order dated 7.4.2001. A writ petition was filed challenging this order. Section 5(a) of the UP Panchayat Act identifies the following persons as disqualified:

> A person who holds any office of profit under a state government or the central government or a local authority, other than a *gram panchayat* or *nyaya panchayat* or a Board, body or corporation owned or controlled by the state government or the Central government.

The petitioner submitted that a board, body or corporation owned or controlled by the state government was excluded from the purview of disqualification. However, the High Court while relying only on the language of the relevant provision including the placement of punctuation marks rather than the intent rejected the contention. The High Court held that an employee of such a corporation was not excluded and would therefore fall under disqualification. This order of the UP High Court is clearly at variance with the judgement in Solanki's case by the Bombay High Court.

Supreme Court

The question whether holding an office of profit, even though the person holding it may be doing so as a temporary or a stopgap arrangement, would still amount to a disqualification, was settled by the Apex Court in a Special Leave Petition from Orissa. In Rabindra Kumar Nayak *versus* Collector, Mayurbanj and others (AIR, 1999 SC 1120/1999 (1) SCALE 564, decided on 19.2.1999), the

Supreme Court considered the matter in some detail. The facts of the case as summarised by the High Court are as follows:

> On August 15, 1995, the appellant, an advocate practising in the court of Cuttack was appointed as Assistant Public Prosecutor provisionally. While so, he contested the election to the Moroda *Panchayat Samiti* as a member and the 4th respondent contested for the seat of a member of Gudigaon *Panchayat Samiti*. After being elected as members, both of them contested in the election to the post of Chairman of the Moroda *Panchayat Samiti*. On February 10, 1997 having lost in the contest the 4th respondent initiated a proceeding against the appellant under Section 45B of the Orissa Panchayat Samiti Act in the court of the District Judge Mayurbanj on the ground that the appellant was holding an office of profit under the government as Assistant Public Prosecutor and so he was not eligible to be a member or a chairman of the Moroda *Panchayat Samiti*. The appellant resisted this proceeding on two grounds; first that his appointment as Assistant Public Prosecutor was a stop-gap arrangement only and as such he was not holding an office of profit and the second was the petition filed by the 4th respondent under Section 45B of the Panchayati Raj Act was not maintainable because after the election was over, the only remedy available to him was to file an election petition under Section 44A. In September 1997, the District Judge held that the petition under Section 45B was maintainable, that the appellant was indeed holding an office of profit under the government and therefore he was disqualified. The appellant challenged the order before the Orissa High Court. In March, 1998 the High Court dismissed the writ petition confirming the said order of the learned District judge. Against that order the appellant moved the Supreme Court by special leave petition.

The Apex Court came to the conclusion that irrespective of the temporary nature of the appointment, the appellant was indeed holding an office of profit. After analysing a catena of cases pertaining to the definition of an office of profit, the Apex Court observed as follows:

> It is contended, the appointment of the appellant was a stop-gap arrangement and that it could not be said that he was holding an office of profit. This contention is devoid of merit. From what is stated above, it is clear that to fulfill the requirements of the said expression, it must be shown that *permanency is attached to the office and not to the term for which a person holds it. Persons who fill the office come and go in succession.* One may succeed the other after a long gap or in quick

> succession. How long one remains in office is irrelevant to decide whether he holds it as office of profit. *We have, therefore, no hesitation in concluding that the appellant was holding office of profit on the relevant date and was not eligible to stand for election of member of Chairman of the Panchayati Samiti* and in view of the provision of clause (i) of sub-section (2) of Section 45 he shall cease to be member or be the Chairman of the *Samiti* (emphasis supplied).

In the result, the order under appeal was confirmed and the Special Leave Petition dismissed.

Pradyut Bordolai *versus* Swapan Roy
(AIR 2001 SC 296/2000(8) SCALE 297) decided on 12.12.2000

This is another case where the issue of an office of profit under the government came up for consideration of the Apex Court. In May and June 1998, a by-election to the Margarita Legislative Assembly, Constituency No.124 was held. Swapan Roy the respondent in the present case had filed a nomination for contesting the election. He was working as a clerk in the North Eastern Coal Fields under Coal India Ltd. On a complaint against his candidature that he was holding an office of profit in the Government Company, the Returning Officer rejected his nomination. Thereafter in the elections held, the appellant Pradyut Bordolai was declared elected. The respondent filed an election petition challenging the appellant's election, stating that his own nomination has been wrongly rejected. The High Court held that the nomination paper was improperly rejected and as such the election of the appellant was void. The matter then came on appeal to the Supreme Court.

Here again the Supreme Court reviewed a number of judgements in earlier cases and relied on the criteria which the apex Court had laid down in Shiv Murthy Swamy Inamdar case (1971(3) SCC 870) commonly known as the Inamdar case. In this case, the Court had laid down various tests to find out whether the office in question is an office of profit under the government. These tests are: (1) whether the government makes the appointment, (2) whether the government has a right to remove or dismiss the holder, (3) whether the government pays the remuneration, (4) what are the functions of the holder and whether he performs them for the government and (5) does the government exercise any control over the performance of those functions. In the present case, the court found that the government was not the appointing or the removal authority and since this basic determinative test having been answered further the probe was not necessary. Accordingly, the Apex Court upheld the order of the High Court.

As mentioned earlier though this decision of the Apex Court was available, it was not followed in the Maharashtra case of M.P. Deulkar discussed earlier where the case involved a Pump Khalasi of the Western India Coal Fields Ltd.

Similarly in Meghraj Singh's case as well as M. Kumar's case discussed earlier, the ratio is not in consonance with Bordolai's case as laid down by the Apex Court. The dissenting judgement in Kumar's case elucidates the intent of the restriction on public servants contesting elections.

It is respectfully suggested that the ratio in Bordolai's case should be used as the touchstone to review the rather contradictory judgements in some of the high court cases mentioned.

Criminal Convictions

Under the Representation of Peoples Act as well as the state laws relating to local body elections, conviction for certain crimes are regarded as a disqualification for specified periods, for contesting elections to the Parliament and state legislatures. Such disqualification applies generally in the case of *panchayat* and municipal elections as well and it is expected that in such cases the nominations will be rejected at the time of filing itself. There is also a regime for disclosure of information about past criminal convictions. In many cases it is seen the facts of past conviction or prosecution are brought out after the elections, which are agitated in election petitions or later on in the High Courts.

Some cases of this nature are discussed here.

Bihar

Lal Rai *versus* State of Bihar and Others, (2003(3) BLJR 1731

In this case the point agitated was that if a candidate elected as *mukhiya* of a *gram panchayat* is subsequently disqualified, whether another candidate who obtained the second largest number of votes could be declared elected as *mukhiya*. In the present case in the elections held in 2001, one Ram Kewal Singh was declared elected as *mukhiya* of Alwalpur *gram panchayat* in Patna district. Subsequently it came to the knowledge of the State Election Commission that at the time of filing his nomination Kewal Singh had concealed the information that he had been convicted and sentenced to undergo imprisonment for seven years which would have acted as a disqualification on him. Accordingly the Commission by its order dated 1.7.2002 unseated him. A writ petition and a further appeal against this order was dismissed. The petitioner in the present case claimed that since Kewal Singh has been unseated and as the petitioner had secured the second largest number of votes for the post of *mukhiya*, he should be declared elected and allowed to function as *mukhiya*. Section 145 of the Bihar Panchayati Raj Act contains a provision that if the Prescribed Authority is of the opinion that but for the votes obtained by the returned candidate by corrupt practices, some other candidate would have obtained a majority of the valid votes, the Prescribed Authority shall declare that person to have been duly elected. The High Court decided that though the petitioners claim appeared to be attractive, it had no substance, as there was no specific provision that the candidate obtaining the second largest number of votes should be declared as *mukhiya*. The facts and circumstances of the instant case were different and therefore the provision under Section 145 would not apply. The petition was accordingly dismissed.

Rajasthan

Hanuman Prasad *versus* District Judge Mirtha and Others (AIR, 2001 RAJ 398) decided on 16.3.2001

In this petition, the order of the Election Tribunal by which the election of the petitioner was declared void and a direction was issued to hold fresh election was challenged. The reason why the tribunal held the election void was because at the time of filing the nomination, there was a criminal charge pending against the petitioner, though subsequently, during the pendency of the election petition itself, he was acquitted. The tribunal had held that since on the relevant date i.e. the date for filing the nomination there was a criminal charge pending, subsequent acquittal could not alter the position.

The High Court took note of several judgements of the Apex Court in this regard and observed that the democratic rights of contesting or voting in the election are statutory rights and have to be exercised in accordance with the statue creating the same. The Court further held that "being charged with a criminal offence of particular description" is an entirely different thing from "conviction of a particular offence." Both are distinct happenings and have to be distinctly considered. If being charged is made statutorily a disqualification, as in the case under relevant Rajasthan law it cannot be wiped of by a subsequent acquittal.

Shiv Ram *versus* State of Rajasthan (AIR 2002 Raj 416)

In this case, disqualification was incurred by the petitioner having been sentenced to imprisonment for six months by a competent court. This provision for disqualification was provided through an amendment in Section 19 of the Rajasthan Panchayati Raj Act, 1994. It was argued on behalf of the petitioner that the Amendment itself was unconstitutional since it was introduced by an Ordinance when there was no emergency in the state or any other compelling reason. Among various other arguments challenging this provision, it was also argued the impugned amendment is hit by Article 14 of the Constitution of India. It was submitted that the provision is arbitrary and unreasonable in as much as, in the case of a sitting MP or an MLA, a person against whom a charge has been framed or a person who has been convicted and sentenced for a period of six months or above was still entitled to contest the election, if the offence is not one of moral turpitude. It was also submitted that selecting the offences punishable with imprisonment of five years or above only in the case of persons to be elected as a *panch* or *sarpanch* is arbitrary in as much as there is no nexus in providing such a cut off line.

It is interesting to note how the Hon'ble Court perceived differing standards of disqualification as prevailing between

Parliament and state legislature on the one hand and *panchayats* on the other. To Quote:

> We are unable to agree with the submission of the learned counsel. As regards election of MPs and MLAs, they are governed by Representation of Peoples Act. Thus to provide such disqualification for MPs and MLAs is within the domain of Parliament. The impugned ordinance/legislation pertains to Rajasthan Legislative Assembly. In our view the impugned Panchayat Act cannot be held to be discriminatory on this ground. We only say that there is no harm in adopting good things of juniors by the seniors. Let the process of purification in democratic governance come from the grassroot i.e. *panch/sarpanch*. Coming to the cut off line of offence punishable with imprisonment for five years, a study of the penal law prevalent in the country especially that contained in the Indian Penal Code, brings out clearly that severity of each punishment sanctioned by law is directly proportionate to seriousness of the offence. We have looked into the schedule appended to the Code of Criminal procedure. All these offences where the punishment is provided above five years are of serious nature. This excludes minor offences.
>
> Thus, it cannot be said that there is no basis for fixing the cut off line of five years for the offences pending trial. In view of this, we find no substance in the third contention as well. In view of the aforesaid, we uphold the constitutional validity of the provisions of Section 19 (g), (gg) and provision (ii). We find no merit in the group of petitions and each of the writ petitions is dismissed being devoid of any merit.

Disclosure by Candidates

While there have been a number of cases filed by contesting candidates themselves or other concerned persons alleging that a candidate has suffered from any disqualification as identified in the RP Act, until recently, information about criminal antecedents of candidates became known only after the elections through the election petitions disputing the outcome. A regime of disclosure by the candidates themselves about their antecedents relating to their educational background, finances and convictions, if any, for criminal offences, has now begun to take shape. This has been made possible because of the landmark decision of the Apex Court in People's Union for Civil Liberties and others *versus* Union of India decided on March 13, 2003. The background to this landmark decision is contained in the following paragraphs.

In 1999, the Association for Democratic Reforms filed a Writ Petition in the Delhi High Court (CWP 7257 of 1999) seeking a directive to the Election Commission to disclose the criminal antecedents, and assets and liabilities of candidates contesting elections to the Parliament and state legislatures. On November, 2, 2000 the Delhi High Court, while allowing the above petition, held that disclosure of this information was also obligated by Article 19(1) (a) of the Constitution, which gave citizens the right to freedom of speech and expression and hence the right to information. The Union of India went in appeal against this judgement. On May 2, 2000, the Supreme Court affirmed and upheld the reasoning of the Delhi High Court and directed the Election Commission to seek information from the candidates on affidavit about their criminal record, assets and, liabilities and educational qualifications as a necessary part of the nomination papers. The court held that this could be done by the Election Commission in exercise of its powers under Article 324 of the Constitution.

On May 14, 2002, the Election Commission requested the Government of India to make appropriate amendments to Rule 4 of the Conduct of Election Rules, 1961 in pursuance of the Supreme Court directive. On June 19, 2002, the Central Government asked the Election Commission to seek extension of time and said that it was convening an all-party meeting on July 8, 2002 to discuss the issue. On June 21, 2002 the Election Commission in its reply asked the Central Government to approach the court on its own for an extension. As no such extension of time was sought or granted by the Supreme Court and as the Election Commission was duty bound to implement the Supreme Court's directive, the Election Commission issued an order on June 28, 2002 requiring candidates to file an affidavit along with the nomination paper disclosing information regarding the aspects mentioned in the Supreme Court judgement.

On July 8, 2002, in the all party meeting convened by the government, it was reported that all the parties unanimously rejected the order of the Election Commission and agreed to the issue of an ordinance to nullify the Supreme Court judgement and the Election Commission's order. On August 16, 2002, the Union Cabinet approved an ordinance to amend the Representation of Peoples Act adding provisions to nullify the Election Commission's notification and sent it to the President for promulgation. On the same day some leading citizens and activists under the aegis of the National Campaign for Electoral Reforms met the President of India and urged him to refer the ordinance to the Supreme Court under Article 143, as some provisions promulgated in the Ordinance clearly affected the citizen's fundamental rights under Article 19(1)(a). On August 23, 2002, the President returned the ordinance to the Cabinet for reconsideration. On August 24, 2002, the government reiterated its recommendation to the President after which the President promulgated the ordinance. The ordinance specifically stated under Section 33B that "notwithstanding anything contained in the judgement of any court or decree or order of any court or any other instructions issued by the Election Commission, no candidate shall be liable to disclose or furnish any such information in respect of his election which is not required to be disclosed or furnished under the Act or the Rules made thereunder." The section also provided that it shall be deemed to have been inserted w.e.f 2nd May 2002 indicating clearly the intention of the government that the Supreme Court judgement of May, 2, 2002 will thus be nullified.

Thereafter several organisations filed a petition before the Supreme Court challenging the Ordinance. The People's Union for Civil Liberties, the Association for Democratic Reforms, the Lok Satta, the Foundation for Democratic Reforms, Movement for Good Government, Centre for Media Studies, Transparency International and Lok Sevak Sangh among others were the petitioners.

After several hearings, the Supreme Court delivered its judgement on March 13, 2003. It is pertinent to mention that during the hearing the government argued that the right to vote was not a fundamental right but only a statutory right subject to statutory restrictions and it was the prerogative of the Parliament to lay down those restrictions. The petitioners argued that even though the right to vote may be a statutory right, exercising that right was part of a citizen's fundamental Right to Expression and the information required for the conscious exercise of that right could not be denied. In its judgement the Supreme Court maintained a distinction between the 'right to vote' and 'freedom of voting' and held that voting was very much a part of a citizen's right to expression and for its proper exercise, the citizen also had the right to information as part of Article 19(1) (a). In the result the Supreme Court struck down the impugned ordinance and directed the Election Commission to take necessary steps for obtaining the information from the candidates.

Though these decisions related to elections to the Parliament and the state legislature, in several states similar disclosure requirements have now been prescribed for elections to *panchayats* and *nagarpalikas* as well. In some states these have been through amendments to the relevant state laws and regulations. In some others they have been prescribed by the State Election Commissioners themselves. As of now in almost all the states such disclosures have been prescribed. In several of the states civil society organisations have formed Election Watch groups, which take on the responsibility of collecting and disseminating the information furnished by the candidates and as required disseminate them among the voters by various meets. A network of these Election Watch groups has also emerged through the initiative of the Association for Democratic Reforms.

While a disclosure regime is thus in position relating to Parliament, Legislature and Local body elections, it remains to be seen how the disclosure statements are monitored or used in election petitions. While convictions for crimes undergone by the candidates have perforce, to be disclosed by the candidates while filing their nominations, such information does not automatically disqualify a candidate. To illustrate, a person convicted for offences listed in Section 8 of the RP Act, 1951 such as promoting enmity between groups (153A of IPC) or importing or exporting prohibited goods, an offence under the Customs Act is disqualified only for a period of six years from the date of conviction. It is upon the official before whom the nomination is filed whether any of the information disclosed by the candidate would be a disqualification and therefore lead to the rejection of the nominations. The disclosure arrangements however make it possible for an election petition to be filed to challenge the election if it comes to light that the disclosure has not been true to facts. Challenges to election based on disclosure have been few and initiated only recently. It remains to be seen how effective the disclosure of criminal antecedents are in deferring candidates.

However, the disclosure statements filed as affidavits along with the nomination papers regarding financial information about the candidates and their dependents as well as significant criminal convictions are very much in the public domain and are well publicised in the newspapers. In the absence of empirical studies it is not possible to say to what extent such information has influenced the choice of candidates of candidates or voting by the electorate.

Related to the disclosure regime is the requirement that after the elections candidates should furnish details of the expenditure incurred by them for contesting. The Election Commission of India has stipulated expenditure norms for this purpose in regard to elections to the Parliament and state assemblies. Similar stipulations have been made in different states by the respective state election commissions. The State laws also provide that failure to furnish expenditure statements may result in the candidates concerned being disqualified to contest elections in the future for specified periods.

The Kerala local government laws contain such provisions. Recently (June '08) as many as 8984 persons were disqualified by the State Election Commission for a period of five years. It remains to be seen whether some of these decisions will be contested in the courts.

Conclusions

In this chapter we have considered the background to the law on disqualifications for contesting local body elections.

(a) The two-child norm has been an important type of disqualification stipulated in some of the states. After reviewing several cases in different state High Courts it has been pointed out that the case law on the matter can be taken as settled in view of the Apex court decision in Javed's case.

(b) In regard to financial interest and a possible conflict of interest arising therefrom the case law on the subject shows that the matter is very much dependent on the definitions, regulations and procedures outlined in the state laws.

(c) Regarding the office of profit a reading of the cases from the different High Courts will show that the state laws relating to the subject are needlessly varied and in some cases overly restrictive. The controversies surrounding the matter appear to be similar to the current debate regarding elections to the Parliament and the legislatures. It is respectfully pointed out that the seemingly contradictory judgements between different High Courts such as Deulkar's case in Maharashtra, Meghraj Singh's case in UP or Janakdhari Prasad's case in Bihar could be resolved by a proper understanding and elucidation of the Apex Court judgement in Rabindra Naik's case.

(d) In regard to criminal convictions the issue brings out the fact that while a disclosure regime has been brought into existence, challenges in the court alleging suppression by candidates of criminal convictions are yet to emerge in a significant manner.

In the next chapter we shall consider the case law relating to post election disputes.

Annexure A-2.1

Javed and Others versus State of Haryana and Others. 2003 8. SCC 369

Before R.C. Lahoti, Ashish Bhan and Arun Kumar JJ

The Judgement of the Court was delivered by R C Lahoti, JJ. Excerpts are given below:

"2. In this batch of writ petitions and appeals the core issue is the vires of the provisions of Sections 175(1)(q) and 177(1) of the Haryana Panchayati Raj Act, 1994 (Act 11 of 1994) (hereinafter referred to as the Act for short). The relevant provisions are extracted and reproduced hereunder:

"175(1) No person shall be a *Sarpanch, Upsarpanch* or a *Panch* of a *Gram Panchayat* or a member of a *Panchayat Samiti* or *Zilla Parishad* or continue as such who—

(q) has more than two living children:

Provided that a person having more than two children on or upto the expiry of one year of the commencement of this Act, shall not be deemed to be disqualified.

177. (1) "If any member of a *Gram Panchayat, Panchayat Samiti* or *Zilla Parishad:*

(a) who is elected, as such, was subject to any of the disqualifi-cations mentioned in Section 175 at the time of his election;

(b) during the term for which he has been elected, incurs any of the disqualifications, mentioned in Section 175, shall be disqualified from continuing to be a member, and his office shall become vacant.

In every case, the question whether a vacancy has arisen, shall be decided by the Director. The Director may give his decision either on an application made to it by any person, or on its own motion. Until the Director decides that the vacancy has arisen, the members shall not be disqualified under sub-section (1) from continuing to be a member. Any person aggrieved by the decision of the Director may, within a period of fifteen days from the date of such decision, appeal to the government and the orders passed by Government in such appeal shall be final:

"Provided that no order shall be passed under this sub-section by the Director against any member without giving him a reasonable opportunity of being heard."

3. Act 11 of 1994 was enacted with various objectives based on past experience and in view of the shortcomings noticed in the implementation of preceding laws and also to bring the legislation in conformity with Part IX of the Constitution of India relating to the *panchayats* added by the Seventy-third Amendment. One of the objectives set out in the Statement

of Objects and Reasons is to disqualify persons for election to *panchayats* at each level, having more than two children after one year of the date of commencement of this Act, to popularise family welfare/family planning programme [vide clause (m) of para 4 of SOR].

4. Placed in plain words, the provision disqualifies a person having more than two living children from holding the specified offices in *panchayats*. The enforcement of disqualification is postponed for a period of one year from the date of the commencement of the Act. A person having more than two children up to the expiry of one year of the commencement of the Act is not disqualified. This postponement for one year takes care of any conception on or around the commencement of the Act, the normal period of gestation being nine months. If a woman has conceived at the commencement of the Act then any one of such couples would not be disqualified. Though not disqualified on the date of election, if any person holding any of the said offices incurs a disqualification by giving birth to a child one year after the commencement of the Act, he becomes subject to disqualification and is disabled from continuing to hold the office. The disability is incurred by the birth of a child which results in increasing the number of living children, including the additional child born one year after the commencement of the Act, to a figure more than two. If the factum is disputed, the director is entrusted with the duty of holding an enquiry and declaring the office vacant. The decision of the Director is subject to appeal to the government. The Director has to afford a reasonable opportunity of being heard to the holder of office sought to be disqualified. These safeguards satisfy the requirements of natural justice.

5. Several persons (who are the writ petitioners or appellants in this batch of matters) have been disqualified or proceeded against for disqualifying either from contesting the elections for, or from continuing in the office of *panchas/sarpanches* in view of their having incurred the disqualification as provided by Section 175(1)(q) or Section 177(1) read with Section 175(1) (q) of the Act. The grounds for challenging the constitutional validity of the above said provisions are very many, couched differently in different writ petitions. We have heard all the learned counsel representing the different petitioners/appellants. As agreed to at the bar, the grounds of challenge can be categorised into five: (i) that the provision is arbitrary and hence violative of Article 14 of the Constitution; (ii) that the disqualification does not serve the purpose sought to be achieved by the legislation; (iii) that the provision is discriminatory; (iv) that the provision adversely affects the liberty of leading personal life in all its freedom and having as many children as one chooses to have and hence is violative of Article 21 of the Constitution; and (v) that the provision interferes with the freedom of religion and hence violates Article 25 of the Constitution.

6. The state of Haryana has defended its legislation on all counts. We have also heard the learned standing counsel for the State. On notice, Shri Soli J Sorabjee, the learned Attorney General for India, has appeared to assist the court and he too has addressed the Court. We would deal with each of the submissions made.

Submission (i), (ii) and (iii)

7. The first three submissions are based on Article 14 of the Constitution and, therefore, are taken up together for consideration.

Is the Classification Arbitrary?

8. It is well settled that Article 14 forbids class legislation; it does not forbid reasonable classification for the purpose of legislation. To satisfy the constitutional test of permissibility, two conditions must be satisfied, namely (i) that the classification is founded on an intelligible differentia which distinguishes persons or things that are grouped together from others left out of the ground and (ii) that such differentia has a rational relation to the object sought to be achieved by the statute in question. The basis for classification may rest on conditions, which may be geographical or according to objects or occupation or the like. (See Constitution bench decision in Budhan Choudhry *versus* State of Bihar). The classification is well defined and well perceptible. Persons having more than two living children are clearly distinguishable from persons having not more than two living children. The two constitute two different classes and the classification is founded on an intelligible differentia clearly distinguishing one from the other. One of the objects sought to be achieved by the legislation is popularising the family welfare/family planning programme. The disqualification enacted by the provision seeks to achieve the objective by creating a disincentive. The classification does not suffer from any arbitrariness. The number of children *viz.* two is based on legislative wisdom. It could have been more or less. The number is a matter of policy decision which is not open to judicial scrutiny.

Does the Legislation not Serve its Object?

9. It was submitted that the number of children which one has, whether two or three or more, does not affect the capacity, competence and quality of a person to serve on any office of a *panchayat* and therefore the impugned disqualification has no nexus with the purpose sought to be achieved by the Act. There is no merit in the submission. We have already stated that one of the objects of the enactment is to popularise family welfare/family planning programme. This is consistent with the National Population Policy.

10. Under Article 243-G of the Constitution, the legislature of a state has been vested with the authority to make law endowing the panchayats

with such powers and authority which may be necessary to enable the *gram panchayats* to function as institutions of self-government and such law may contain provisions for the devolution of powers and responsibilities upon *panchayats*, at the appropriate level, subject to such conditions as may be specified therein. Clause (b) of Article 243-G provides that *gram panchayats* may be entrusted the powers to implement the schemes for economic development and social justice including those in relation to matters listed in the Eleventh Schedule. Entries 24 and 25 of the Eleventh Schedule read:

"24. Family welfare

25. Women and child development"

In pursuance of the powers given to the State Legislatures to enact laws, the Haryana Legislature enacted the Haryana Panchayat Raj Act, 1994 (Haryana Act 11 of 1994). Section 21 enumerates the functions and duties of *Gram Panchayat*. Clause XIX (1) of Section 21 reads:

XIX. Public Health and Family Welfare

(1) Implementation of family welfare programme

Family welfare would include family planning as well. To carry out the purpose of the Act as well as the mandate of the Constitution the legislature has made a provision for making a person having more than two living children ineligible to either contest for the post of *panch* or *sarpanch*. Such a provision would serve the purpose of the Act as mandated by the Constitution. It cannot be said that such a provision would not serve the purpose of the Act.

11. In our opinion, the impugned disqualification does have a nexus with the purpose sought to be achieved by the Act. Hence, it is valid.

Is the Provision Discriminatory?

12. It was submitted that though the state of Haryana has introduced such a provision of disqualification by reference to elective offices in *panchayats*, a similar provision is not found to have been enacted for disqualifying aspirants or holders of elective or public offices in other institutions of local self-governance and also not in state legislatures and Parliament. So also all the other states have not enacted similar laws, and therefore, it appears that people aspiring to participate in Panchayati Raj governance in the state of Haryana have been singled out and meted out hostile discrimination. The submission has been stated only to be rejected. Under the constitutional scheme there is a well-defined distribution of legislative powers contained in Part IX of the Constitution. Parliament and every state legislature has power to make laws with respect to any of the matters which fall within its field of legislation under Article 246 read with the Seventh Schedule of the Constitution. A legislation by one of the states

cannot be held to be discriminatory or suffering from the vice of hostile discrimination as against its citizens simply because Parliament or the legislatures of other states have not chosen to enact similar laws. Such a submission, if accepted, would be violative of the autonomy given to the Centre and the states within their respective fields under the Constitutional scheme.

Two laws enacted by two different governments and by two different legislatures can be read neither in conjunction nor by comparison for the purpose of finding out if they are discriminatory. Article 14 does not authorise the striking down of a law of one state on the ground that in contrast with a law of another state on the same subject, its provisions are discriminatory. When the sources of authority for the two statutes are different, Article 14 can have no application. So is the view taken in Bar council of UP *versus* State of U.P., State of T.N. Vs Ananthi Ammal and Prabhakaran Nair *versus* State of T.N.

15. Incidentally it may be noted that so far as the state of Haryana is concerned, in the Haryana Municipal Act, 1973 (Act 24 of 1973) Section 13-A has been inserted to make a provision for similar disqualification for a person from being chosen or holding the office of a member of a municipality.

16. A uniform policy may be devised by the Centre or by a State. However, there is no constitutional requirement that any such policy must be implemented at one go. Policies are capable of being implemented in a phased manner. More so, when the policies have far-reaching implications and are dynamic in nature, their implementation in a phased manner is welcome for it receives gradual willing acceptance and invites lesser resistance.

The provisions, if it violates Article 21 or 25

21. Before testing the validity of the impugned legislation from the view point of Articles 21 and 25, in the light of the submissions made, we take up first the more basic issue—whether it is at all permissible to test the validity of a law which enacts a disqualification operating in the field of elections on the touchstone of violation of fundamental rights.

22. Right to contest an election is neither a fundamental right nor a common law right. It is a right conferred by a statute. At the most, in view of Part IX having been added in the Constitution, a right to contest an election for an office in a *panchayat* may be said to be a constitutional right—a right originating in the Constitution and given shape by a statute. But even so, it cannot be equated with a fundamental right. There is nothing wrong in the same statute which confers the right to contest an election also to provide for the necessary qualifications without which a person cannot offer his

candidature for an elective office and also to provide for disqualifications which would disable a person from contesting for, or holding, an elective statutory office.

23. Reiterating the law laid down in N.P. Ponnuswami vs. Returning Officer, Namakkal Constituency and Jagan Nath *versus* Jaswant Singh this Court held in Jyoti Basu vs. Debi Ghosal (SCC p.696, para 8)

"8. A right to elect, fundamental though it is to democracy, is, anomalously enough, neither as a fundamental right nor a common law right. It is pure and simple, a statutory right. So is the right to be elected. So is the right to dispute an election. Outside of statute there is no right to elect, no right to be elected and no right to dispute an election. Statutory creations they are, and therefore, subject to statutory limitation."

25. In our view, disqualification on the right to contest an election by having more than two living children does not contravene any fundamental right nor does it cross the limits of reasonability. Rather it is a disqualification conceptually devised in national interest.

26. With this general statement of law which has application to Articles 21 and 25 both, we now proceed to test the sustainability of attack on constitutional validity of the impugned legislation separately by reference to Articles 21 and 25.

The Disqualification, if Violates Article 21?

27. Placing strong reliance on Maneka Gandhi *versus* Union of India and Kasturi Lal Lakshmi Reddy *versus* State of J&K it was forcefully urged that the fundamental right to life and personal liberty emanating from Article 21 of the Constitution should be allowed to stretch its span to its optimum so as to include in the compendious term of the article all the varieties of rights which go to make up the personal liberty of man including the right to enjoy all the materialistic pleasures and to procreate as many children as one pleases.

28. At the very outset we are constrained to observe that the law laid down by this court in the decisions relied on is either being misread or read divorced of the context. The test of reasonableness is not a wholly subjective test and its contours are fairly indicated by the Constitution. The requirement of reasonableness runs like a golden thread through the entire fabric of fundamental rights. The lofty ideals of social and economic justice, the advancement of the nation as a whole and the philosophy of distributive justice – economic, social and political – cannot be given a go-by in the name of undue stress on fundamental rights and individual liberty. Reasonableness and rationality, legally as well as philosophically provide colour to the meaning of fundamental rights and these principles are deducible from those

very decisions, which have been relied on by the learned counsel for the petitioners.

41. To say the least, it is futile to assume or urge that the impugned legislation violates right to life and liberty guaranteed under Article 21 in any of the meanings, howsoever expanded the meanings may be.

The Provision if it Violates Article 25 ?

42. It was then submitted that the personal law of Muslims permits performance of marriages with four women, obviously for the purpose of procreating children and any restriction thereon would be violative of the right to freedom of religion enshrined in Article 25 of the Constitution. The relevant part of Article 24 reads as under:

"25. Freedom of conscience and free profession, practice and propagation of religion: (1) subject to public order, morality and health and to the other provisions of this Part, all persons are equally entitled to freedom of conscience and the right freely to profess, practise and propagate religion, (2) Nothing in this article shall affect the operation of any existing law or prevent the State from making any law:

(a) regulating or restricting any economic, financial, political or other secular activity which may be associated with religious practice;

(b) providing for social welfare and reform or the throwing open of Hindu religious institutions of a public character to all classes and sections of Hindus."

43. A bare reading of this article deprives the submission of all its force, vigour and charm. The freedom is subject to public order, morality and health. So the article itself permits a legislation in the interest of social welfare and reform which are obviously part and parcel of public order, national morality and the collective health of the nation's people.

44. Muslim law permits marrying four women. The personal law nowhere mandates or dictates it as a duty to perform four marriages. No religious scripture or authority has been brought to our notice which provides that marrying less than four women or abstaining from procreating a child from each and every wife in case of permitted bigamy or polygamy would be irreligious or offensive to the dictates of the religion. In our view, the question of the impugned provision of the Haryana Act being violative of Article 25 does not arise. We may have a reference to a few decided cases.

Some Incidental Questions

62. It was submitted that the enactment has created serious problems in the rural population as couples desirous of contesting an election but having living children more than two, are feeling compelled to give them in

adoption. Subject to what has already been stated hereinabove, we may add that disqualification is attracted no sooner a third child is born and is living after two living children. Merely because the couple has parted with one child by giving the child away in adoption, the disqualification does not come to an end. While interpreting the scope of disqualification we shall have to keep in view the evil sought to be cured and purpose sought to be achieved by the enactment. If the persons sought to be disqualified are responsible for or have given birth to children more than two who are living then merely because one or more of them are given in adoption the disqualification is not wiped out.

63. It was also submitted that the impugned disqualification would hit women the worst, in as much as in the Indian society they have no independence and they almost helplessly bear a third child if their husbands want them to do so. This contention need not detain us any longer. A male who compels his wife to bear a third child would disqualify not only his wife but himself as well. We do not think that with the awareness which is arising in Indian womenfolk, they are so helpless as to be compelled to bear a third child even though they do not wish to do so. At the end, suffice it to say that if the legislature chooses to carve out an exception in favour of females it is free to do so merely because women are not excepted from the operation of the disqualification it does not render it unconstitutional.

Conclusion

65. The challenge to the constitutional validity of Sections 175(1)(q) and 177(1) fails on all the counts. Both the provisions are held *intra vires* of the Constitution. The provisions are salutary and in public interest. All the petitions which challenge the constitutional validity of the above said provisions are held liable to be dismissed.

3

Post Election Cases

We have noted that in the pre-election phase once a notification for election had been issued the jurisdiction of the courts is excluded under Article 243-0. This article as well as sub-article (d) also stipulate that no election to any *panchayat* shall be called in question except by an election petition presented to such authority and in such manner as is provided for, by, or under any law made by the Legislature of a state. An identical provision is contained in part (b) of Article 243ZG in regard to elections to any municipality. We have noted that by and large the courts have observed a self-imposed restraint in exercising their jurisdictions under Article 226. However, given the widespread nature and very large number of persons involved in *panchayat* and municipal elections in the country, it is inevitable that such elections also result in a large number of disputes challenging the results. These disputes cover a wide variety of issues such as mistakes in electoral rolls, defects or irregularities in the acceptance of nomination papers, actual conduct of the polls, counting of votes, jurisdiction of the authorities hearing the election petitions, violations in the procedure for filing the petitions etc.

Such cases are not new and have been agitated frequently in regard to the Parliament and assembly elections as well. The jurisprudence or case law on the subject is not significantly different in the case of *panchayat* and municipal elections. Nevertheless it is useful to have a sense about the kind of disputes raised. Generally, the High Courts have adhered to the provisions of Articles 243-O and 243ZG and in most cases have restrained themselves from entering into the merits of an election petition. On the contrary, the High Courts have called for adherence to the procedures for considering election petitions as laid down in the concerned laws and the rules thereunder as well as adherence to the principles of natural justice; We may now consider the cases adjudicated in the different states relating mainly to the counting of votes and the common points emerging therefrom.

Andhra

Smt. S K Khasim B Versus State Election Commissioner, Andhra (WP 24001 of 1995) decided on 19.12.1995

This is one of the early cases to be considered by the AP High Court wherein issues of counting and recounting were raised. The petitioner and the fourth respondent contested the office of *sarpanch* in the elections to the Mangalagiri Padu *gram panchayat* held on 27.6.1995. The counting of votes was to begin on 27.6.1995 and it was informed that the petitioner got 512 votes, the fourth respondent received 509 votes and 51 were declared to be invalid. The Election Officer did not declare the result in view of a stay granted by the court in a batch of writ petitions. In one of the writ petitions, the court also passed an order to this effect that the result of the election would be subject to the verdict in the writ petition. Separately the State Election Commissioner had issued an order one day prior to counting, directing the Election Officers to undertake recount of votes in certain constituencies including cases where the margin of victory is less than 1 per cent of the total polled votes. These orders of the SEC were duly notified. Accordingly, recounting of votes was undertaken in regard to Mangalagiri Padu *gram panchayat* on 21.1.1995. In the recount the petitioner got 510 votes, the fourth respondent got 513 votes, 42 votes were invalid and 7 ballot papers were found to be missing. Smt. S.K. Khasim assailed the action of the recount through writ petition no.24001.

In deciding the petition, the High Court held that though its writ jurisdiction under Article 226 cannot be abrogated, the High

Court had imposed self-limitations and declined to interfere with the election process, because problems in this regard can effectively be agitated before the election tribunals. However, where the constitutional validity of an act or a rule affecting the election is challenged, or where the exercise of such jurisdiction is malafide and not in compliance with the rules of natural justice, the High Court has got ample power under Article 226. In this case the High Court found that the SEC's notification directing recounting where the margin was less than 1 per cent, was against Rule 37 of the Conduct of Election Rules which clearly lists and specifies the grounds on which recounting could be done. Accordingly the High Court regarded the recounting against the law and revoked the same.

Y. Venkat Reddy versus *District Munsif (1998(4) ALT 495 (DB) decided on 3.7.1998*

This case also related to recounting. Elections to the office of *Sarpanch* of Kalvel *panchayat* were held on 3.7.1995. Counting was held on the same day and it was found that a total of 948 votes were polled. Of these Shri Venkat Reddy secured 428, Shri Pratap Reddy 431 votes, and 89 votes were declared invalid. The petitioner submitted a petition for recounting. The Election officer recounted the votes but found no change. As happened in Smt. S.K. Khasim's case the Election Officer could not announce the results in view of the orders of the High Court staying the declaration of the election results. Thereafter on the basis of the SECs notification dated 26.7.1995 mentioned in Khasim's case *supra,* a recount was conducted on 21.10.1995. The recounting revealed that 949 votes were polled out of which the petitioner Venkat Reddy secured 430 votes and the contesting respondent Pratap Reddy received 426 votes. Thereupon the petitioner was declared elected. Questioning the said election, the contesting respondent filed an election petition. The election tribunal cited the judgement of the AP High Court in Khasim's case and held the SECs notification as illegal and as such the recounting done on 21.10.1995 was not warranted. The Division bench of the AP High Court upheld its earlier decision that the SECs directions for recounting of votes was not in keeping with the relevant laws and the rules.

Bathina Baby Jyotsna *versus* Government of AP (2002 (2) ALT 158 (DB) decided on 28.1.2002. In this case the appellant alleged certain irregularities in the elections to the office of the *sarpanch* of Chandurthi *gram panchayat* in East Godavari district. The Election Officer who agreed for recounting of the votes on the representation made by the appellant recounted only the invalid votes. After verification only four votes were declared as valid but this did not alter the results. The appellant then made a representation to the District Collector who passed an order asking the appellant to approach the Competent Appellant Authority. The appellant then filed a writ petition in the AP High Court. The learned Single Judge dismissed the petition as not maintainable and directed the petitioner to make the challenge before the election tribunal. The present writ appeal was filed impugning the above order.

A Division Bench of the AP High Court held that in the present case the Election Officer had not complied with the provisions of the Act and rules made thereunder in regard to the recounting of the votes and therefore the appellant was entitled to challenge the order passed by the Election Officer and the further order passed by the District Collector before the prescribed authority.

Bihar

Bambhola Rai versus State Election Commission and Others, CWJC No. 2012 of 2003 decided on 27.2.2004 (2004-03 BLJR 1818)

The writ petition was filed for quashing the order dated 24.1.2003 passed by Sub Judge IV Vaishali at Hajipur, in Election Case No. 228 of 2001 whereby an amendment petition filed by the plaintiff/respondent No.4 was allowed after the case was partly heard. The case of the plaintiff/respondent No.4 was that he filed nomination form for the post of Member of *panchayat samiti* of Brahampur *gram panchayat*. The Election was held on 11.4.2001. He lost the election and the defendant/petitioner was elected as member of the *panchayat samiti*. The respondent No.4 then filed the election petition stating that the election was vitiated by large scale booth capturing, firing, violence etc. The election for booths No.74-75 were cancelled and re-poll was conducted. The respondent wanted to add a few more polling booths for consideration as part of his petition so that the fair conduct of the poll could be assessed. The question arose as to whether such an amendment could be better allowed in an election petition. In the Bihar *Panchayat* Election Rules 1959, there is a provision for amendments to an election petition to certain extent but in the Bihar *Panchayat* Election Rules of 1995, no such provision has been made. In the case of Sarachandra Mandal *versus* Phai Bhushan Singh and Others (AIR, 1974 Patna 40) a Full Bench of the Bihar High Court had held that the election tribunal has power to amend defective verification, but it cannot afford an opportunity to the election petitioner for amending the petition for removal of major and fatal defects. In the instant case the Panchayat Act, 1993 and the Election Rules, 1995 would apply. There is no provision either under the Act, 1993 or rule for amendment of the election petition. The detailed procedure of Civil Procedure Code will not apply in this case. Besides, the evidence was almost complete and six witnesses of defendant/petitioner had been examined before the amendment petition was filed. Accordingly the High Court held that the amendment to the election petition allowed by the sub judge was not lawful and set aside the same.

Himachal Pradesh

Vimla Devi versus State of Himachal Pradesh,
C.W.P No. 753 of 1998 decided on 24.3.1999 (AIR 1999 HP 38)

The petitioner and respondent No.4 contested for the office of *pradhan, gram panchayat* Nanj in the year 1995. The votes were counted on 18.12.1995. The respondent No.4 secured 350 valid votes whereas the petitioner secured 349 valid votes and respondent No.4 was declared as elected for the office of *pradhan* by the Returning Officer. This was challenged by means of an election petition before the Authorised officer under Section 161 of the Himachal Pradesh Panchayati Raj Act, 1994 read with Rule 94 of Himachal Pradesh Panchayati Raj Election Rule 1994. The Authorised officer concluded that there was improper reception of a proxy vote in favour of the returned candidate i.e. respondent No.4 which materially affected the result of the election. The appellant authority set aside the orders of the authorised officer that there was no positive and convincing evidence to support his conclusion that the proxy vote was materially affecting the result.

A writ petition challenging the decision of the appellate authority was filed. The High Court held that it was a settled proposition of law that the person who has challenged the election of the elected candidate, has to prove the allegations made in the election petition by cogent and convincing evidence and unless this heavy burden is discharged by the person concerned the election petition cannot be accepted. The High Court accordingly refused to interfere with the decision of the appellant authority.

Madhya Pradesh

In Madhya Pradesh several cases came up before the High Court regarding the recounting of votes.

Lakhan Lal Patel versus State of M.P. and Others L.P.A. No. 46 of 2002, decided on 3.4.2002

Shri Ram Prakash Srivastava, respondent No.4 in this case was declared elected as *sarpanch* of Natwara *gram panchayat*, district Jabalpur. The election was held on 28.1.2000. As many as 14 persons including the appellant Lakhan Lal Patel participated in the election. In the result which was declared after the election, respondent No.4 secured 323 votes and was declared elected whereas the appellant secured only 259 votes. He filed election petition under Section 122 of M.P. Panchayati Raj Adhiniyam, 1993 challenging the election of respondent No.4. The Election Tribunal after considering the evidence and material before it directed for re-counting of votes vide order dated 26.2.2001. Recounting of votes was undertaken which showed that while the appellant Lakhan Lal Patel secured 249 votes, the respondent No.4 Ram Prakash secured only 245. Accordingly, by the order dated 24.3.2001 the appellant was declared elected. Aggrieved by this order, respondent No.4 filed W.P. No. 1603 /2001 and the learned single judge vide order dated 4.10.2001 allowed the petition and quashed the impugned order. In the appeal which followed it was held that recounting of votes can be permitted only if a written request is made to the Returning Officer immediately after announcement of the election result. Filing of written application is, therefore, a mandatory condition for claiming recounting under Rule 80 of the Election Rule M.P. Panchayat Election Rule 1994. Having not complied with this rule, the appeal was dismissed.

Chander Bhan Singh versus State of M.P. Writ Petition No. 2349/2000, decided on 31.3.2001 (2001 AIHC 2961)

Shri Chander Bhan Singh and Shri Rao Khetsingh contested the election to the post of President, *zila panchayat* Damoh held on March 1, 2000. Shri Chander Bhan Singh was declared elected and granted certificate under Rule 17 of M.P. Panchayat Nirvachan Niyam, 1995. Shri Rao Khetsingh immediately approached the election tribunal and obtained a stay against the issuance of notification under Rule 22 of 1995. The election tribunal entertained the election petition and stayed the issuance of notification. Finally the election of Shri Chander Bhan Singh was set aside. This order of the election tribunal passed was challenged through this writ petition. The court came to the conclusion that the election dispute cannot be raised before the election tribunal on the basis of certificate granted under Rule 17 of Rules 1995. The election petition can be filed before the election tribunal after the notification has been published under Rule 22 of Rules 1995. After making this observation the court remanded the matter back to the single judge for decision on merits.

Punjab & Haryana

Gurdev Kaur and Others versus Dy. Commissioner, Patiala and Others Civil Writ Petition No. 2941 of 1993, decided on 6.5.1993

This is a group of petitions challenging the result of the election held for the *panchayat* in the state of Punjab in regard to the women *panches* as also the co-option of women panches. Sub-section 4 of section 6 of the Punjab Gram Panchayat Act, 1952 provides that in every *gram panchayat* there shall be at least two women *panches*. It also provides for the manner of the co-option of women *panches* in case no woman is deemed to have been elected. Sub-section 4 reads as follows:

"In every *gram panchayat* there shall be at least two women *panches* and if only one woman or no woman is elected as a *panch* and the number of unsuccessful contesting women candidates is two or more, then one woman or two women, as the case may be, securing the highest number of valid votes from amongst unsuccessful women candidates shall be deemed to have been elected as *panches*:

"Provided that if only one woman or no woman is deemed to have been elected then one woman or two women, as the case may be, shall be co-opted by the *gram panchayat* in the prescribed manner from amongst members of the *gram sabha* qualified to be elected as *panch*."

Sub-clause (3) of Article 15 of the Constitution of India empowers the state government to make any special provision for women and children.

On 31.12.1992 the state of Punjab issued a notification establishing a *gram sabha* for the area of village Bakshi Wala, in district Patiala. Elections were scheduled to take place on 18th January 1993. The petitioners Gurdev Kaur and Har Devi contested but were not successful. On 15th February 1993 a meeting of *panches* was held for co-opting lady *panches*. The petitioners filed the present writ petition seeking the relief that they be declared to have been deemed to be elected as woman *panches* and no other women *panches* should be co-opted.

The Court held as follows:

> We hold that (1) in case one woman *panch* has been elected and there is one unsuccessful contesting woman candidate then the said unsuccessful woman candidate shall be deemed to have been elected as a *panch*; (2) if there is no woman candidate who has been elected and the number of unsuccessful women candidates are two then both the unsuccessful women candidates shall be deemed to have been elected; (3) if there are more than two unsuccessful candidates then the two women candidates who have the highest number of valid votes shall be deemed to have been elected as *panches*; (4) if only

one woman candidate contests the election and she is unsuccessful then the said woman candidate would be deemed to have been elected and one more would be co-opted under the proviso; and (5) if no woman candidate contests the election then both the women candidates have to be co-opted under the proviso.

In the result, writ petition No.2941 of 1993 is allowed and, both the petitioners are declared as deemed to have been elected as women *panches* for *gram panchayat* Bakhshi Wala, and the respondents are restrained from interfering with the petitioners functioning as such in the *gram panchayat* in question. In those petitions where women *panches* have been co-opted contrary to the decision taken by us, the said co-option is quashed and the co-opted women *panches* are restrained from functioning as such in the *gram panchayat* in question.

This case brings out the fact that in such matters of detail like co-option of woman members it should really be the responsibility of the state to frame rules and regulations failing which the court will be forced to step in and fill the gap, which may or may not reflect the intent of policy and law.

Uttar Pradesh

Badan Singh versus Election Commissioner, 2003(4) AWC 2898 decided on 9.5.2003

On 30.6.2000 elections to a *panchayat* were held. The petitioner Badan Singh was shown to have received 597 votes whereas respondent No.6 received 585. The Election Officer issued a certificate to the petitioner stating he is elected. It is alleged that subsequently under the political pressure of the President of the *Zilla Panchayat*, the Returning Officer declared respondent No. 6 as elected without informing the petitioner. The petitioner accordingly moved a representation to the Election Commission. Not satisfied with the result thereon, the present petition was moved in the Allahabad High Court. The High Court held that once the election result is declared the only remedy is to file an election petition. In the present case, the concerned authority after declaring the petitioner elected as *pradhan* subsequently declared respondent No.6 elected as *pradhan*.

The two Judge bench of the High Court observed in this regard as follows:

"It is well-settled that once the election result is declared, the only remedy is to file an election petition vide Shambhu Singh *versus* State Election Commissioner, 2000 (4) AWC 2777: 2000 (41) ALR 111 and Smt. Ram Kanti *versus* D.M. and Others., 1995 AWC 1465, under the relevant statutory provision, which is Section 12C of the U.P. Panchayat Raj Act. The remedy of the respondent No.6 was to file an election petition. In this case the concerned authority after declaring the petitioner as elected *Pradhan* subsequently declared respondent No.6 as elected *Pradhan*. In our opinion this was clearly illegal. Hence, we allow the writ petition and direct that the petitioner shall be allowed to function as *Pradhan* and shall be given oath of *Pradhan*."

Supreme Court

In some of the States, for elections to the positions of chairpersons, the practice of 'single transferable vote' is adopted. This is the position in regard to UP *kshettra panchayats* and *Zilla Panchayats*. The single transferable vote system is based on what is internationally known as the Hare and Clark system. In Lalit Mohan Pandey *versus* Pooran Singh and Others (2004) 6 SCC626/ Air 2004 SC2303 decided on 27.4.2004), the correctness of the application of this particular system came up for consideration.

The facts of this case are briefly stated. For the post of *Adhyaksha* of *Zilla Panchayat* Champawat district situated now in the state of Uttaranchal, there were three candidates in the contest. The appellant Lalit Mohan Pandey received six first preference votes, respondent 1 received five first preference votes and the third candidate received only one. On elimination of the third candidate, both appellant and the respondent obtained six votes each. The Returning Officer declared the office to be vacant on the ground that both contesting candidates received equal votes and that none of them secured the quota of votes which was mandatory in nature. In the election petition filed, the district judge allowed the same. Aggrieved by this, an appeal was filed there by the respondent before the High Court of Uttaranchal, Nainital upheld this decision. This judgement was challenged in the appeal before the Supreme Court. The Supreme Court held that as there was only one vacancy and three candidates, the principle of transferring the votes of the eliminated candidate alone was applicable. The Apex Court further held that the High Court committed a manifest error in interpreting statutory provisions laying down procedures for declaration of results. Since the appellant received the highest number of first preference votes, the Returning Officer should have adhered to the system instead of declaring the post vacant. The judgement also contains a very useful elucidation of the principles of the single transferable vote system and its application. The relevant extracts from the judgement are contained in the Annexure A-3.1.

Conclusion

In this chapter we have considered the various cases adjudicated in the different states relating to disputes arising after the elections are held. Disputes relating to counting of votes have been a significant category. It is worth noting that Article 243-O and 243ZG of the Constitution stipulates that election disputes relating to *panchayats* and municipalities shall be agitated only through an election petition before the authorities designated for this purpose and the Civil Courts in general are barred from entertaining the same. While election petitions themselves have been undoubtedly numerous, only a few where important questions were involved have been agitated before the High Courts. It also appears that since case law regarding election disputes pertaining to Parliament and assembly elections have evolved over a much longer period, the norms and procedures relating to them have been a general guidance in settling disputes pertaining to *panchayat* and municipal elections as well.

Duration of the elected bodies and timeliness in holding elections when their tenure ends are the matters considered in the next chapter.

Annexure A-3.1

Extracts from the Judgement of the Supreme Court in Lalit Mohan Pandey versus Pooran Singh and Others

AIR 2004 SC 2303 (V.N. Khare, C.J., S.B. Sinha and S.H. Kapadia, JJ)

Hare and Clark Principle

21. Whereas the election of office by majority is the normal rule, a single transferable vote system was developed in Denmark and Britain and is known as the Hare system, named after Thomas Hare, and Englishman, one of its developers. Andrew Inglis Clark, Tasmanian Attorney-General, 1888 and a member of the Tasmani an Parliament, introduced a modified version of the Hare system into Tasmanian law in 1896. This system is now known as the Hare-Clark electoral system.

22. Every voter under the Hare system has a single vote. On the ballot paper, the voter has to rank all or any of the competing candidates giving them preferences 1,2,3 and so on. A quota is fixed which is the minimum number of votes which cannot be secured by more candidates than the number of seats. When a candidate secures votes equal to this quota, he is declared elected. If a candidate receives more votes than the quota, then he is declared elected and his surplus votes (votes exceeding the quota) are transferred to other candidates in proportion of second preference indicated in his ballot papers. After surplus votes of all candidates are transferred, if all seats are not filled in then the candidate who has polled the lowest number of votes would be considered. This process goes on till all seats are filled in by completion of quota or candidates remaining do not exceed seats still to be filled in. This system ensures actual use of maximum number of votes polled.

23. The system poses a complex system and is difficult for use where a large number of voters are illiterate. In a complex society like India where divergent, religious, linguistic or cultural groups and large number of political parties exist, use of single transferable system in election to legislatures and other bodies is although advocated but the method of voting and computations in this system sometimes renders it unsuitable for an election involving the masses. One does not know if feeling of segregation from other groups which is already there may be aggravated if this system is employed. (See *Law of Elections* by Narendra Chapalgaonker, 2nd edition)

24. The purpose of the Hare system is intended to secure representation of every shade of the electorate's opinion in direct proportion to its numerical strength.

Application of the Rule

25. The Hare-Clark electoral system is a type of proportional representation system also known as the Single Transferable Vote (S.T.V.) method. Under this system, electors vote by showing preferences for individual candidates. In order to be elected a candidate needs to receive a quota of votes. Each elector has a single vote, which can be transferred from candidate to candidate according to the preferences shown, until all the vacancies are filled.

26. As to how the Single Transferable Vote works, has been explained by Vernon Bogdanor at page 81 of his book title "What is Proportional Representation" as follows:

a) In that system, voters mark preferences for candidates in the order of their choice by using the numbers 1,2, 3, 4, 5 and so on. If there are five vacancies, voters are instructed to show five preferences; if there are seven vacancies, voters are instructed to show seven preferences.

b) In order to get elected a candidate has to receive a quota of votes. However, he may be elected without a quota. This can happen when the number of candidates remaining in the count, who have not been elected or excluded (continuing candidate) is equal to the number of vacancies that remain to be filed. Suppose there are two vacancies, for the said two vacancies, suppose there are five candidates, one of them attains the exact quota, then he stands elected. However, the remaining candidates do not secure the quota. Therefore, one vacancy out of two remains unfilled. For that vacancy, the candidate with the smallest number of votes is excluded and his votes are distributed to continuing candidates according to the remaining preferences. The eliminated candidate with smallest number of votes is called an "excluded candidate." Votes of such excluded candidates are distributed to the continuing candidates. If in the process, any continuing candidate secures the quota, he fills up the remaining vacancy. However, if despite the addition of transferred votes, the remaining continuing candidates do not secure the quota then the Returning Officer has to continue to apply the principles of elimination till the number of continuing candidates in the count is equal to the vacancy that remains to be filled. Therefore, even under the Hare system, a candidate can be elected without a quota. It operates at two levels. In cases where a candidate receives votes in excess of the quota the said system prevents wastage of surplus votes by transfer of surplus in favour of continuing candidates. In cases where the quota cannot be attained, it eliminates the candidates having the least number of votes, by principle of elimination and the votes of such excluded candidates are distributed to the remaining continuing candidates so that the resultant number is equal to the vacancy which remain to be filled.

27. In short, the Hare system works on two principles, namely, transfer of surplus votes and transfer of votes of eliminated candidates. In the present case, we are concerned with only one vacancy and three candidates and therefore the principle of transferring the votes of eliminated candidates alone is applicable.

How is a Candidate Elected?

28. A candidate is elected when his/her total number of votes equals or exceeds the quota.

What is the Quota?

29. The quota is the lowest number of votes a candidate needs to be certain of election.

30. To calculate the quota, the number of formal votes is divided by one more than the number of candidates to be elected (rounded up to the next whole number).

31. If five candidates each receive a quota (just over one sixth of the formal vote) then less than one quota of the votes remain.

Is a Quota Rule Mandatory?

32. The system states that it is always not necessary to get a quota.

33. In the House of Assembly elections, it is common that the last elected member in a division is elected without obtaining a quota. In some cases the last two elected members in a division are elected without each obtaining a quota.

34. During the distribution of preferences, some votes are "lost" from the count. A small number are lost due to rounding of fractional numbers. A more significant number of votes are "exhausted" towards the end of the count, as many ballot papers do not show a preference for any remaining candidate.

35. Where the contest for the last seat is close, it is common for the remaining two candidates to both have less than a quota. The candidate with the least votes is excluded, and the other candidate elected without reaching the quota. The more votes that are lost during the scrutiny, the more likely that not all elected members will obtain the quota.

36. A less common situation occurs where remaining three candidates are contesting the last two seats. In this case, the candidate with the least votes is excluded, and the other two candidates are elected without either reaching the quota.

4

Regularity of Elections

In this chapter, we shall consider the following:

(i) The clear purpose and intent of the constitutional amendments to ensure regular elections thereby conferring a 'right to live' on *panchayats* and municipalities.

(ii) Timeliness in holding elections and the measures necessary to avoid a hiatus.

(iii) The duration and tenure of the elected bodies and their chairpersons; and

(iv) Some issues of uncertainty still pending for adjudication.

The Constitutional Objectives

It is pertinent to mention, the inclusion of the two chapters on *panchayats* and municipalities in the Constitution of India was a deliberate action to secure and strengthen democracy at the grassroot levels. The Constitutional mandate makes it abundantly and unambiguously clear that there should be regularity of elections and consequent smooth transfer of power to the newly elected body by its predecessor. This was acknowledged in the Statement of Objects and Reasons when the Bill to amend was moved in Parliament on 11.9.1991. The provisions with respect to timely conduct of elections in the 74th Amendment are as follows:

"243E. Duration of *panchayats*, etc.

(1) Every *panchayat,* unless sooner dissolved under any law for the time being in force, shall continue for five years from the date appointed for its first meeting and no longer.

"(2) No amendment of any law for the time being in force shall have the effect of causing dissolution of a *panchayat* at any level, which is functioning immediately before such amendment, till the expiration of its duration specified in clause (1).

"(3) An election to constitute a *panchayat* shall be completed-

(a) before the expiry of its duration specified in clause (1);

(b) before the expiration of a period of six months from the date of its dissolution;

Provided that were the remainder of the period for which the dissolved *panchayat* would have continued is less than six months, it shall not be necessary to hold any election under this clause for constituting the *panchayat*.

"(4) A *panchayat* constituted upon the dissolution of a *panchayat* before the expiration of its duration shall continue only for the remainder of the period for which the dissolved *panchayat* would have continued under Clause (1) had it not been so dissolved.

"243U. Duration of Municipalities etc.

"(1) Every municipality, unless sooner dissolved under any law for the time being in force, shall continue for five years from the date appointed for its first meeting and no longer;

Provided that a municipality shall be given a reasonable opportunity of being heard before its dissolution.

"(2) No amendment of any law for the time being in force shall have the effect of causing dissolution of a municipality at any level, which is functioning immediately before such amendment, till the expiration of its duration specified in clause (1).

"(3) An election to constitute a municipality shall be completed-

(a) before the expiry of its duration specified in clause (1);

(b) before the expiration of a period of six months from the date of its dissolution.

"Provided that where the remainder of the period for which the dissolved municipality would have continued is less than six months, it shall not be necessary to hold any election under this clause for constituting the municipality for such period.

"(4) A municipality constituted upon the dissolution of a municipality before the expiration of its duration shall continue only for the remainder of the period for which the dissolved municipality would have continued under clause (1) had it not been so dissolved."

It is obvious from these provisions that every *panchayat* or municipality shall continue for five years from the date of its first meeting. But it can be dissolved earlier in accordance with the procedure prescribed by state law but that dissolution can last only for six months and fresh elections must take place before the expiry of the above period. A *panchayat* or a municipality reconstituted after premature dissolution (i.e. before the expiry of the full period of five years) shall continue only for the remainder of the period. But if the remainder of the period is less than six months, it shall not be necessary to hold elections. The word "supercession" is not used which practice was in vogue before the amendments. It is also worth noting as mentioned before that the statement of objects and reasons, when both the *Panchayat* and *Nagarpalika* Amendment Bills were introduced, specifically mentions that "in many states, local bodies have become weak and ineffective on account of a variety of reasons including the failure to hold regular elections, prolonged supercession and inadequate devolution...it is considered necessary that provisions are incorporated in the Constitution....for ensuring regular conduct of elections."

These provisions make it abundantly clear that the continuity of a *panchayat* or a municipality is a principal intent and purpose of the Constitution. Nevertheless the implementation of even this single most important provision has had to be agitated before various High Courts and the Apex Court to obtain positive verdicts in line with the constitutional mandate. Despite these judgements, the timely conduct of elections continues to be fraught with uncertainties. A hiatus occurs, often man made, rather than supervening forces of nature in the timely conduct of elections. It is necessary to understand the case law on the issue including the facts of the cases so that one is forewarned about the possible array of omissions and commissions creating such hiatus and be better prepared to seek judicial intervention as necessary. For this chapter, we shall consider the cases in a chronological sequence rather than state wise. This will also give an indication of the progress of the case law on the issue.

Anugrah Narain Singh and Another *versus* State of UP and Others (1996) 6 SCC 303)

In 1996 itself, just four years after the amendment of the Constitution, in Anugrah Narain Singh and Another *versus* State of UP and Others (1996) 6 SCC 303) the Supreme Court dealt with the aspect of timely conduct of elections. Since no municipal elections had taken place in the state of Uttar Pradesh for 10 years, pursuant to the writ petition moved by the appellant, the High Court directed the state government to conclude the elections by 31.11.1995. Notification for the election was issued accordingly on 11th and 13th October, 1995. Ten persons filed writ petitions in the High Court and fifteen similar petitions before the Lucknow Bench, challenging this notification on the grounds of defects in the electoral rolls, delimitation of constituencies and arbitrary reservation. The High Court dismissed these petitions on the ground that in view of the bar imposed by Article 243-ZG of the Constitution, the writ jurisdiction of the court could not be invoked to stall the election process. This judgement of the Lucknow Bench of the High Court (comprising two Judges) and the other connected cases was placed before the Allahabad High Court. A Division Bench passed the impugned order stopping the election process regardless of the judgement and order passed by the Lucknow Bench of the High Court barely one week before the voting was scheduled to commence.

The Supreme Court in appeal held that in terms of Article 243-ZG of the Constitution there is a complete and absolute bar in considering any matter relating to municipal election on any ground whatsoever after the publication of the notification for holding municipal elections. The bar imposed by Article 243-ZG was twofold. Validity of laws relating to delimitation and allotment of seats made under Article 243-ZA could not be questioned in any court. No election to a municipality can be questioned except by an election petition. Moreover, it is well settled that if the election is imminent or well under way, the court should not intervene to stop the election process. If this is allowed to be done, no election will ever take place because someone or the other will always find some excuse to move the court and stall the elections. It was held that the High Court overlooked the fact that no municipal election had been held in the state for nearly ten years and the dates of the elections were fixed under the direction given by the High Court in another case. If elections are allowed to be stalled on the complaint of a few individuals, then grave injustice will be done to crores of other voters who have a right to elect their representatives to the local bodies.

The Supreme Court further held that so far as preparation of the electoral roll is concerned, there were sufficient safeguards in the Act against any abuse or misuse of power. In view of the provisions for filing objections and also the right of appeal against inclusion, deletion and correction of names and also to the constitutional authority of the Election Commission to give directions in all matters pertaining to elections, there was hardly any scope for a court to intervene and correct the electoral rolls under Article 226 of the Constitution. Therefore, the Court should not have intervened at all on the basis of allegations as to preparation of electoral rolls. It was held that if this is allowed to be done, every election will be indefinitely delayed and it will not be possible to comply with the mandate of the Constitution that every municipality shall have a life span of five years, or less, if dissolved earlier, and thereafter fresh elections will have to be held within the time specified in clause (3) of Article 243-U.

The Apex Court's decisions were reinforced in another important public interest litigation regarding timely conduct of elections. In Rural Litigation and Entitlement Kendra and another *versus*

Government of UP and others (Writ Petition (C) No.719 of 1995) passed a series of orders and finally held on 12.8.1997 as follows:

> Before we part, we may, however, indicate that the 73rd amendment of the Constitution was made with the stated object of continuity of *panchayat* bodies regulating the tenure. Article 243 M of the Constitution envisages that the tenure of the *panchayat* shall be five years from the date appointed for its first meeting and shall continue no longer than that. Even a *panchayat* constituted upon premature dissolution of the earlier one, shall not continue beyond the tenure of five years. Article 243-E also provides that election of the *panchayat* shall be held before the expiry of the said tenure of five years or within six months of its dissolution as the case may be. In order to ensure holding of election of *panchayats*, Article 243-M of the Constitution provides that laws relating to *panchayats* in the states inconsistent with the 73rd Amendment shall continue in force only for a year from the commencement of the Seventy Third Amendment unless the competent legislature has repealed or suitably amended such laws in the meantime. It is necessary to emphasise that various clauses of Article 243 are to be followed in letter and spirit. The concerned states cannot be permitted to withhold election of *panchayats* except in cases of genuine supervening difficulties to hold such election e.g. unforeseen natural calamities in the state like floods, earthquakes etc. or extremely urgent situation prevailing in the state for which election of the *panchayats* cannot be held within the time frame. It will be unfortunate if the concerned states remain insensitive to the constitutional mandate of holding election of *panchayats* in time and my unjustified inaction, allows old bodies to continue in the office of the *panchayats*. We hope and expect that the state government will be alive and sensitive to the duties and responsibilities flowing from the mandates of the Constitution in holding *panchayat* elections.

B.K. Chandrashekhar and Another *versus* State of Karnataka (W.P. No.3679 of 1999 and W.P. No.3826 of 1999), AIR, 1999 KAR 461, decided on 17.3.1999

One of the early and prominent cases with respect to timely conduct of elections was heard by the High Court of Karnataka. In B.K. Chandrashekhar and Another *versus* State of Karnataka (W.P. No.3679 of 1999 and W.P. No.3826 of 1999), AIR, 1999 KAR 461, decided on 17.3.1999. Pursuant to the 73rd Amendment about 5660 *gram panchayats* were organised in Karnataka and elections to the same were held in March/April 1994. Fresh elections were therefore due in March/April 1999. The State Election Commission started making preparation for the same from mid 1998. A new government which had come into power in the state wanted to make some structural changes in the *panchayat* set up such as reducing the number of *gram panchayats* by increasing their population yardstick, removing the provisions for compulsory rotation of reserved constituencies etc. In January 1999, the government issued an ordinance to bring about these changes. The writ petitions challenged the *vires* of this ordinance and alleged it was for the ostensible purpose of not holding elections and thereby violating the constitutional mandate. The Karnataka High Court in a well reasoned judgement of a Division Bench held that though the state government has the competence to legislate on the subject, if by giving effect to the ordinance the constitutional requirement of holding timely elections is defeated, the state law has to yield before the Constitution. Extracts of the judgement are reproduced below *in extenso*.

"There is a constitutional compulsion to create and keep alive the *panchayats* which are the institutions of local self-governance. The power of the State Legislature is reduced and is to be so exercised as to subserve the constitutional mandates newly engrafted by the 73rd Amendment. The *panchayats* which were creatures of state legislatures have now attained the status of constitutional institutions and their composition etc., are governed by constitutional provisions which provide that the population ratio has to be uniform throughout the state. Seats can only be filled up by direct elections. Under Article 2453-E duration of the *panchayat* has been constitutionally limited to 5 years. Dissolution is permissible but not extension. Elections to new *panchayats* have to be completed before the expiry of the duration of the outgoing *panchayat* and in the case of dissolution before the expiry of six months from the date of its dissolution. Elections are completely in the hands of the Election Commission. The State Election Commissioner is an independent constitutional functionary.

"No doubt the State Legislature has the power to amend Sections 4 and 5 of the Panchayati Raj Act. The object with which they are sought to be amended may be laudable and may result in a more efficacious way of governance of the *panchayat*. But if the same results in flouting the constitutional mandate to conducting the elections within the time frame set out in the Constitution, then the same has to be ignored. Article 243-E mandates that every *panchayat* unless sooner dissolved under any law for the time being in force, shall continue for five years from the date appointed for its first meeting and no longer. The maximum period for which a *panchayat* can function is five years. The use of the word 'shall' and thereafter 'no longer' regarding continuation of an existing *panchayat* under Article 243E shows that the duration of the *panchayat* is constitutionally limited to five years. Its dissolution may be permissible under given circumstances but there can be no extension of this period. Article 243E of the Constitution is mandatory and not directory. In the context of subject matter and the importance of the provision to the general object intended to be secured by the 73rd Amendment Article 243E had to be held to be mandatory and not directory as suggested by the Advocate-General. The state legislature would lack the legislative competence to enact any provision which seeks to nullify or modify the mandate of Article 243E providing for the duration of *panchayat* and holding of the next elections. Article 243E brooks no defiance of its mandate and would brush aside any unconstitutional obstacles and hurdles put in its way.

"Since the subject of term of the *panchayat* is taken care of specifically and exclusively by Article 243E by necessary implication, the subject stands excluded from the field covered by Entry 5 of List II. It can neither expressly or incidentally trench upon the mandate of the Constitution for holding the election within five years of the expiry of the term of the outgoing *panchayat*."

The court had also considered the possible consequences of the ordinance on the election schedule. To quote: "During the course of arguments we had asked Mr. Acharya, learned Counsel appearing for State Election Commission as to within how much time the Election Commission would be able to hold elections, if the ordinance is given effect to. According to him it will take in all atleast seven months to hold the elections as fresh notifications under Section 5(1), (2) and (5) have to be issued. On the expiry of the period of five years, the present elected bodies would become functus officio. The *gram panchayats* will not be having an elected body which would result in breakdown of the democratic set up envisaged by the Constitution. In order to prevent such a situation it would be necessary to direct the respondents to hold elections to the *Gram Panchayats* in the state of Karnataka immediately. We are not holding that the state legislature does not have the competence to amend Sections 4 and 5 of the Panchayat Raj Act. If it has the power to enact it has necessarily the power to amend those provisions as well. But as the amendment results in nullifying the mandate of the Constitution of India specially when the process of election had begun, the same is held to be not applicable to the present elections to *gram panchayats* due to be held in the month of March/April 1999. If there is conflict between the mandatory provision of the Constitution and the right of the state legislature to enact laws which falls within its legislative competence and which results in nullifying the mandate of the Constitution then in such a case provision of the Constitution would take precedence. If such a view is not taken then the mandate of the Constitution can be flouted with impunity by the state legislature on one pretext or the other. The Constitution is supreme and the laws by the legislature have to enacted subject to the provisions of the Constitution of India and therefore subservient to it. Press Note at Annexure-B issued by the Election Commission attached in W.P.No.3826 of 1999 is quashed."

State of Haryana and Another *versus* Surjit Singh and Others (JT 2000(7) SC 320) decided on 1.2.2000

The attention of the Apex Court was drawn to the question of timely election once again in the State of Haryana and Another Vs. Surjit Singh and Others (JT 2000(7) SC 320) decided on 1.2.2000. The case related to the holding of elections to the Municipal Corporation, Faridabad as well as other municipal councils, *gram panchayats, panchayat samitis* and *zilla parishads*. Citing dissolution of the Haryana Assembly and the elections to be held thereafter in

February 2000, the Haryana government contended it would be possible to hold elections to rural and urban local bodies by the end of February 2006 and some more time was required for the purpose. The High Court in its orders of December 1999 and 21st January 2000 made in the review application have directed the state government and the State Election Commission to hold these elections on time. Upon an appeal by the State government in the Supreme Court, the Apex Court reviewed a tentative time schedule proposed by the government but felt the same was not reasonable. Accordingly with the consent of all the parties to the proceedings, the Apex Court directed that elections to the *panchayats* should be completed by 31.3.2000 and to the Municipalities by 7th April 2000. The Court expressed the considered opinion that the democratic process of election should not be postponed unduly.

Prem Lal Patel *versus* State of UP, through the Secretary, *Panchayati Raj* and Another (W.P. No.1371 of 2000)

The High Court of Uttar Pradesh on 3.4.2000 passed an important judgement similar to the RLEK case in Prem Lal Patel *versus* State of UP, through the Secretary, Panchayati Raj and Another (W.P. No.1371 of 2000). The petitioner challenged the validity of the Ordinance through which amendments to the Uttar Pradesh Panchayati Raj Act, 1947 were carried out. The Ordinance inserted a new sub-section 3A, according to which elections to the *Panchayat* could be deferred due to unavoidable circumstances or in the public interest. In addition, this ordinance also inserted sub-section 3 under Section 12BB whereby the State Government in consultation with the State Election Commission by notification could appoint the date for holding general election or bye-election to the office of the *pradhan, up-pradhan* or members of a *gram panchayat*. It was held that the Ordinance in question was unconstitutional and *ultra vires* of the provisions of Articles 243E and 243K of the Constitution. It was also held that such an ordinance was not only violative of Article 234K of the Constitution but also invalidated the powers of the State Election Commission. It was further held that if the state government does not abide by the Constitutional mandate and issues an ordinance which goes against the constitution and delays holding of elections the state government is to be blamed for the same.

State Election Commission *versus* the State of Andhra Pradesh and Another, W.P. No 2481 of 2000 decided on 21.4.2000

Around the same time an extraordinary litigation was being considered in the AP High Court when the State Election Commission itself was seeking the court's intervention to ensure the state government's compliance with the constitutional mandate. State Election Commission *versus* the State of Andhra Pradesh and Another, W.P. No 2481 of 2000 decided on 21.4.2000 along with various accompanying petitions including an Intervention Application from the Institute of Social Sciences, Delhi). Timely elections in the state of Andhra Pradesh were sought to be impeded by the promulgation of the Andhra Pradesh Mandal Parishad and Zilla Parishad (Transitional Arrangements) Ordinance 2000, through which arrangements were made providing for the administration of *mandal parishad* and *zilla parishad* till the next ordinary elections to these bodies were held. The petitioners challenged the said ordinance and sought to quash the same as being untenable and repugnant to Article 243-E (3) of the Constitution of India. The High Court took into account Section 153(5) read with Section 154 of the A.P. Panchayati Raj Act, 1994 which stated that the term of office of the President or Vice-President of a *mandal parishad* who is elected in an ordinary election shall be five years from the date appointed by the State Election Commissioner for the first meeting of a *mandal parishad* after the ordinary elections. Similarly, under sub-section(6) of Section 181 read with Section 182 of the A.P. Panchayati Raj Act, 1994, the term of office of the Chairman or Vice-Chairman of a *zilla parishad* who is elected at an ordinary election shall be five years from the date appointed by the State Election Commissioner for the first meeting of the *zilla parishad* after the ordinary election. It was noted that elections were held to the *mandal parishads* and *zilla parishads* in the state of Andhra Pradesh on 6.3.1995 and 10.3.1995 and their term was to expire on 17.3.2000 and 19.3.2000. The High Court invalidated the said ordinance and the consequent orders. It rejected the request of some of the writ petitioners in the accompanying petition to continue the elected members to these bodies beyond their term of five years till ordinary elections are held and directed the State Election Commission to complete the entire process of elections to the Panchayati Raj bodies within a time-bound period.

As in the Chandrasekhar case, the AP High Court also referred to the Apex Court's decision in the RLEK case. It then proceeded to analyse whether any of the grounds mentioned in the ordinance promulgated by the AP government for not holding elections to the *Panchayat* bodies could be considered as 'supervening difficulties.' It came to the conclusion that the provisions of Article 243E of the Constitution are mandatory and not directory. There is no escape for a state government from holding elections to the local bodies on the ground that an amendment proposed to Article 243C is pending before the Parliament. Anticipating an amendment cannot be a ground for postponement. While recognising that the state government's decision to revert to a different structure of the Panchayati Raj system may be a genuine effort, anticipating a constitutional amendment to bring about such an altered system and postponing elections because of avoidable financial burden in holding them could not be accepted as supervening difficulties.

The AP High Court also specifically took up the query of the State Election Commission whether it was justified in approaching the High Court for seeking its intervention in ensuring timely elections. To quote: "when the State Election Commission which is a constitutional functionary is confronted with a situation against the backdrop of promulgation of ordinance No.3 of 2000 by the state government, making transitional arrangement and the consequent communication dated 10.2.2000 sent to it by the state government indicating the desire of the government to postpone the elections, the Election Commission which is an authority under Article 243-K of the Constitution for holding elections to *Panchayati Raj* bodies was placed in a precarious situation. The State Election Commission cannot function and discharge its duties without the cooperation of the state government. However, in the backdrop of promulgation of Ordinance No.3 of 2000 dated 5.2.2000 and in the absence of the state government identifying the seats/offices reserved for SCs, STs, BCs and women and forwarding such list to the Election Commission, the State Election Commission cannot proceed with the conduct of elections to these bodies. Having regard to these circumstances, we are of the view, the State Election Commission is justified in approaching this Court seeking appropriate directions. We answer this issue accordingly."

This is an important observation of the High Court which has been reiterated by a few other High Courts as well such as Gujarat in the *Panchayat Parishad* case. The SEC is a constitutional authority mandated to carry out timely elections. It cannot be a mute witness if other executive authorities fail to perform the tasks for which they are responsible and thereby defeat or undermine the SEC's constitutional mandate. Six years later the Constitution Bench of the Supreme Court found it necessary to reiterate these points with significant force.

State of Maharashtra and Others *versus* Jalgaon Municipal Council and Others (2003 9 SCC 731) decided on 14.2.2003

Are there some exigencies where a hiatus is inevitable resulting in delay in holding elections which were due? This issue became prominent in State of Maharashtra and Others *versus* Jalgaon Municipal Council and Others (2003) 9 SCC 731) decided on 14.2.2003. The proposal for converting Jalgaon city from a Municipal Council to a Municipal Corporation was under consideration of the state government. Notice of the same was issued on 16.10.2001 inviting objections within two months. An ordinance was issued before the expiry of the said two months reducing it to 30 days. Later on two notifications were issued, published in the official gazette dated 15.11.2001, amending the notification dated 16.10.2001 and limiting the period for making objections till 21.11.2001. The said ordinance was repealed and replaced by an Act having the same contents. The objections received highlighted two issues; firstly that the development activity in progress and undertaken by the municipal council would be hampered by switching over to a municipal corporation and secondly, the constitution of a municipal corporation would result in imposition of newer and higher taxes.

There was no dispute on the population crossing the benchmark of three lakh requiring the constitution of a Municipal Corporation. While the final notification was yet to be issued several writ petitions came to be filed in the High Court laying challenge to the proposal of the state government. The matter was taken up and consequently the process of constitution of the municipal corporation was stalled. However, in between, the State Election Commission announced elections for the next municipal council to be held on 9.12.2001, which were held and the newly elected municipal council assumed office on 17.12.2001. Eventually, the writ petitions challenging the setting up of a corporation were allowed and notifications/ proclamations dated 16.10.2001 and 15.11.2001 were quashed. The High Court also refused to stay the operation of its judgement as the new municipal council had already been elected. The rationale behind the judgement of the High Court was that there should be no interregnum or hiatus between the dissolution of the municipal Council and the date of the municipal corporation into existence; for such hiatus would necessarily involve a government officer being appointed an administrator and that will be subversive of the principles of democracy and local self-governance. Reliance was also placed on the provisions of Article 243-U (3) (a) which mandates that an election to constitute a 'Municipality' shall be completed before the expiry of its duration specified in clause (1) of Article 243-U.

The judgement of the High Court was challenged by the state of Maharashtra in the Supreme Court. The appeals were allowed and it was held that a hiatus is an unavoidable event, which must take place in the process of conversion of municipal council into a municipal corporation, and Article 243-U cannot be relied on for challenging hiatus in conversion. The use of expression 'a municipality' in sub-Article (3) of Article 243-U in the context and in the setting in which it is empowered suggests and means the duration of the same type of municipality coming to an end and the same type of successor municipality taking over as a consequence of term of the previous municipality coming to an end. Article 243-U cannot be applied to a case where the area of one description is converted into an area of another description and one description of municipality is ceased by constituting another municipality of a better description. Article 243-U (3) cannot be pressed into service to base a submission on that an election to constitute a Municipal Corporation is required to be completed before the expiry of duration of a municipal council. The constitution of municipal corporation would require notification of a larger urban area and a municipal corporation to govern it. The area shall have to be divided into wards with the number of corporations specified and reservations made. The corporation would need to nominate councillors. The territorial limits may need to be altered. The State Election Commission cannot conduct elections without specifying numbers and boundaries of wards. New rules, by-laws etc., shall need to be framed and the municipal tax structure may need to be recast. The statutory provisions do not contemplate a situation where the same area may be called a smaller and a larger area simultaneously and the process of constitution of the municipal corporation being commenced and completed though the municipal council continues to exist. Such an action would result in anomaly and confusion if not chaos. Care has been taken by the legislature by engrafting Section 452A into the body by the Bombay Provincial Municipal Corporation (Amendment and Validation) Act, 1995 at Maharashtra Act 4 of 1995).

The court further held that the Administrator once appointed shall not continue to stretch and unreasonably extend his term of office and may not be instrumental in obstructing the elections being held. The law does not permit any officer serving as an Administrator beyond the first meeting of the Corporation or a period of six months from the date of specification of an area as a larger urban area. Thus, the maximum period for which an Administrator may be in office shall be six months and within this much period the state government and the State Election Commission shall positively bring the Municipal Corporation into existence so as to take over the administration from the Administrator.

A. Kadirappa and Others *versus* Government of AP and others decided on 27.3.2003; 2003(3 ALT 270)

Hiatus between the end of the term of one body and the succession by another body through election came up in a case before the AP High Court, i.e., A. Kadirappa and Others *versus* Government of AP and Others decided on 27.3.2003; 2003(3 ALT 270). The question of extending the duration of an intermediate level *panchayat* and deferring the elections for that body came up for adjudication. Ordinary elections to *mandal parishads* (*panchayats* at the intermediate level) in the Anantapur district of AP were held during 1995. In respect of one *mandal parishad* however, Bukkarayasamudram the *parishad* could not function because of certain government orders and the first meeting of this *parishad* was held on 27.2.1997. Ordinary elections became due in respect of all the *parishads* in the district in 2000. The term of the elected representatives were to expire on 17.3.2000 but the elections could not be held in the state due to other reasons already discussed in the other case of State Election Commission *versus* State of AP. To cover the contingency, the AP government promulgated an ordinance providing for administration of the *mandal parishads* by the special officers. Some of the elected members of the Bukkarayasamudram *parishad* challenged this, claiming that they should have continued in office for five years from their first meeting i.e. 27.2.2002 and under the ordinance they had to relinquish their post 18 months earlier. When the case was in progress the AP government issued orders allowing them to continue. While this petition thus became infructuous there was another petition, which challenged such continuation. The sole question remaining for determination was about the competency of the government, in having issued the order permitting the *mandal parishad* members to continue. The court held as follows:

"In the instant case the *mandal parishad* was not dissolved by any order. In fact the *mandal parishad* could not work because of certain government orders issued by the government but later, on realising the mistake, another proceeding was issued by virtue of which members of the *mandal parishad* continued to function till

27.2.2002. There is neither any provision in the Act nor any authority vests in the government which enables it to issue government order like the one dated 24.4.2002 extending the term of the office of the members of the *mandal parishad* beyond the period of the last date *viz.*, 27.2.2002 which has necessarily to be fixed with reference to the first meeting of the *mandal parishad* after the election. The date cannot be extended in any circumstances. The learned Additional Advocate-General contended that there is no prohibition in the Act prohibiting the government from extending the time and the impugned government order is legal and valid. We cannot accept this submission in view of the provisions contained in Clause (1) of Article 243-E of the Constitution which says that the *panchayat* shall continue for 5 years and no longer from the date appointed for its first meeting."

Junagadh Municipality *versus* State of Gujarat (2003(3) GLR 2663) decided on 8.10.2003

At about the same time that the Jalgaon case was being considered by the Apex Court, another case under somewhat similar circumstances arose in the neighbouring state of Gujarat i.e., Junagadh Municipality *versus* State of Gujarat (2003(3) GLR 2663) decided on 8.10.2003. In this case important issues regarding the Constitution of a municipal corporation replacing an existing municipality when the tenure of that municipality had still not come to an end as well as the satisfaction of the 'Governor' as distinct from the 'government' in arriving at the decision to constitute a corporation and other related issues were raised. Briefly stated, the Junagadh Municipal Board had come into existence after elections held and a party different to the ruling party in the state obtained a two-thirds majority in the elections. The first meeting was held during 1999-2000 and therefore the elected municipality was entitled to continue upto 19.1.2005. In April 2002 a proposal was made to include 8 *gram panchayats* adjoining the Junagadh municipality and constitute them into a corporation. These *gram panchayats* opposed the move. Later on in July 2002, the state government decided to constitute a municipal corporation for Junagadh comprising the existing Junagadh municipality as well as 11 village *panchayats*. By a further notification issued in September 2002 an Administrator for the said corporation was appointed for a period of 2½ years or the date of the first election of the new corporation whichever is earlier. A writ petition was filed challenging these orders. Given the pace and spread of urbanisation, replacing municipalities by corporation with enlarged boundaries and jurisdiction will take place frequently. It is important to understand the legal implications of such a change; the arrangements to be made during the transition and ensuring that the constitutional requirements are not infringed. In regard to the present Junagadh case, the sequence of events preceding these orders as well as the decisions of the court in some of the petitions which related to these orders and earlier development are best recounted in the orders of the court itself. Appropriate extracts from the judgement are contained in the Annexure A-4.1.

In the event the High Court did uphold the orders of the government but several important aspects pertaining to constitution of municipal corporations and related issues also came up for consideration. One was that in the matter of constituting a municipal council, a municipal corporation or similar institutions, it is not the personal satisfaction of the Governor but due consideration of the matter by the Council of Ministers on whose advice the Governor is to act. The second was that the constitution of a municipal area is essentially an activity of a legislative nature and as such the procedures of natural justice do not apply. Unless the state laws dealing with the creation of a municipal corporation specifically provide for inviting objections or public hearing providing such opportunities is not obligatory. Thirdly the contention that replacing a municipality by a municipal corporation did not amount to the dissolution of a municipality was not agreed to. This contention in the instant case has a considerable significance because in the normal course of events the expectation is that before making any changes in the area or a rural local body an opportunity would be given to the citizens of the area to be heard. The cases of Sundar Das Kanhaiyalal Bhatija and Tehal Singh referred in this case vide paras 26 and 27 of the judgement does give considerable powers to a state government in these matters.

Unless the opportunity for public hearing or objection is specifically provided for in the relevant state laws, the state government would be free to act as it considered appropriate in the guise of legislative action.

The court, however, did add one direction. This was regarding the extension of the term of the Administrator beyond the period of one year. The court considered it unfortunate that elections for the newly constituted municipal corporation had not been held within that year. The court accordingly directed the state government to take up the matter with the State Election Commission for holding the election of the Corporation within a period of three months and if in the event of any supervening difficulties, it would not be done. The elected members of the erstwhile Junagadh municipality would be considered to be the councillors of the Junagadh Municipal Corporation.

It is respectfully submitted that this direction does appear to be fair and equitable and is intended to spur the state government to action. Nevertheless, the constitutional provision requires a corporation to be composed of representatives elected for that purpose. The Hon. Court's direction, it is respectfully submitted, does not also appear to be congruous with the stand taken by the State government and agreed to by the court itself that upon creation of the corporation, the erstwhile municipality stood automatically abolished/abrogated/extinguished.

Despite the decisions of the High Courts and the Apex Court on the timely conduct of elections, issues kept recurring and elections were delayed in many cases. We may now consider three cases decided recently. Two pertain to Gujarat and one to Karnataka, decided in 2005 and 2006 respectively. In all these cases failure to complete or undertake delimitation of the territorial constituencies on the basis of the latest census figures have been important issues.

Babubhai Karsanbhai Raika *versus* Gujarat State Election Commission decided on 21.9.2005

In Babubhai Karsanbhai Raika *versus* Gujarat State Election Commission decided on 21.9.2005 (Special Civil Application No.19047 of 2005, four councillors of Surat, Vadodara, Rajkot and Bhavnagar municipal corporation prayed for a writ to direct the Gujarat State Election Commission to hold elections for constituting the municipal corporations for the respective cities before the expiry of their term in 2005. It was noted that the State Election Commission itself had commenced preparations for this purpose and was reminding the state government repeatedly to determine the number of seats to be reserved and other related matters so that the commission could proceed with its own work of delimitation. There was also a complicating factor because for Parliament and assembly constituencies a separate Delimitation Commission had been set up with countrywide jurisdiction. This Commission had asked all the states not to alter the existing administrative boundaries including municipal wards until its exercise of delimitation had been completed. The court discussed extensively the constitutional requirements about timely elections including revision of electoral rolls. A time schedule for holding the elections was furnished by the state government. Eventually the court directed the Election Commission and other concerned authorities to organise elections according to the programme submitted before the court so as to complete the process by December 2005. The court further observed that *"before parting with the matter, we cannot help observing and expressing our confidence that once the State Election Commissioner reads the propositions laid down and the observations made by us in paragraphs 14 to 18 of this judgement, there would be no occasion for any citizen to file a petition for timely conduct and completion of elections to institutions of local self-government like municipal corporations, municipalities and panchayats in the state of Gujarat. Just in case there has to be any such petition, we hope that it will be one filed by the State Election Commissioner."* (emphasis supplied).

Gujarat Pradesh Panchayat Parishad and Hiteshbhai Kantilal Barot *versus* State Election Commission and Others (Special Civil Application Nos. 10602 and 10603 to 10605 of 2005)

Another judgement quickly followed on 29.9.2005 in Gujarat Pradesh Panchayat Parishad and Hiteshbhai Kantilal Barot *versus* State Election Commission and Others (Special Civil Application

Nos. 10602 and 10603 to 10605 of 2005). Here again the appellants were seeking directions of the court to the SEC and others for timely elections to the *panchayats* including some which as a result of population increase were to become *nagar panchayats*. The discussion on the constitutional requirements were extensive in this case as well. Reference was made to an earlier decision of the same Court's Division Bench while interpreting the provisions of parts IX and IXA of the Constitution when the Bench enunciated the following principles:

"It will be seen that the provisions of parts IX and IXA do not contemplate any hiatus. The elections are required to be regularly held and the only time that an unelected body can exist is when it is superseded. Even then it is incumbent to hold the elections within six months of the supercession. Whereas under Article 83 and Article 172 the duration of the Parliament and the state legislatures can be extended due to the proclamation of Emergency, in the case of local authorities no such contingency is contemplated by part IX and IXA of the Constitution and election schedule has to adhere to the provisions of Articles 243-E and 243-U of the Constitution. Therefore, any attempt on the part of the executive or the state legislature not to hold elections cannot be permitted."

The court also considered whether the time limit for elections should or should not be enforced when they seemingly contradict the right of fair representation which is the essence of a delimitation exercise. The court considered four sets of issues in relation to (i) the circumstances requiring delimitation (ii) reasons for the delay/ inaction on the part of the authorities in commencing/completing the delimitation exercise (iii) when a court is moved for issuing a writ of *mandamus* for timely elections and (iv) onus on the authorities to undertake and complete delimitation and other requirements for election.

Regarding the circumstances requiring delimitation, the court delineated the following:

(a) Where there is a change of status of a local body from one category to another (e.g. Jalgaon Municipal Council case).

(b) Where new areas are brought within the territorial limits of an existing local body.

(c) Where any areas are taken out or excluded from the territorial limits of an existing local body.

(d) Where the latest census figures are published.

In regard to the second category the court's view was that "when the delay in conducting and completing elections is attributable to natural calamities like floods, earthquakes etc., then certainly the Election Commission or the courts would not insist on compliance with the time limit because the law does not compel one to do that which one cannot possibly perform.

Regarding the third category about when a petition can be moved for a writ, the court explained that if the petition is filed at the last moment the court may decline to exercise its jurisdiction. In this connection the court referred to the Special Civil Application No.19047 of 2005, referred to in para 5.5.1 above which was decided on the 21st September, 2005. The petition was dismissed because it was filed only on the 16th September though the state government had issued notifications on 8th June itself re-determining the number of wards and the number of reserved seats and the revised voters list were to be published on 29th December.

In regard to the fourth category namely the onus on the authorities the court held "when the constitutional provisions stipulate mandatory time limits for holding elections.....it is for the authorities including the state government and the Election Commission to show what steps have been taken by them for timely completion of elections. It is therefore, not at all necessary for the petitioners to allege, much less to prove, malafides. Elucidating on compliance with statutory provisions, the court summarised the legal and constitutional positions as follows:

(a) when there is no Parliamentary legislation or rule made under the said legislation, the State Election Commission is free to pass any orders in respect of the conduct of elections,

(b) where there is an Act and express rules made thereunder, it is not open to the Commission to override the Act or the rules and pass order in direct disobedience to the mandate contained in the Act or the rules. In other words, the powers of the Commission are meant to supplement rather than supplant the law (both statute and rules) in the matter of superintendence, direction and control as provided by Article 324,

(c) where the Act or the rules are silent, the Commission has no doubt plenary powers under Article 324 to give any direction in respect of the conduct of elections, and

(d) where a particular direction by the Commission is submitted to the government for approval, as required by the rules, it is not open to the Commission to go ahead with the implementation of it at its own sweet will even if the approval of the government is not given.

In conclusion the court directed the State Election Commission to hold elections to the *taluk* and district *panchayats* and complete the same by October 2005 without waiting for completion of the delimitation exercise on the basis of the 2001 Census figures. The operating paragraph of the judgement is reproduced below.

"As regards the status of the 60 areas converted from *gram panchayats* into *nagar panchayats* by government notification dated $10^{th}/12^{th}$ August 2005 and determination of number of seats for different *taluka panchayats* and district *panchayats* and reservation of seats, we direct that for the purposes of holding elections to 209 *taluka panchayats* and 23 district *panchayats* in October 2005, the State Election Commission shall hold elections for the constituencies already determined on the basis of the 1991 census without waiting for completion of the delimitation exercise on the basis of the 2002 census figures and these elections shall be conducted on the basis of electoral rolls revised in 2004. The 60 areas in question will be treated as parts of the respective *taluka panchayats* and district *panchayats* for the purpose of the ensuing elections but this direction shall not preclude the state government and the State Election Commission from undertaking or completing the exercise of demarcation of the boundaries of those areas, delimitation of their constituencies and preparation for the electoral rolls for those constituencies for the purpose of holding elections to the municipal boroughs in those areas."

It will thus be seen that while generally the High Courts have held that though delimitation and determination of reserved constituencies are important preliminary steps and also pre-requisites under relevant state laws, failure to perform these actions should not result in breaching the constitutional obligation to hold timely elections. When delimitation has been or is likely to be delayed due to various reasons, an attempt was also made by the Rajasthan Government to hold timely elections by providing in law, that elections could be held on the basis of previous delimitation. However, this initiative did not succeed.

Patta Ram Bheel *versus* State of Rajasthan, (RLW 2005(1) Raj 415) decided on 20.10.2004

In Patta Ram Bheel *versus* State of Rajasthan, (RLW 2005(1) Raj 415 decided on 20.10.2004), the holding of municipal elections in Rajasthan was challenged on the ground that delimitation on the basis of the 2001 census had not been done. The State Election Commission contended that though the Commission and the state government were prepared to undertake the delimitation, they were prevented from doing so because of the ban imposed by the Delimitation Commission of India. During the pendency of the case the Rajasthan government amended Section 9 of the Rajasthan Municipalities Act, 1959 as follows:

"Provided further that such determination of seats on the basis of latest census shall take effect from such date as the state government may, by order, specify and until such determination of seats take effect any election to the municipalities may be held on the basis of the territorial limits of board or wards existing before such determination."

Though this particular amendment brought about by Ordinance No.10 of 2004 is very similar to the provisos to Article 82 and 170, the Rajasthan High Court held this to be in contravention of the constitutional provision in Article 243P(g) and as such *ultra vires*. The point emphasised by the court was that re-adjustment or delimitation on the basis of the latest available census is the norm and exceptions are to be provided in the Constitution itself and not by mere state law.

It appears from Patta Ram Bheel case that so far as *panchayat* and municipal elections are concerned, once the census figures are published there is no escape from undertaking delimitation and if such a delimitation is not undertaken and completed, elections cannot be held. However, as cited in the cases from the Gujarat and Karnataka High Courts if a state law stipulates delimitation but that activity results in delaying the elections beyond the tenure of a *panchayat* or a municipality that also amounts to contravening the Constitution which the courts have held as not tenable. There is therefore a need for a harmonious interpretation of the provisions of the Constitution in regard to the obligations of periodical delimitation on the one hand and holding timely elections on the other.

Bharamraj S. Parmaj *versus* State of Karnataka, WP No. 8003 of 2006, decided on 21.6.2006

The High Court held that the constitutional requirement of timely elections would override any state law requiring periodical delimitation of wards. As discussed in Chapter 2, in this petition filed by ex-corporators of the Belgaum Municipal Corporation and the Gulbarga Municipal Corporation it was urged that until fresh delimitation on the basis of the 2001 census was completed elections should not be held. The court was of the view that even though, in the absence of fresh delimitation, parity in the ratio of constituency population would not be the same across the corporation area and such delimitation was provided for in the states laws. Besides, the State Election Commission had already taken steps for conducting elections, the constitutionally required time schedule should take precedence. Accordingly the writ petitions were dismissed.

Anugrah Narain Singh and Another *versus* State of UP and Others (1996(6) SCC 303 which was decided on 10.9.1996

Delays in delimitation became the central issue in another litigation in UP. It has been mentioned in Chapter 1 how elections to the municipal corporations in UP required intervention of the Apex Court itself in Anugrah Narain Singh and Another *versus* State of UP and Others (1996(6) SCC 303 which was decided on 10.9.1996. Subsequently elections were held for municipalities and municipal corporation in UP sometime in November, 2000. The tenure of these bodies was to expire on various dates between November 2005 and January 2006 depending on when the first meeting was held. In November 2002, the Delimitation Commission of India wrote to the state governments not to alter the boundaries of various administrative units, as they existed on 1.8.2002. Between 2002 and 2004 there was an exchange of correspondence between the State Election Commission of UP and the Delimitation Commission of India about the extent of ban on altering administrative boundaries, relaxation thereon, reimposition of the ban etc. In August 2004, The State Election Commission proposed to the State government that in view of the embargo imposed by the Delimitation Commission, elections to the municipalities/ municipal corporations could be held on the basis of previously demarcated municipal wards. The state government accepted the proposal and notifications for holding the elections on the 22nd and the 24th November 2005 were issued. In the meantime writ petition no.59093 of 2005 (Kamlesh Singh and Another *versus* State of UP and Others) was moved before the Allahabad High Court alleging that it would be violative of the constitutional provisions and a mockery of democracy if elections to the municipal corporations are held without delimitation on the basis of the 2001 census. The Allahabad High Court by its decision of 28.10.2005 held that the State Election Commission has been misled by the letters of the Delimitation Commission as the work of the Delimitation Commission of India and State Election Commission were operating in different fields. The High Court drew attention to the requirement under Article 243-U to complete the elections before the expiry of the term of municipalities but refused to pass orders since that may have the effect of delaying the elections.

In November 2005, the state legislature passed an amendment to the UP urban local self-government laws providing for the appointment of Administrators to take over functioning of the municipalities till such time as the elections are held. The state government also issued orders appointing Administrators. A few days later a petition was filed by the veteran litigant Anugrah Narain Singh challenging the constitutional validity of this amendment. A Division Bench of the Allahabad High Court eventually issued a judgement upholding the constitutional validity of the Amendment Act but quashed the government orders and directed the respective Administrators to hand over the charge back to the erstwhile Mayor and the elected corporators of *Nagar Nigams* in the state for the unexpired portion of their original tenure. This order of the Allahabad High Court upholding the Amendment Act providing for appointment of administrators was challenged before the Supreme Court.

Eventually notifications for elections to the municipalities and municipal corporations were issued in September 2006 and elections were completed in October 2006. This has meant a delay of about one year during which these corporations have been without any elected body. The appeal before the Apex Court was also not heard as a similar matter relating to regularity of elections was pending before a Constitution bench.

Delimitation and other issues which may cause a significant change in the character or continuance of a local body have certainly to be accepted as a ground reality but there is no reason why actions in dealing with these realities cannot be taken within a stipulated time limit. After all the change of a council to a corporation or a change of its boundaries can well be anticipated and adjustment to constituency boundaries need not be left to be initiated only in the last minute or only when a few months are left for fresh elections to take place. It is also worth noting what statutory relief is available where delimitation has not been possible due to extraneous circumstances. In regard to the Lok Sabha and assemblies, the delimitation of constituencies on a periodical basis after the results of each census are published, is an important feature of the Constitutional scheme. This process however, was affected by the Constitution's 42nd Amendment 1976 which put the delimitation process into a freeze until the census figures of 2001 are published. As a consequence, elections to the Parliament and the assemblies have been held for the past three decades on the basis of the 1971 census. This freeze has since been removed and the delimitation process was recommenced in 2002. However, the amendment, while lifting the initial freeze, has substituted a fresh freeze until the year 2026. In other words, the Delimitation Commission which commenced its work in 2002 will be a one time exercise based on the 2001 census but there will be no decadal adjustments in future until 2026. The proviso in Articles 82 and 170 by the Constitution's 42nd Amendment Act, is the reason why elections to the Lok Sabha or the assemblies have not been challenged on the ground that constituencies were not delimited on the basis of the latest census.

In regard to *panchayats* and municipalities, Articles 243 (f) and 243P(g) define population as what is 'ascertained at the last preceding census of which the relevant figures have been published.' Unfortunately though much of the language in parts IX and IXA was taken from the relevant provisions of Chapter II of part 5 and Chapter III of part 6 of the Constitution and though the contingency of delay in readjustment or delimitation was anticipated and covered by the proviso brought about by the 42nd Constitutional Amendment, a similar proviso was not included in parts IX and IXA. This has resulted in challenges which continue to be against the holding of *panchayat* and municipal elections without delimitation on the basis of the latest census. Matters were further complicated when the Delimitation Commission of India imposed a virtual ban on the delimitation of municipal and *panchayat* constituencies until its own exercise was completed.

Postscript

The harmonious interpretation of the requirements of holding timely elections and other measures in preparation for the same has since become available, thanks to a very recent judgement of the Supreme Court in Kishansingh Tomar *versus* the Municipal Corporation of Ahmedabad and Others (appeal civil 5657 of 2005). This judgement was delivered on 19.10.2006 by a Constitution Bench comprising the Chief Justice and four other Judges. The object and purpose of Article 243U specifies that every municipality unless sooner dissolved shall continue for "five years from the date of its first meeting and no longer" has been clearly interpreted. The judgement states that barring Acts of God no other calamities or no other circumstances will justify the delay in holding elections. It follows that all acts like revision of electoral rolls, fresh delimitation, boundary adjustments, reservation of constituencies or any similar matter which are man made though required under the relevant state laws, cannot override the clear purpose and patent expression of the Constitutional provision under Article 243U which is "five years and no longer." The logic of the Constitution Bench's judgment applies with equal force in the case of *panchayats* as well, since the intent and language of Article 243E(i) about the duration of *panchayats* are identical.

The judgement also contains some salutary directions to the state governments as well as the State Election Commissions in ensuring timely elections. It is hoped that this most recent judgement will set at rest the pending issues. Extracts of this judgement are contained in Annexure A-4.2.

In the next chapter we may consider the case law relating to reservation in the election of representatives and chairpersons.

Annexure A-4.1

High Court of Gujarat at Ahmedabad: Extracts of the Judgement in Special Civil Application

No.9243 of 2002 with Civil Application No.6110 of 2003 decided on 8.10.2003. (2003 (3) GLR2663).

Appellants: Junagadh Municipality *versus* State of Gujarat (Hon'ble Judge K A Puj, J)

1. The present petition is filed under Article 226 of the Constitution of India challenging the action of the state government to constitute the Junagadh Municipal Corporation before the tenure/duration of the petitioner No.1 municipality is over and that too, without dissolving the municipality and without giving a reasonable opportunity of hearing to the petitioner municipality. During the pendency of this petition, the petitioner has also moved a draft amendment whereby the petitioner has prayed for quashing and setting aside the Notification No.KV-125/02/MNA/1001-CMR-41(i)P dated 13.09.2002 constituting the municipal corporation for the city of Junagadh and appointing the Collector as Administrator of the municipal corporation.

4. The brief facts giving rise to the present petition are that the petitioner No.1 is a municipality duly constituted under the provisions of the Gujarat Municipalities Act, 1963. The petitioner municipality was having a duly elected body for the period of five years and the tenure of that body expires in 2005. The *Taluka* Development Officer, Junagadh has sent letters on 01.04.2002 to 8 *gram panchayats* calling upon them to pass necessary resolutions regarding their inclusion in the proposed Municipal Corporation for the city of Junagadh. All the *panchayats* have unanimously passed resolutions on or around 05.04.2002 expressing their displeasure and objection to any proposed inclusion into the proposed municipal corporation limits. Some of the *gram panchayats* apprehended that the corporation would be constituted, have preferred S.C.A. No. 4714/2002 before this court and the same came to be disposed of by this court (Quorum: M.S. Shah, J) on 10.05.2002 directing that the representation dated 05.04.2002 made by the said *gram panchayats* shall be considered before issuance of any notification by the state government for constituting a municipal corporation for the city of Junagadh.

5. So far as petitioner No.1 municipality is concerned, the party governing the same, prior to the constitution of municipal corporation for the city of Junagadh has got 2/3rd majority in the election and is different from the ruling party in the state and it was apprehended by the said party that the state government by using and resorting to undemocratic means, was making all attempts to ensure that the present body having a majority was undemocratically thrown out. With a view to achieve this object, a show

cause notice was issued under Section 263 of the Gujarat municipalities Act for dissolution of the municipality. The said notice was challenged by the municipality before this court in S.C.A No.6354/2002 which came to be disposed of by an order dated 18.07.2002 (Coram:-D.A. Mehta, J) directing the respondent authorities to take into consideration the reply that would be filed by the petitioner on merits and after giving an opportunity of being heard, if so demanded, it would be open to the respondents to pass an appropriate order within a reasonable time. It was also made very clear that if any order of suspension is passed by the respondents, the same would not be implemented for a period of ten days from the date of its receipt by the municipality.

6. Some of the *gram panchayats* have earlier filed S.C.A No.4174/2002 before this court and again approached to this court by way of filing S.C.A No.6490/2002 which was dismissed by this court vide order dated 170.07.2002 holding that the petition could not be entertained at that stage, against which the said *panchayats* have preferred LPA No.543/2002 before this court and the division bench of this court has issued notice on 06.08.2002. During the pendency of this LPA, the state government has issued a notification constituting the municipal corporation for the city of Junagadh.

8. Mr. N.D. Nanavati, learned senior advocate appearing for the petitioners along with learned advocate Mr. Hriday Buch submits that the action of constituting the municipal corporation for the city of Junagadh is nothing but flouting the constitutional mandate and disregarding the statutory provisions. He has submitted that Article 243-U of the Constitution of India contains a constitutional mandate that every municipality shall continue for five years from the date of its first meeting. The only exception permissible under the Constitution of India to curtail the tenure of a municipality is when the municipality is dissolved under any law for the time being in force. However, under proviso to Article 243-U(1) of the Constitution of India, there is a constitutional mandate that before effecting any dissolution of the municipality, the municipality shall be given a reasonable opportunity of being heard. He had further submitted that the petitioner No.1 municipality's first meeting was convened on 20.01.2000 and under the constitutional mandate, the petitioner No.1 municipality is entitled to continue upto 19.01.2005. He has submitted that the constitution of a municipal corporation inevitably has the effect of dissolution of the petitioner No.1 municipality and such dissolution is not only contrary to the constitutional mandate contained in Article 243-U of the Constitution of India but is apparently contemptuous and in willful disregard of the order passed by this Court.

11. Mr. Nanavati has further submitted that under the Constitution, except those powers which are required to be exercised by the Governor

himself in his own discretion, remaining powers are required to be exercised as per the aid and advice of the Council of Ministers and such decision of the Council of the Ministers are required to be expressly taken in the name of the Governor. A perusal of Articles 163, 166 and 243-O(2) of the Constitution of India makes it abundantly clear that the powers to constitute a Municipal Corporation are conferred exclusively upon the Governor of the State which the Governor is required to exercise directly as per his own discretion and after satisfying himself about the existence of the factors mentioned in Article 243-Q(2) of the Constitution of India.

12. It is in the above light of the Constitutional Provisions, Mr Nanavati has invited the court's attention to the factual matrix of the case. The Cabinet in its meeting held on 10.07.2002 has taken a decision on the note placed before it to constitute a municipal corporation for Junagadh comprising therein the existing municipal areas of Junagadh municipality and the areas comprised in 11 village *panchayats*. The only formality left was publication of a notification in that behalf and constitution of a nominated Corporation as provided under Clause 22 0f Part IV of Appendix-IV of the BPMC Act.

23. Mr K.B. Trivedi, learned Additional Advocate General appearing for the respondents submits that as per the provision of Articles 154, 163 and 166 of the Constitution, it is the satisfaction of the Council of Ministers on whose aid and advice the Governor exercises all his powers and functions under the Constitution barring a very small area of exercise of his own personal discretion, wherever it is so expressly provided under the Constitution. In this view of the matter, wherever the Constitution requires the satisfaction of the Governor for the exercise of any power or function by the Governor, the satisfaction required by the Constitution is not the personal satisfaction of the Governor but is the satisfaction of the Governor in the constitutional sense under the Cabinet system of government and that therefore executive action taken in the name of the Governor is the executive action of the state. He has therefore submitted that the exercise of the power under Article 243-Q(2) of the Constitution for declaration of any larger urban area is not a matter of the personal discretion of the Governor but is the exercise of the said power in the constitutional sense in the Cabinet System of the Government i.e. the satisfaction of the council of Ministers on whose aid and advice, the Governor is to exercise the said power. He has further submitted that despite this constitutional provision, as far as the present case is concerned, the whole matter was in fact placed before the Governor and he has considered and thereafter the notifications were issued. In support of his submission, Mr Trivedi has relied on the decision of the Hon'ble Supreme Court in the case of Samsher Singh *versus* State of Punjab and Another, 1974(2)SCC 831 wherein it is held as under:

"The Governor is the constitutional or formal head of the state and he exercises his powers and functions conferred on him by or under the Constitution on the aid and advice of his Council of Ministers save in spheres where the Governor is required by or under the Constitution to exercise his functions in his discretion."

26. Mr. Trivedi has also relied on the decision of the Hon'ble Supreme Court in the case of Sundarjas Kanyalal Bhatija and others *versus* Collector, Thane, Maharashtra and Other, 1989(3) SCC 396 wherein it is held as under:

> The function of the government in establishing a corporation under the Act is neither executive nor administrative. It is a legislative process. No judicial duty is laid on the government in discharge of the statutory duties. The only question to be examined is whether the statutory provisions have been complied with. If they are complied with, then the court could say no more. In the present case, the government did publish the proposal by a draft notification and also considered the representation received. It was only thereafter, a decision was taken to exclude Ulhasnagar for the time being. That decision became final when it was notified under section 3(2). The court cannot sit in judgement over such decision. It cannot lay down norms for the exercise of that power. It cannot substitute even "its juster will for theirs.
>
> The government in the exercise of its powers under Section 3 is not subject to the rules of natural justice any more than is legislature itself. The rules of natural justice are not applicable to legislative action plenary or subordinate. The procedural requirement of hearing is not implied in the exercise of legislative powers unless hearing was expressly prescribed.
>
> The principles and precedents thus do not support the view taken by the High court. The government is only expected to act and must act in a way, which would make it consistent with good administration. Is they, and no one else who must pass judgement on this matter.

27. Mr. Trivedi has further relied on the decision of the Hon'ble Supreme Court in the case of State of Punjab *versus* Tehal Singh and others, 2002(2) SCC 7 wherein it is held as under.

> The principles of law which are pertinent in this context are: (1) where provisions of a statute provide for legislative activity i.e. making of a legislative instrument or promulgation of general rule of conduct or a declaration by a notification by the government that a certain place or area shall be part of a *gram sabha* and on issue of such a declaration certain other statutory provisions come into action forthwith which provide for certain consequences; (2) where the

> power to be exercised by the government under provisions of a statute does not concern the interest of an individual but relates to the public in general or concerns a general direction of a general character and is not directed against an individual or to a particular situation; and (3) lays down future course of action, the same is generally held to be legislative in character.
>
> The provisions of Sections 3 and 4 of the Act which provide for declaring territorial area of a *gram sabha* and establishing a *gram sabha* for that area are not concerned with the interest of an individual citizen or a particular resident of that area. Declaration contemplated under Section 3 of the Act relates to an area inhabited by the residents which is sought to be excluded or included in a *gram sabha*. The declaration under Section 3 of the Act by the Government is general in character and not directed to a particular resident of that area. Further, the declarations so made under Sections 3 and 4 of the Act do not operate for past transactions but for future situations. Under the aforesaid situation, when declarations by issue of notifications by the government are made under Sections 3 and 4 of the Act respectively determining the territorial area of a *gram sabha* and establishing a *gram sabha* for that area, such declarations become operative at once.

29. Mr. Trivedi has further submitted that there was never a dissolution of the erstwhile institution of the Junagadh municipality as sought to be contended, in as much as an institution having perpetual existence, never gets dissolved, but its body of members may get dissolved under certain circumstances and the institution awaits a new body to come in. He has further submitted that in the present case, consequent upon the exercise of the constitutional mandate constituting a new institution i.e. Municipal Corporation of the city of Junagadh, the erstwhile institution of Junagadh municipality got extinguished/abolished/annihilated, with the result the body of members also stood automatically abolished/abrogated/extinguished.

34. This Court has extensively set out hereinabove the facts and contentions of the parties, relevant statutory and constitutional provisions and the judicial decisions on the subject. The question which falls for the Court's consideration is, though, in a narrow compass, it raises an interesting issue concerning the powers of the state government to have the desired result by and through using the constitutional office and position of the Governor. It is an admitted position that the process of constituting the municipal corporation for the city of Junagadh started much earlier. However, the state government started taking steps from April, 2002. By that time, duly elected body for Junagadh municipality was at the helm of affairs and its five years' tenure would have come to an end on 19.01.2005.

Before that, the *Taluka* Development Officer, sent a communication-dated 01.04.2002 to eight *gram panchayats* to know their inclination to be joined in the larger urban area for the city of Junagadh. This was challenged before this Court in S.C.A. No.4714 of 2002 and while disposing of the said petition on 10.05.2002, this court has directed the authorities to consider the representation dated 05.04.2002 from this *panchayat* and, thereafter to take appropriate decision in the matter. Subsequent events show that the said proposal appears to have been dropped. Then, comes the show-cause notice issued under Section 263 of the Act on 13.06.2002 proposing to dissolve Junagadh Municipality. This was also challenged before this Court in S.C.A No.6354 of 2002, which came to be disposed of by this court on 18.07.2002, with a direction that if any order of supercession was passed by the respondents, the same would not be implemented for a period of 10 days from the date of its receipt by the municipality. No dissolution of the Municipality took place, pursuant to the show-cause notice dated 13.06.2002. At this stage, the state government has come forward with three impugned notifications dated 13.09.2002 constituting the municipal corporation for the city of Junagadh, specifying 15th September, 2002 as the date on which the remaining provisions of the BPMC Act came into effect and appointing Mr. R.K. Pathak, IAS as the Administrator and Municipal Commissioner of the Junagadh Municipal Corporation for a period of 2 and 1/2 years or the date of first election of the said corporation, whichever is earlier.

35. The above sequence or chronology of events, in no uncertain terms, demonstrates that what the state government could not do directly by adopting other course, could very well do by bringing the Office of the Governor to its rescue, in the form of impugned notifications. Mr. Nanavati has strenuously and vigorously urged that the whole exercise is nothing but flouting the constitutional mandate, disregarding statutory provisions, violating or by-passing this court's order in connected proceedings and sheer abuse or malafide exercise of powers. The court, though is in agreement with the petitioner to some extent and finds force in the submissions of Mr. Nanavati, cannot, however, overlook or ignore the relevant constitutional and/or statutory provisions as interpreted by the Hon'ble Supreme Court as this court is bound by the said precedents and judicial pronouncements.

36. Article 243Q of the Constitution of India refers to the constitution of municipalities, which inter alia, includes a municipal corporation for a larger urban area. Under Article 243 Q(2), the Governor of the state may constitute a 'larger urban area' having regard to the population of the area, the density of the population therein, the revenue generated for local administration, the percentage of employment in non-agricultural activities, the economic importance or such other factors as he may deem fit. The question, therefore, arises as to whether discretion exercised by the Governor should

be based on his own personal satisfaction or the satisfaction of the Council of Ministers. Article 154 of the Constitution of India states that the executive powers of the state shall be vested in the Governor and shall be exercised by him either directly or through officers subordinate to him in accordance with the Constitution. Article 163(1) of the Constitution makes it clear that there shall be a Council of Ministers with the Chief Minister at the head to aid and advise the Governor in the exercise of his function except in so far as he is by or under the Constitution required to exercise his functions or any of them in his discretion. Along with this, Article 166(1) of the Constitution, requires to be noted, which says that all executive action of the government of a state shall be expressed to be taken in the name of the Governor. In Samsher Singh's case (*Supra*), the Hon'ble Supreme Court has observed that wherever the Constitution requires the satisfaction of the President or the Governor for the exercise by the President or the Governor of any power or function, the satisfaction required by the Constitution is not the personal satisfaction of the Governor in the constitutional sense in the cabinet system of government, but is, satisfaction of his Council of Ministers on whose aid and advice the President or the Governor generally exercises all his powers and functions. In the case of State of U.P. and Others *versus* Pradhan Sangh Kshettra Samiti and Others (*Supra*), the Hon'ble Supreme Court had an occasion to deal with Article 243(g) of the Constitution, which requires the Governor to specify the village by a public notification and in this context, it is observed that in view of the provisions of Article 154 and 163 read with 166 of the Constitution, Governor means the Government of the state. On the basis of this reasoning, the discretion to be exercised by the Governor within the meaning of Article 243 Q(2) of the Constitution, can as well be construed as the discretion to be exercised by the government of the state.

37. One of the grievances raised by Mr. Nanavati is that the municipal corporation was constituted without affording any opportunity of being heard. In this context, in the case of Sundarjas Kanyalal Bhatija and others (Supra), the Hon'ble Supreme Court has observed that the function of the government in establishing a corporation under the Act is neither executive nor administrative. It is a legislative process and as held by the Hon'ble Supreme Court in the case of Tulsipur Sugar Co. Ltd (*Supra*), an authority which has to exercise a legislative function need not follow the principles of natural justice before discharging such function. This is also reiterated by the Hon'ble Supreme Court in the case of State of Punjab *versus* Tehal Singh and Others (*Supra*), by holding that on making of declaration under Section 3 of the Act determining the territorial area of a *gram sabha* and therefore, establishing a *gram sabha* for that area is an act legislative in character in the context of the provisions of the Act and where the legislature in its wisdom has not chosen to provide for any opportunity of hearing or

observance of principles of natural justice before the issue of a declaration either under Section 3 or Section 4 of the Act, the resident of the area cannot insist on an opportunity of hearing before the area where they are residing is included in another *gram sabha* or local authority, in this view of the matter, the petitioner's grievance of non-granting of opportunity of being heard before issuance of notification dated 13.09.2002 constituting municipal corporation for the city of Junagadh, does not seem to be justified.

38. With regard to other issues raised by the petitioner, this court is of the view that upon issuance of the notification dated 13.09.2002 in exercise of powers conferred under Section 3 of Section 1 of the BPMC Act, 1949, the provisions of the BPMC Act were made applicable to the City of Junagadh and as a consequence thereof, the provisions of Chapter XXXI dealing with 'Repeals and Amendments' of the BPMC Act, came into force and resultant effect thereof, as envisaged in Section 490 of the BPMC Act is that the Gujarat Municipalities Act, 1963 shall cease to apply to any area included in the city. Here, in the present case, the whole city area of erstwhile Junagadh Municipality is now considered to be the area of Junagadh Municipal Corporation and is now governed by the BPMC Act. The Court, therefore, finds substance in Mr Trivedi's submissions that *consequent upon the exercise of the constitutional mandate constituting a new institution i.e. Municipal Corporation of the city of Junagadh, the erstwhile institution of Junagadh got extinguished/abolished/annihilated. The court, therefore, is in conformity with the view taken by the Patna High Court in the case of Kamakhya Narain Singh Vs. State of Bihar and Others (Supra) that the legislature has given power to the state government to include any area in order to constitute a corporation, may be a municipality or Notified Area Committee, joining the area with such area as the state government may think fit and proper.* (emphasis supplied)

39. As far as other issues raised by the petitioners are concerned, they are of minor nature and they are taken care of by subsequent notifications dated 16.12.2002 and 12.02.2003. By notification dated 16.12.2002, the state government, while exercising powers conferred by paragraph 22(a) read with paragraph 22(B) read with paragraph 23 in Part IV of Appendix IV to the BPMC Act, has clarified and directed that the Administrator has been appointed to exercise all the powers and perform all the functions and duties of all the authorities referred to in items (i) to (iv) of sub-paragraph (a) of paragraph 22 in part IV of appendix IV of the BPMC Act, during and from the period of his appointment as Administrator and Municipal Commissioner. Similarly, by notification dated 12.02.2003, the state government has substituted the word 'one year' in place of the words 'two and a half years' as mentioned in notification No. KV-127-2000-MNA-100-CMR-41(iii)-P dated 13.09.2002. In this view of the matter, it cannot be said that the action was taken without any application of mind. On the contrary, the record shows

that the concerned file was placed before the Governor. He has perused the file, put his endorsement and, thereafter, decision regarding constitution of the Junagadh Municipal Corporation for the city of Junagadh was taken.

40. However, the notification dated 10th September, 2003 causes some concern to the court. By virtue of this notification, the state government appointed Shri R.K. Pathak as Administrator and continued him as Municipal Commissioner of the Junagadh Municipal Corporation, effective from 15th September, 2003 for a further period upto the date immediately preceding the date of the first meeting, after first election of the municipal corporation of the city of Junagadh, and also clarified and directed that the Administrator has been appointed to manage affairs of the Junagadh Municipal Corporation and to exercise all the powers and perform all the functions and duties of the municipal authorities as specified under Section 7 A of the BPMC Act. It is worthwhile to note here that the notification dated 10.09.2003 was issued at a time when the tenure of one year was about to expire on 15.09.2003 and the petitioner has moved Civil Application No.6110 of 2003 in the pending petition i.e. S.C.A. no.9243 of 2002 on 29.08.2003 praying for stay against Mr. R.K. Pathak, IAS, restraining him to work as Administrator and Municipal Commissioner of Junagadh Municipal Corporation with effect from 14th September, 2003 and alternatively, praying for direction to the respondent No.1 to declare the election for the Junagadh municipal corporation immediately upon expiry of the period of one year as prescribed under the Act. Though the said notification has not been challenged, the same was placed on the record of this court, by the learned Additional Advocate General, Shri K.B. Trivedi, along with his note containing chronology of important events, legal propositions and authorities.

41. It is very unfortunate that during the period of one year, the state government has not taken any action for holding the election of the newly constituted Junagadh municipal corporation and allowed the Administrator as well as Municipal Commissioner to function and now his tenure has been extended for indefinite period by virtue of the notification dated 10.09.2003. It is contrary to the democratic principles and in violation of the legitimate right of the people of Junagadh to have a duly elected body representing the need of the people. The Court is normally not interfering in the legislative-cum-executive function of the State Government and precisely for this reason, the Court has not interfered with the notifications issued by the state government for constitution of the Junagadh municipal corporation. However, when the term of the Administrator and Municipal Commissioner is extended without any justifiable reason, the court cannot ignore the intention of the state government which can be gathered from circumstantial evidence and sequence of events taken place, which would ultimately result in denying the people at large, to have their duly elected body at the helm

of affairs of the corporation. Precisely for these reasons, this court issues the direction to the state government to take up the matter with the Election Commission for holding the election of the Junagadh Municipal Corporation as far as possible, within a period of three months from today and see to it that in any case, the said election shall be held on or before 31.01.2004. It is made clear that unless there are certain unforeseen circumstances such as natural calamities, riots or compelling reasons because of which it will not be possible to hold the election within the above time limit prescribed by this court, if the election is not held, the elected members of the erstwhile Junagadh municipality would be considered to be the councillors of the Junagadh municipal corporation till their tenure as the members of the Junagadh municipality expires or till the election of the Junagadh municipal corporation is held, whichever is earlier. This court is constrained to give this direction, despite the fact that the institution of the Junagadh municipality got extinguished/abolished/annihilated by virtue of the constitution of the Junagadh municipal corporation, as the court would not allow anybody to keep out the elected members for an indefinite period and thwart any democratic process by taking shelter of some executive orders or instructions.

42. Subject to the aforesaid direction, S.C.A. No.9243 of 2002 is dismissed. Rule discharged without any order as to costs.

43. In view of the direction given in the main petition, Civil Application No.6110 of 2003 would not survive and it is accordingly disposed off.

Annexure A-4.2

Case No.: Appeal (civil) 5756 of 2005

Petitioner: Kishansing Tomar

Respondent: Municipal Corporation of the City of Ahmedabad and Ors

Date of Judgment: 19/10/2006

Bench: Y.K. Sabharwal CJI, K.G. Balakrishnan and S.H. Kapadia, C.K. Thakkar, P.K. Balasubramanyan

Judgment: K.G. Balakrishnan, J.

This appeal is directed against the judgment of the Division Bench of the High Court of Gujarat. The appellant filed a Special Civil Application No. 9847 of 2005 praying for a writ of *mandamus* or any other appropriate writ or direction to the respondents in the writ petition, namely, the municipal corporation of the city of Ahmedabad, the state of Gujarat and the Gujarat State Election Commission, to take all steps necessary for the purpose of holding elections for constituting the municipal corporation of the city of Ahmedabad before the expiry of the duration of the municipal corporation constituted pursuant to the elections held in October, 2000. The appellant, who was the writ petitioner before the High Court, was the Chairman of the Standing Committee of the Ahmedabad Municipal Corporation (hereinafter referred to as 'AMC'). The elected body of the AMC was constituted for the relevant period pursuant to an election held in October, 2000 and its term was due to expire on October 15, 2005. The appellant apprehended that the authorities may delay the process of election to constitute the new municipal body and therefore filed the aforesaid writ petition on 23rd August, 2005. The AMC filed an affidavit before the High Court stating that it was the responsibility of the third respondent, namely, the State Election Commission, to conduct the elections in time. The State Election Commission, in a separate affidavit in reply, submitted that under the provisions of the Bombay Provincial Municipal Corporations Act, 1949, the state govt. had issued a notification on 8th June, 2005 determining the wards for the city of Ahmedabad by which the total number of wards had been increased from 43 to 45 and in view of the increase in the number of wards, the commission was required to proceed with the exercise of delimitation of the wards of the city of Ahmedabad in accordance with the provisions of the Bombay Provincial Municipal Corporation (Delimitation of Wards in the City and Allocation of Reserved Seats) Rules, 1994 and that the commission had issued a circular requiring the Collectors and the Designated Officers to furnish the details and to make proposals for delimitation of the wards. The commission contended that it would take two months' time to complete the process of delimitation as the preparation of voters' lists in each ward had to be revised in accordance with the Bombay Provincial Municipal Corporation (Registration of Voters) Rules, 1994. It was alleged by the Commission that it was required to consult the political parties to carry out the delimitation of the wards and that it would take at least six months' time for completing the process of election and the Commission could act only after the State Govt. issued the notification. The state govt. produced a chart showing the detailed steps taken by the state govt. at various stages culminating in the issue of notification dated 8th June, 2005.

The appellant contended before the single judge that in view of Article 243-U of the Constitution, the authorities were bound to complete the process at the earliest and the elections should have been held before the expiry of the term of the existing municipal corporation. The learned single Judge accepted the timeframe suggested by the State Election Commission and directed that it should be strictly followed and the process of elections must be completed by 31st December, 2005, and that no further extension for holding the elections would be permissible.

Aggrieved by the decision of the single judge, the appellant filed a Letters Patent Appeal before the High Court and the Division Bench of the High Court by the impugned judgment held that the timeframe given by the State Election Commission was perfectly justified and the Election Commission was directed to begin and complete the process as per the dates given in its affidavit and the L.P.A. was dismissed. Aggrieved thereby, the present appeal is preferred before us by the appellant.

We heard the appellant's counsel as also the counsel for the respondents. The main thrust of the arguments of the appellant's counsel was that in view of the various provisions contained in part IX of the Constitution of India, it was incumbent on the part of the authorities to complete the process of election before the expiry of the period of five years from the date appointed for first meeting of the municipality. The counsel for the respondents, especially the counsel for the State Election Commission contended that every effort was made by the Election Commission to conduct the elections before the stipulated time, but due to unavoidable reasons, the elections could not be held and the preparation of the electoral rolls and the increase in the number of wards had caused delay in the process of election and under such circumstances the delay was justified in conducting the elections.

The question that arises for consideration is whether Article 243-U of the Constitution, by which the duration of the municipality is fixed, is mandatory in nature and any violation could be justified in the circumstances stated by the respondents. (Articles 243U, 243ZA and 243T are then cited)

Provided that a municipality shall be given a reasonable opportunity of being heard before its dissolution.

(2) No amendment of any law for the time being in force shall have the effect of causing dissolution of a municipality at any level, which is functioning immediately before such amendment, till the expiration of its duration specified in clause (1).

(3) An election to constitute a municipality shall be completed,—

(a) before the expiry of its duration specified in clause (1);

(b) before the expiration of a period of six months from the date of dissolution:

The provisions contained in the Bombay Provincial Municipal Corporations Act, 1949 also are relevant to be noted here. (Section 6 of the Act is reproduced).

It may be noted that Part IX-A was inserted in the Constitution by virtue of the Seventy Fourth Amendment Act, 1992. The object of introducing these provisions was that in many states the local bodies were not working properly and the timely elections were not being held and the nominated bodies were continuing for long periods. Elections had been irregular and many times unnecessarily delayed or postponed and the elected bodies had been superseded or suspended without adequate justification at the whims and fancies of the state authorities. These views were expressed by the then Minister of State for Urban Development while introducing the Constitution Amendment Bill before the Parliament and thus the new provisions were added in the Constitution with a view to restore the rightful place in political governance for local bodies. It was considered necessary to provide a constitutional status to such bodies and to ensure regular and fair conduct of elections. In the statement of objects and reasons in the Constitution Amendment Bill relating to urban local bodies, it was stated:

"In many states, local bodies have become weak and ineffective on account of a variety of reasons, including the failure to hold regular elections, prolonged supercessions and inadequate devolution of powers and functions. As a result, urban local bodies are not able to perform effectively as vibrant democratic units of self-Government.

Having regard to these inadequacies, it is considered necessary that provisions relating to urban local bodies are incorporated in the Constitution, particularly for:

(i) putting on a firmer footing the relationship between the state government and the urban local bodies with respect to :

  (a) the functions and taxation powers, and

  (b) arrangements for revenue sharing.

(ii) ensuring regular conduct of elections.

(iii) ensuring timely elections in the case of supercession; and

(iv) providing adequate representation for the weaker sections like Scheduled Castes, Scheduled Tribes and women.

Accordingly, it has been proposed to add a new part relating to the Urban Local Bodies in the Constitution to provide for:

(f) fixed tenure of five years for the municipality and re-election within a period of six months of its dissolution."

The effect of Article 243-U of the Constitution is to be appreciated in the above background. Under this Article, the duration of the municipality is fixed for a term of five years and it is stated that every municipality shall continue for five years from the date appointed for its first meeting and no longer. Clause (3) of Article 243-U states that election to constitute a municipality shall be completed:

(a) before the expiry of its duration specified in clause (1), or (b) before the expiration of a period of six months from the date or its dissolution. Therefore, the constitutional mandate is that election to a municipality shall be completed before the expiry of the five years' period stipulated in Clause (1) of Article 243-U and in case of dissolution, the new body shall be constituted before the expiration of a period of six months and elections have to be conducted in such a manner. A proviso is added to Sub-clause (3) Article 243-U that in case of dissolution, the remainder of the period for which the dissolved municipality would have continued is less than six months, it shall not be necessary to hold any election under this clause for constituting the municipality for such period. It is also specified in Clause (4) of Article 243-U that a municipality constituted upon the dissolution of a municipality before the expiration of its duration shall continue only for the remainder of the period for which the dissolved municipality would have continued under Clause (1) had it not been so dissolved.

So, in any case, the duration of the municipality is fixed as five years from the date of its first meeting and no longer. It is incumbent upon the Election Commission and other authorities to carry out the mandate of the Constitution and to see that a new municipality is constituted in time and elections to the municipality are conducted before the expiry of its duration of five years as specified in Clause (1) of Article 243-U.

The counsel for the respondents contended that due to multifarious reasons, the State Election Commission may not be in a position to conduct the elections in time and under such circumstances the provisions of Article 243-U could not be complied with *stricto sensu*.

A similar question came up before the Constitution Bench of this court in Special Reference No. 1 of 2002 with reference to the Gujarat Assembly elections matter. The Legislative Assembly of the State of Gujarat was dissolved before the expiration of its normal duration. Article 174(1) of the Constitution provides that six months shall not intervene between the last sitting of the Legislative Assembly in one session and the date appointed for its first sitting in the next session and the Election Commission had also noted that the mandate of Article 174 would require that the Assembly should meet every six months even after dissolution of the House and that the Election Commission had all along been consistent that normally a Legislative Assembly should meet at least every six months as contemplated by Article 174 even where it has been dissolved. As the last sitting of the Legislative Assembly of the State of Gujarat was held on 3.4.2002, the Election Commission, by its order dated 16.8.2002, had not recommended any date for holding general elections for constituting a new Legislative Assembly for the State of Gujarat and observed that the Commission will consider framing a suitable schedule for the general election to the State Assembly in November-December, 2002 and therefore the mandate of Article 174(1) of the Constitution of India to constitute a new Legislative Assembly cannot be carried out. The Reference, thus, came up before this court.

Speaking for the Bench, Justice Khare, as he then was, in paragraph 79 of the Answer to the Reference, held: "However, we are of the view that the employment of the words "on an expiration" occurring in Sections 14 and 15 of the Representation of the People Act, 1951 respectively shows that the Election Commission is required to take steps for holding elections immediately on expiration of the term of the Assembly or its dissolution, although no period has been provided for. Yet, there is another indication in Sections 14 and 15 of the Representation of Peoples Act that the election process can be set in motion by issuing of notification prior to expiry of six months of the normal term of the House of the People or Legislative Assembly. Clause (1) of Article 172 provides that while promulgation of emergency is in operation, Parliament by law can extend the duration of the Legislative Assembly not exceeding one year at a time and this period shall not, in any case, extend beyond a period of six months after promulgation has ceased to operate.

The aforesaid provisions do indicate that on the premature dissolution of the Legislative Assembly, the Election Commission is required to initiate immediate steps for holding elections for constituting a Legislative Assembly on the first occasion and in any case within six months from the date of premature dissolution of the Legislative Assembly."

Concurring with the foregoing opinion, Pasayat, J. in paragraph 151, stated as follows:

"The impossibility of holding the election is not a factor against the Election Commission. The maxim of law *impotentia excusat legem* is intimately connected with another maxim of law *lex non cogit ad impossibilia. Impotentia excusat legem* is that when there is a necessary or invincible disability to perform the mandatory part of the law that *impotentia* excuses. The law does not compel one to do that which one cannot possibly perform. "Where the law creates a duty or charge, and the party is disabled to perform it, without any default in him." Therefore, when it appears that the performance of the formalities prescribed by a statute has been rendered impossible by circumstances over which the persons interested had no control, like an act of God, the circumstances will be taken as a valid excuse. Where the act of God prevents the compliance with the words of a statute, the statutory provision is not denuded of its mandatory character because of supervening impossibility caused by the act of God. (See Broom's Legal Maxims, 10th ed., at pp 1962-63 and Craies on Statue Law, 6th Edn. p. 268.) These aspects were highlighted by this court in Special Reference No. 1 of 1974. Situations may be created by interested persons to see that elections do not take place and the caretaker government continues in office. This certainly would be against the scheme of the Constitution and the basic structure to that extent shall be corroded."

From the opinion thus expressed by this court, it is clear that the State Election Commission shall not put forward any excuse based on unreasonable grounds that the election could not be completed in time. The Election Commission shall try to complete the election before the expiration of the duration of five years' period as stipulated in Clause (5). Any revision of electoral rolls shall be carried out in time and if it cannot be carried out within a reasonable time, the election has to be conducted on the basis of the then existing electoral rolls. In other words, the Election Commission shall complete the election before the expiration of the duration of five years' period as stipulated in Clause (5) and not yield to situations that may be created by vested interests to postpone elections from being held within the stipulated time. (emphasis supplied)

The majority opinion in Lakshmi Charan Sen and Others *versus* A.K.M. Hassan Uzzaman and Others (1985) 4 SCC 689 held that the fact that certain claims and objections are not finally disposed of while preparing the electoral rolls or even assuming that they are not filed in accordance with law cannot arrest the process of election to the legislature. The election has to be held on the basis of the electoral rolls which are in force on the last date for making nomination. It is true that Election Commission shall take steps to prepare the electoral rolls by following due process of law, but that too, should be done timely and in no circumstances, it shall be delayed so as to cause gross violation of the mandatory provisions contained in Article 243-U of the Constitution.

It is true that there may be certain man-made calamities, such as rioting or breakdown of law and order, or natural calamities which could distract the authorities from holding elections to the municipality, but they are exceptional circumstances and under no circumstance the Election Commission would be justified in delaying the process of election after consulting the state govt. and other authorities. But that should be an exceptional circumstance and shall not be a regular feature to extend the duration of the municipality. Going by the provisions contained in Article 243-U, it is clear that the period of five years fixed thereunder to constitute the municipality is mandatory in nature and has to be followed in all respects. It is only when the municipality is dissolved for any other reason and the remainder of the period for which the dissolved municipality would have continued is less than six months, it shall not be necessary to hold any elections for constituting the municipality for such period.

In our opinion, the entire provision in the Constitution was inserted to see that there should not be any delay in the constitution of the new municipality every five years and in order to avoid the mischief of delaying the process of election and allowing the nominated bodies to continue, the provisions have been suitably added to the Constitution. In this direction, it is necessary for all the state governments to recognise the significance of the State Election Commission, which is a constitutional body and it shall abide by the directions of the Commission in the same manner in which it follows the directions of the Election Commission of India during the elections for the Parliament and state legislatures. In fact, in the domain of elections to the panchayats and the municipal bodies under Part IX and Part IX A for the conduct of the elections to these bodies they enjoy the same status as the Election Commission of India (emphasis supplied).

In terms of Article 243 K and Article 243 ZA (1) the same powers are vested in the State Election Commission as the Election Commission of India under Article 324. The words in the former provisions are in *pari materia* with the latter provision.

The words, 'superintendence, direction and control' as well as 'conduct of elections' have been held in the 'broadest of terms' by this Court in several decisions including in Re: Special Reference No. 1 of 2002 (2002) 8 SCC 237 and Mohinder Singh Gill's case (1978) 1 SCC 405 and the question is whether this is equally relevant in respect of the powers of the State Election Commission as well.

From the reading of the said provisions it is clear that the powers of the State Election Commission in respect of conduct of elections is no less than that of the

Election Commission of India in their respective domains. These powers are, of course, subject to the law made by Parliament or by state legislatures provided the same do not encroach upon the plenary powers of the said Election Commissions. (emphasis supplied)

The State Election Commissions are to function independent of the concerned state governments in the matter of their powers of superintendence, direction and control of all elections and preparation of electoral rolls for, and the conduct of, all elections to the *panchayats* and municipalities.

Article 243 K (3) also recognises the independent status of the State Election Commission. It states that upon a request made in that behalf the Governor shall make available to the State Election Commission "such staff as may be necessary for the discharge of the functions conferred on the State Election Commission by clause (1). It is accordingly to be noted that in the matter of the conduct of elections, the concerned government shall have to render full assistance and co-operation to the State Election Commission and respect the latter's assessment of the needs in order to ensure that free and fair elections are conducted.

Also, for the independent and effective functioning of the State Election Commission, where it feels that it is not receiving the cooperation of the concerned state government in discharging its constitutional obligation of holding the elections to the panchayats or municipalities within the time mandated in the Constitution, it will be open to the State Election Commission to approach the High Courts, in the first instance, and thereafter the Supreme Court for a writ of mandamus or such other appropriate writ directing the concerned state government to provide all necessary cooperation and assistance to the State Election Commission to enable the latter to fulfill the constitutional mandate. (emphasis supplied)

Taking into account these factors and applying the principles of golden rule of interpretation, the object and purpose of Article 243-U is to be carried out. (emphasis supplied)

As the elections to the Ahmedabad Municipal Corporation have already been held and the new Municipal body constituted, no further direction is required in the matter. With these observations, we dispose of the appeal with no order as to costs.

5

Reservation of Posts and Seats

Reservation or providing for a certain percentage of seats in the legislature as well as educational institutions and jobs in departments of the government and organisations owned by the government has been a special feature of the Constitution and other laws in India. While Article 14 of the Constitution specifically proclaims equality before the law or equal protection of the laws to all citizens, Article 330 of the Constitution contains a special clause for reservation of seats in the House of the People for the SCs and STs. The basis of this reservation is to be the proportion of the population of the SCs or the STs. There are of course some exclusions in regard to some parts of the country but for our purposes it is sufficient to note that population proportion is the main basis of reservation. Until 1961, there were double member constituencies of which one was reserved for SC or the ST candidates as the case may be. By an Act in 1961, the double member constituencies were abolished. It was further provided that initially the reservation of seats would be for a period of ten years but the period has been extended from time to time. The 62nd Constitutional Amendment of 1982 has stipulated a period of 60 years for the system to continue from the commencement of the Constitution i.e. until 2011.

Since population is the basis, the Constitution provided that after every census which takes place once in 10 years, a delimitation of the assembly and Parliament constituencies will take place on the basis of the published census. Since population growth rates vary significantly between the states, delimitation would have inevitably resulted in the loss of some Lok Sabha seats for those states where due to population planning measures pursued growth was less than some others. In response to the political outcry from some of these states, the southern states, in particular, the 42nd Amendment to the Constitution in 1976 put a freeze on delimitation. The Parliament and assembly constituencies have thus remained frozen on the basis of the 1971 census when the last delimitation exercise took place.

The provisions regarding reservation of seats for SCs and STs were repeated in the 73rd and the 74th Amendments. Additionally, under Articles 243D and 243T one-third of the seats in the *panchayats* and *nagarpalikas* at every level as well as one-third of the posts of chairpersons at every level have been reserved for women. The 73rd and the 74th Amendments further enable the states to organise the delimitation of constituencies on the basis of published census figures. The provisions do not stop here. There is a further stipulation under Articles 243D and 243T which enables state legislatures to provide for reservations in favour of other backward classes, OBC for short. Unlike the Census which provides SC/ST population figures, no such data on the OBCs is uniformly available in the country. The application of the term and the listing of the OBCs vary between states and each state has to devise special arrangements to determine the numbers of OBC population.

International experience does show that even with data availability and transparent criteria, measures of affirmative action or reservation, whether for seats in the legislature, education or jobs is not easy to implement and is rarely free from dispute. The limited experience of applying reservation in the case of *panchayats* and *nagarpalikas* gained in India during the past decade shows that the situation is replete with controversies. The situation is further complicated by the fact that though a Delimitation Commission for the country was set up in 2002 and has substantially completed its work, its formulations based on the Census figures of 2001 have been notified only in May 2008. As a result elections to the state assemblies even after the delimitation process started have been held only on the basis of the 1972 delimitation which as noted earlier is based on the 1971 census figures. On the other hand, the law enjoins that for *panchayats* and *nagarpalikas* delimitation has to be done periodically. To say the least, this does not enable appropriate methodologies to be evolved for delimitation, reservation or rotation of the reserved constituencies. It does not also help the public or polity to understand how electoral districts are to be adjusted in keeping with demographic changes. These factors have to be kept in mind while considering the case law on reservation of posts and seats in the *panchayats* and the *nagarpalikas*.

In this chapter we shall deal with the following:

(i) The scope and extent of the reservation provisions.

(ii) The case law pertaining to reservation of seats in *panchayats* and municipalities as well as posts of chairpersons.

(iii) The case law relating to rotation of the reserved seats and posts.

It may be noted that these issues are very much interrelated and cannot be dealt with separately or in a given chronological order. The cases have therefore been presented according to the different High Courts and the Apex Court.

The relevant Article 243D in the Constitution of India reads as follows:

> Reservation of seats.
>
> (1) Seats shall be reserved for:
>
> (a) the Scheduled Castes; and
>
> (b) the Scheduled Tribes,
>
> In every *panchayat* and the number of seats so reserved shall bear, as nearly as may be, the same proportion to the total number of seats to be filled by direct election in that *panchayat* as the population of the Scheduled Castes in that *panchayat* area or of the Scheduled Tribes in that *panchayat* area bears to the total population of that area and such seats may be allotted by rotation to different constituencies in a *panchayat*.

(2) Not less than one-third of the total number of seats reserved Scheduled Castes or, as the case may be, the Scheduled Tribes.

(3) Not less than one-third (including the number of seats reserved for women belonging to the Scheduled Castes and the Scheduled Tribes) of the total number of seats to be filled by direct election in every *panchayat* shall be reserved for women and such seats may be allotted by rotation to different constituencies in a *panchayat*.

(4) The offices of the Chairpersons in the *panchayats* at the village or any other level shall be reserved for the Scheduled Castes, the Scheduled Tribes and women in such manner as the legislature of a state may, by law, provide:

Provided that the number of offices of Chairpersons reserved for the Scheduled Castes and the Scheduled Tribes in the *panchayats* at each level in any state shall bear, as nearly as may be, the same proportion to the total number of such offices in the *panchayats* at each level as the population of the Scheduled Castes in the State or of the Scheduled Tribes in the state bears to the total population of the state:

Provided further that not less than one-third of the total number of offices of Chairpersons in the *panchayats* at each level shall be reserved for women:

Provided also that the number of offices reserved under this clause shall be allotted by rotation to different *panchayats* at each level.

(5) The reservation of seats under clauses (1) and (2) and the reservation of offices of Chairpersons (other than the reservation for women) under clause (4) shall cease to have effect on the expiration of the period specified in Article 334.

(6) Nothing in this part shall prevent the legislature of a state from making any provision for reservation of seats in any *panchayat* or offices of Chairpersons in the *panchayats* at any level in favour of backward class of citizens."

The language in Article 243T pertaining to the reservation of seats in municipalities is nearly identical to Article 243D. Both Articles seek reservation of Scheduled Castes and Scheduled Tribes in proportion to their population in the relevant area of the *panchayat* or the municipality. Both articles stipulate that one-third of the seats shall be reserved for woman. Both articles also contain an enabling provision to allow the legislature of a state for making a provision for reservation of seats in favour of backward classes. However, between the two articles, two points of difference may be noted; one is that under Article 243ZD, reserved seats for SCs and STs as well as women *may* be allotted by rotation to different constituencies in a *panchayat*. But in the proviso of clause IV of Article 243D, states the number of offices of chairpersons reserved *shall* be allotted by rotation. In the case of Article 243T while reserved seats for SC/ST and woman may be allotted by rotation, there is no specific provision regarding chairperson's offices to the effect that these shall be allotted. However it is now settled law that there is no distinction between the words *may* or *shall* and whether a provision is mandatory or discretionary will have to be determined in the context and purpose of the relevant provision of law (Chandrika Prasad Yadav *versus* State of Bihar (2004(5) SC 159 decided on 5.4.2004). Another difference between Articles 243D and 243T is that under clause 4 of Article 243D, the number of offices of chairpersons reserved for SC and ST in the *panchayat* at each level shall bear the same proportion to the total number of such offices in the *panchayats* at each level as the SC/ST population bears to the total population of the state. Such a specific arithmetical provision has not been made in the case of Article 243T.

It also needs to be mentioned that the Constitution has enabled the state legislature to extend the system of reservation to the backward classes. So far nine states i.e. Andhra Pradesh, Gujarat, Haryana, Karnataka, Madhya Pradesh, Maharashtra, Punjab, Rajasthan and Uttar Pradesh have made such reservations. Some states like Tamil Nadu because of the large proportion of backward classes (BC) population have not found it necessary to make the reservation. It is also to be noted that while the Census of India contains figures of SC/ST population, the Census does not carry figures of backward classes. The definition of backward classes itself varies from one state to another in a few cases. Furthermore, there being no census of backward classes, substitutes such as data obtained from sample surveys or other means for specific schemes of financial assistance to backward classes are used. The procedures regarding the identification and certification of people belonging to backward classes also vary. Given these factors, it is not surprising that the litigation in regard to reservation issues has been high.

We nay now proceed to consider some important cases in the High Courts of different states in alphabetical order.

Andhra

Balaji and Another versus Government of AP 2002 (3) ALT14 (DB) decided on 23.11.2001

This case relates to the election of the President of *mandal parishad*, Singarani which falls in a scheduled area. Since the area is predominantly tribal and in the area of the *mandal panchayat* concerned, 12 out of 13 villages are within the scheduled with seats reserved for ST, the post of the Chairperson cannot be reserved for a backward class woman only because one particular village falls outside the scheduled area. The court observed that the object of the constitutional mandate would be completely defeated if a chairperson from a backward class is allowed to run the *mandal panchayat* despite the fact that 12 out of 13 villages form part of a scheduled area. It was accordingly held that the post of the *mandal parishad* Chairperson should also be reserved in favour of an ST.

Prakasam District Sarpanches Association and Others versus Government of AP (2001(1) ALT 138) decided on 13.12.2000

Section 202 (a) of the AP Panchayati Raj Act, 1994 permits the state government to make reservations in favour of backward classes to the extent of 34 per cent for the office of the chairperson and members of the *gram panchayats. Mandal parishads* and *zilla parishads* on the basis of the population figures gathered in the Socio-Economic Survey conducted by the AP Backward Classes Finance Corporation Ltd. Under Rule 9 of the Panchayati Raj Act, 1995, reservation of offices for SCs/STs, BCs and women shall be made by rotation as far as practicable. Since no population figures in respect of BCs are available, the reservation was sought to be applied through draw of lots using the figures of Backward Classes Finance Corporation. The court held that the reservation of seats in favour of backward classes by the process of draw of lots would defeat the object of reservation. In the absence of any constitutional requirement providing specific percentage of seats for the BCs, it cannot be said that there is discrimination between BCs on the one hand and SC/STs on the other. The state government was directed to identify the BC voters from the existing voters list and on such identification reservation of seats in favour of BCs should be made in descending order in rotation.

Assam

Bhabish Dihingia versus State of Assam
(2004 (1) GLT 161) decided on 26.3.2004

The question for determination in this case was whether under Section 33 of the relevant Assam Act, there could be any reservation for Women Commissioners in respect of the post of Chairman of Dhemaji Town Committee. The provision contained in Section 33 of the Act was considered unambiguous, meaning that the post of chairperson in respect of municipalities and town committees amounting to 30 per cent shall be reserved for women irrespective of belonging to Scheduled Castes and Scheduled Tribes. In the earlier term, the post of Chairman was occupied by a woman Commissioner who was, incidentally, from the ST community. It was submitted on behalf of the respondents that since this could be treated as fulfilling the requirement of reservation for ST, and therefore the same would not operate as a bar for appointment of a woman commissioner of the general category as Chairman of the Dhemaji Town Committee. The court held that this argument could not be accepted in view of the express provision in Section 33 of the Assam Act. The impugned notification could not ignore the concept of rotation. The post of Chairman having been occupied by a woman commissioner on the earlier term was coincidental. Provision having been made for rotation so as to maintain number of woman chairman in 30 per cent of the Municipalities and Town Committees by way of rotation, the post of Chairman of Dhemaji Committee having been held by a woman on an earlier occasion could not be held to be fulfilling the provisions in law for rotation. Provisions in a statute cannot be set aside by consensus.

Bihar

Krishna Kumar Mishra and Another versus State of Bihar and Others (AIR 1996, Patna 112) decided on 19.3.1996

In this case various provisions relating to reservation in the Bihar Panchayati Raj Act, 1993 in the context of the 73rd Amendment were examined.

Since various sections of the Bihar Panchayati Raj Act were involved, a summary of the decisions of the Patna High Court are reproduced below:

(a) Reservation of one-third of seats in favour of SC/ST or women does not violate any provision of the Constitution much less its basic structure.

(b) Limiting the period of reservation to that prescribed in Article 334 is not *ultra vires.*

(c) Combined reservation in Section 13(1) in favour of SC/ST and Backward Classes which will be in excess of the permissible limit of 50 per cent is *ultra vires.*

(d) Similarly reservation for the post of *pramukhs* of *panchayat samiti* under Section 38(2) (a) on the basis of proportionate total population of SC/ST/BC being in excess of 50 per cent is unconstitutional.

(e) Similarly section 63(1) in regard to reservation of seats in the *zilla parishad* combined in favour of SC/ST and BC being more than 50 per cent is unconstitutional

(f) Reservation of the post of *Adhyaksha* of *zilla parishad* , *pramukh* of a *panchayat samiti* or *mukhiya* of a *panchayat* will be unconstitutional as this amounts to 100 per cent reservation. Section 65(2) (9) of the Act is unconstitutional.

The decision of the Patna High Court that the reservation of the post of chairpersons at the village, intermediate and District level *panchayat* amounts to a hundred per cent reservation rests on the interpretation that each such *panchayat* is to be held as a single entity and totalling the number of *panchayats* at each level as a group within which reservation of a prescribed quantum for certain classes of people is unconstitutional.

This decision is similar to another decision of the Calcutta High Court referred to subsequently. However, this view has not been held by some other High Courts. The decision of the Bihar High Court is on appeal before the Supreme Court and the same has been referred to a 9 Judge Bench for hearing, which is still awaited. The matter is pending for nearly a decade. Until a clear interpretation is available from the Apex Court challenges to the system of reserving posts of chairperson may continue to be made.

Haryana and Punjab

Desh Raj versus Surjit Kaur (Appeal No.125 of 1999) decided on 4.1.2001

The High Court of Punjab and Haryana in the case of Desh Raj *versus* Surjit Kaur (Appeal No.125 of 1999 decided on 4.1.2001), upheld the view that when the government issues a notification then the election has to be conducted according to that notification. Facts of the case are presented below, *in extenso*, to give an idea of the complexities in the actual application of the reservation system.

The government issued a notification for holding elections to *gram panchayats*. As per notification, depending upon number of voters, some posts of *panches* in each village were kept reserved for General or Scheduled Caste candidates with further reservation for males or females. As regards notification in respect of village Shekhupur Khurd of district Sangrur, out of 5 posts of *panches*, 2 were reserved for male general category, 2 for female general category, whereas 1 for Scheduled Caste male.

One Surjit Kaur polled more votes than the appellant Des Raj but was still declared defeated. She filed an election petition under the Punjab State Election Commission Act, 1994. It was, *inter alia*, pleaded in the election petition that she as also Des Raj are permanent residents of village Shekhupur Khurd and belonging to the Ramdasia community and that they stood for election of *panches* from the reserved category. The election from *gram panchayat* for village Shekhupur Khurd was held on 21.6.1998 and the result was declared on the same date. From the result, as was declared by the Presiding Officer, she ought to have been declared elected but when she objected to the result, she was told that the same has been done at the instance of the Returning Officer. She further pleaded that injustice has been caused to her, as despite the fact that she had secured more votes than Des Raj, she had not been declared elected. The appellant Des Raj filed a written statement contesting her cause and pleaded therein that even though it may be true that the petitioner Surjit Kaur and he belonged to the Ramdasia community, she stood for the election of *panch* against a general category candidate whereas he had contested the election of *panch* against reserved category. He further pleaded that in *gram panchayat* of village Shekhupur Khurd total seats of *panches* were 5, out of which 2 seats were reserved for general category male, 2 seats were reserved for general category female, whereas 1 seat was reserved for Scheduled Caste 'male'. He was the only contesting candidate against Scheduled Caste 'male category' and, thus, was declared elected *panch*. The election tribunal upheld the plea of Surjit Kaur-respondent no.1 and declared her elected, whereas the election of the appellant Des Raj as *panch* was declared void and consequently set aside. This order was upheld by the learned single Judge in FAO No.2612 of 1998. Thereafter the matter went on appeal to a Division Bench.

The appellant vehemently contended before the Division Bench that the election pertaining to village Shekhupur Khurd was to be held strictly according to the notification. Respondent No.1 Surjit Kaur may be a Ramdasia, belonging to a Scheduled Caste but her candidature as a Scheduled Caste candidate could not possibly be accepted. Her candidature had to be considered as a general category candidate and therefore she had to compete with those who had contested the election against the general category. The notification of the election itself could not be challenged in an election petition and in fact the same was not challenged and yet a finding has been returned by the learned single judge that under the scheme of the Constitution and even under the Punjab State Election Commission Act, 1994, there cannot be any reservation for male, as also that in view of Section 13 of the General Clauses Act, 1897, masculine gender shall be taken to include females.

The decision of the Division Bench is presented in the following extract.

> Time is now ripe to consider as to whether without there being any challenge to the notification issued by the government calling upon a constituency to elect members, the grounds on which the election of the appellant has been set aside by the learned single judge, could at all be gone into. We may mention once again the learned single judge has held that under the scheme of the Constitution and even under the Punjab State Election Commission Act, 1994, there could not be any reservation for male and further that by virtue of Section 13 of the General Clauses Act, 1897, which specifically makes it clear that unless there is anything repugnant in the subject or context, words importing the masculine gender shall be taken to include females and therefore the very reference to reservation for males would include females.
>
> Perusal of the relevant provisions of the Act of 1994, manifest that the *sine qua* non of holding election is a notification calling upon a constituency to elect a member or members. In other words, elections cannot be held till such time notification for that purpose is issued by the government. .... The Election Commission has jurisdiction to hold election in accordance with the notification issued by the government and if that be so, no election can be challenged by way of election petition that may detract from that notification issued by the government on any ground. As election had to be held in strict compliance with the notification issued by the government, it will be futile to go to the questions raised by the learned Counsel representing the appellant as also to comment anything on the findings returned by the learned single Judge, reference whereof has been given above.
>
> In view of the discussion made above, we allow this appeal. Consequently, the order passed by the election tribunal dated 26.10.1998 and the judgement dated 2.7.1999 passed by the learned single judge are set aside. The appeal, as mentioned above shall be allowed.

Satbir Singh and Another versus Ajit Singh and Another (AIR 2001 P&H 146)

In a case which followed soon after, the issue whether an election will be void in the absence of reservation was raised and dealt with.

In Satbir Singh and another *versus* Ajit Singh and Another (First Appeal From Order No.4156 of 2001) (AIR 2001 P&H 146 decided on 5.2.2002), it was held that if no provision is made regarding the reservation of seats for Scheduled Castes, Scheduled Tribes or Backward Classes, the election tribunal cannot declare the whole election null and void on the ground such failure amounted to a violation of the Constitution of India. The facts of the case are as follows:

Election to the office of *panches* and *sarpanch* in village Palti Jhikki, Tehsil and District Nawanshahar, was held on June 21, 1998. Appellants 1 to 6 and proforma respondents 7 and 8 were declared elected accordingly. The total election of the *panches* and *sarpanch* was questioned in the election petition filed before the election tribunal, Nawanshahar on the following among other grounds:

(i) That no reservation has been made for the scheduled caste candidates though 1/3rd of the seats of the candidates should have been reserved for the aforesaid category and that out of them, 1/3rd further should have been reserved for the Scheduled Caste women candidates.

(ii) That an additional list of voters has been issued without any verification having been made in the village. The names of the persons having votes in municipality and other villages have also been included in the list pertaining to the village in question.

(iii) That one of the returned candidates belongs to a Scheduled Caste but he has been allowed to contest as a general category candidate.

The tribunal set aside the election and the matter went on appeal.

The decision in the appeal was as follows:

> The election tribunal has fallen into error while setting aside the election. Admittedly, the notification issued by the government pursuant to which the State Election Commission has issued notification under Section 35 of the Punjab State Election Commission Act, for holding election to the offices of *panches* and *sarpanch*, has not been challenged anywhere. Counsel for the respondents has fairly admitted that the notification issued by the government is bad

> because it does not provide for reservation as per the rights protected under the Constitution of India and the definition in respect thereof under Section 11 of the Punjab Panchayati Raj Act. If the election is to be held again it would be in pursuance of the notifications issued by the Government of Punjab and the State Election Commission wherein no reservation has been provided. The election tribunal is not competent to go into the legality or illegality of the notification issued by the Government of Punjab. The forum is elsewhere. Unless and until the notification issued by the government of Punjab is questioned and a finding in that regard is obtained, the election tribunal was not justified in setting aside the election as a whole.
>
> In view of the above, the appeal is accepted and impugned order dated 4.10.2001 is set aside. However, the parties are at liberty to challenge the legalities of the notification issued by the government of Punjab.

Karnataka

Karnataka is one of the states where in addition to reservations for SC/ST and women, the state law enables reservation for backward classes as well. Disputes have arisen in the application of the reservation provisions particularly for the election of *Adhyaksha* and *Upadhyaksha* at various levels of the *panchayat*.

Mahalakshmi and Another versus the Deputy Commissioner, Bellary (2000(6) KAR LJ 559/ILR 2000 KAR 3576)

In this case the issue was whether in the election for the office of *Adhyaksha* reserved for women in general category members belonging to a reserved category were entitled to contest. The petitioners were belonging to Scheduled Castes. Their case was that they were elected to the *Panchayat* in respect of seats for the category of women (general) during the elections held in March 2000. Subsequently in April 2000, the offices of *Adhyaksha* and *Upadhyaksha* in respect of 40 *gram panchayats* in Bellary district were notified for reservation. In the case of the Karekallu *gram panchayat*, the office of the *adhyaksha* was reserved for women (general) and the office of *upadhyaksha* was reserved for backward classes category B. The petitioners sought a direction from the Respondent Deputy Commissioner to hold elections to the office of *adhyaksha* only among the women members belonging to the category of women (general) and not to accept nomination of women belonging to other categories.

For a proper understanding of the case the relevant sections of the Karnataka Panchayati Raj Act of 1993 are reproduced below:

Section 5(4) of the Karnataka Panchayati Raj Act, 1993 reads as follows:

> (4) Not less than one-third of the seats reserved in each category, for persons belonging to the Scheduled Castes, Scheduled Tribes and Backward Classes and of the non-reserved seats in the *gram panchayat* shall be reserved for women:
>
> Provided that the seats reserved under sub-sections (2), (3) and (4) shall be allotted by rotation to different constituencies in the *panchayat* area:
>
> Provided further that nothing contained in this section shall be deemed to prevent a woman or a person belonging to the Scheduled Castes and Scheduled Tribes or Backward Classes for whom seats have been reserved in a *gram panchayat* from standing for election to any non-reserved seat in such *gram panchayat*.

Section 44 of the Karnataka Panchayati Raj Act, 1993 reads as follow:

> 44. Election of *adhyaksha* and *upadhyaksha*:
>
> (1) Every *gram panchayat* shall, within one month from the date of publication of names of elected members under sub-section (8) of Section 5, choose two members of the *gram panchayat* to be respectively. *Adhyaksha* and *upadhyaksha*. In the event of occurrence of any vacancy by reason of death, resignation, removal or otherwise in the Office of *adhyaksha* of *upadhyaksha*, the *gram panchayat* shall choose another member to be the *adhyaksha* or the *upadhyaksha*, as the case may be.
>
> (2) Subject to the general or special order of the State Election Commission, the Deputy Commissioner shall reserve:
>
> (a) Such number of offices of *adhyaksha* and *upadhyaksha* of *gram panchayats* in the state for the Scheduled Castes and Scheduled Tribes and the number of such offices bearing as nearly as may be the same proportion to the total number of the offices in the state as the population of the state.
>
> (b) Such number of offices of *Adhyaksha* and *Upadhyaksha* of the *Gram Panchayats*, which shall as nearly as may be, one-third of the

total number of offices of *Adhyaksha* and *Upadhyaksha* in the state for the persons belonging to the Backward Classes:

Provided that out of the offices reserved under this clause eighty per cent of the total number of such offices shall be reserved for the persons falling under category 'A' and the remaining twenty per cent of the offices shall be reserved for the persons falling under Category 'B' and vice versa;

(b) Not less than one-third of the total number of offices of *Adhyaksha* and *Upadhyaksha* of *Gram Panchayats* in the state from each of the categories which are reserved for persons belonging to the Scheduled Castes, Scheduled Tribes and Backward Classes and of those which are non-reserved, for women;

Provided that the offices reserved under this sub-section shall be allotted by rotation to different *gram panchayats;*

Explanation: For the removal of doubts it is hereby declared that the principle of rotation for purposes of reservation of offices under this section shall commence from the first election to be held after the commencement of the Karnataka Panchayati Raj Act, 1993.

Considering the complicated provisions, it is useful to provide extracts of the judgement of the High Court as below:

A combined reading of clauses (a), (b) and (c) of sub-section (2) of Section 44 showed that reservations have been made to the office of *Adhyaksha* and *Upadhyaksha* (Chairperson and Vice-Chairperson) for Scheduled Castes, Scheduled Tribes, Backward Classes and also to women belonging to the said categories to the extent of not less than one-third of the total number of offices of *Adhyaksha* and *Upadhyaksha* of *gram panchayats* in the state. The language employed in clause (c) of sub-section (2) of Section 44 while providing for reservation for women belonging to reserved category, made it amply clear that there was no reservation made for women belonging to the non-reserved category.

The language employed in clause (c) in so far as reservation made for women was concerned states, that not less one-third of the non-reserved seats of *Adhyakshas* and *Upadhyakshas* of *gram panchayats* in the state shall be reserved for women.

The language used was "for women." The words "for women," included women belonging to all categories of persons including Schedules Castes, Scheduled Tribes and Backward Classes. Therefore, from the plain reading of clause (c) of sub-section (2) of Section 44 of the Act, in respect of one-third of the seats reserved for women, all

> women irrespective of the category to which they belong, whether any reservation has been made in their favour or not, were entitled to contest to the offices of *Adhyaksha* and *Upadhyaksha* (emphasis supplied). If the object of the reservation made in the Act was understood in the backdrop of the preamble given to the Constitution and amendments made to the Constitution by means of the Seventy-third Amendment and the provisions contained in the Directive Principles of State Policy there was no escape to take a view other than the one holding that the persons belonging to reserved categories i.e., Scheduled Castes, Schedules Tribes and Backward Classes and women (general) were entitled to contest to the Office of *Adhyaksha* and *Upadhyaksha* in respect of the general seats. The object was to provide the minimum guarantee to the reserved sections of the society. It cannot be understood as taking away the benefit provided in a legislation. If one-third of the seats were reserved for women for the post of *Adhyaksha* and *Upadhyaksha*, it meant that all women irrespective of the category to which they belonged, were entitled to contest for the office of *Adhyaksha* and *Upadhyaksha*.

This judgement indicates how complicated the provisions in regard to reservation can become requiring even more complex interpretation. It also provides an insight into how the measures for affirmative action can create sharp divisions among the candidates and the voters.

Channigappa and Another versus State of Karnataka and Others (2000(6) KARLJ 163 (DB)

Initially the powers for delimitation of territorial constituencies including reserved constituencies were exercised by the State Election Commission. In the year 2000, the Karnataka government amended the laws and instead of the State Election Commission the powers of delimitation were vested in the state government, which meant in effect the Deputy Commissioner of the district concerned. A challenge was laid to this amendment in this particular case but importantly the procedure for readjustment for rotation of the reserved constituencies was also challenged. The facts of the case and the judgement of the Division Bench of the High Court are reproduced below.

"This petition was filed by way of public interest challenging the constitutional validity of Section 124(c) and Section 163 of the

Karnataka Panchayati Raj Act, 1993 as amended by Act 8 of 2000 praying for a *mandamus* directing the State Election Commission not to accept the lists sent by the government and Deputy Commissioners of the state or notifications issued by the government and Deputy Commissioners of the State identifying the reservation of constituencies to Scheduled Castes, Scheduled Tribes, Backward Classes and for women to *Taluka Panchayats* and to *Zilla Panchayats* in the State of Karnataka and not to hold elections to *Taluka Panchayats* and to *Zilla Panchayats* as per notifications issued by the government and the Deputy Commissioners of the state dated 17.4.2000, 20.4.2000, 22.4.2000, 24.4.2000, 26.4.2000 and 28.4.2000. Petitioners also sought for a direction to constitute a commission or committee consisting of retired judges of the High Court and Director of Backward Classes and Minorities, Director of Scheduled Castes, Scheduled Tribes, and the local MLAs of the District to assist the State Government in the matter.

"The petitioners primarily contended that the Amendment Act 8 of 2000 was unconstitutional, invalid and illegal due to the reason that the power vested with the State Election Commission was taken away by the government contrary to Article 243. By virtue of the amendment the power was entrusted to the Deputy Commissioner/ government, which could not be done in terms of the constitutional mandate according to the petitioners. Sections 124 and 163 of the Karnataka Panchayati Raj Act, 1993 which provide for delimitation of territorial constituency were involved in the present case.

"Held: Sections 123 and 124 of the Act provide for delimitation subject to the general or special order of the State Election Commission by the Deputy Commissioner. Section 163 provides for a delimitation of territorial constituency, subject to general or special orders of the State Election Commissioner. The State Government amended these provisions by Act 8 of 2000. Section 7 of the amended Act provides for the substitution of the word "Government" for the word "State Election Commission" in Sections 121, 122 and 123 of the Principal Act. In substance the power vested with the State Election Commission was taken away and was given to the Deputy Commissioner and the government. Article 243-K (4) provided for law being made with respect to all matters relating to or in connection with the election to the *Panchayat*. Law relating to delimitation/adjustment to a constituency also can be made by the legislature since it was a matter relating to or in connection with the election to the *panchayat*. The delimitation and adjustment of constituencies was an act of precedence in the matter of conduct of elections, *and it cannot be said to be a part of the electoral process*. The delimitation or the adjustment was an act preceding the preparation of the electoral rolls and conduct of elections and therefore it could not be held that in terms of the amended Act the Deputy Commissioner/government cannot also work with respect to delimitation or adjustment (emphasis supplied)."

The Hon'ble Court further held that Rule 3 of the rules provide for seats being reserved in favour of Scheduled Castes, Scheduled Tribes, Backward Classes and women and amendment of the rules were in conformity with the amended Act thereby providing for the power to the Deputy Commissioner and the state government instead of the State Election Commission. Retrospective amendment of laws is a well-known process of legislation. Section 311(2) of the Act provides for a rule under this Act being made with retrospective effect. A careful reading of Section 311(2) would show that every rule made under this Act with retrospective effect shall have the effect as if enacted in this Act. It would mean that a retrospective rule if so made has the approval of the statute. The rules were amended in conformity with the Act providing for the powers to the Deputy Commissioner and the state instead of the State Election Commission retrospectively which was permissible under the Act.

The court also held that it was a well-settled proposition of law that an opportunity to the affected parties for hearing had to be provided whenever civil consequences occur. In the case on hand the government in exercise of its statutory rotation power had readjusted certain constituencies after amendment or rules without calling for objections from the general public. Natural justice had to be observed as and when this regrouping was changed/done by the state government through the Deputy Commissioner. Though in the present case this was not done, in the absence of factual evidence, the court did not strike down the notification of reservation on this ground alone but directed that such opportunity for hearing be given in the future.

Smt. Soubhagya versus Returning Officer, Horalavadi Gram Panchayat and Others (2001(5) Kar L.J 216), decided on 2.8.2001

The issue which arose in this case is that in the event members are not available from the reserved category to get elected for the post of *Adhyaksha* or *Upadhyaksha* whether members belonging to other reserved categories can contest for the same.

Petitioner in this case sought for issuance of a writ of *certiorari* quashing the Notification No. ELN.GP. 46/99-2000, dated 10.3.2000 and also rejection of the nomination of the petitioner to the post of *Adhyaksha* and for issuance of a writ of *mandamus* directing respondents 1 and 2 to reserve the post of *Adhyaksha* of 3rd respondent *Gram Panchayat* in favour of SC women by rotation by following the order of the Election Commissioner dated 16.2.2000 and as provided under Article 243-D(4) of the Constitution of India and to hold election for the said post by providing the said reservation and further to direct the respondents to accept the nomination of the petitioner for the post of *Adhyaksha* which is reserved in favour of persons belonging to ST Women of Mullur-II constituency of the third respondent and to fill up the said post of *Adhyaksha* from the other reserved categories urging various facts and legal contentions.

The claim of the petitioner was seriously contested contending that under Section 5 of the Karnataka Panchayati Raj Act, 1993, if no person belonging to the Scheduled Caste is available the seats reserved for the said category shall also be filled up by the persons belonging to the Scheduled Tribes, but under Section 44 of the Act 1993 which relates to the election of the *Adhyaksha* and *Upadhyaksha,* there is no such provision and as such it is stated that the petitioner has no statutory right under Section 44 of the Act and the relief sought for by the petitioner cannot be granted.

Section 5 of the Karnataka Panchayati Raj Act, 1993 reads as follows:

5. Constitution of the *Gram Panchayat*:

(1) The *Gram Panchayat* shall consist of such number of elected members as may be notified from time to time by the (State Election Commission), at the rate of one member for every four hundred population or part thereof of the *panchayat* area:

Provided that the determination of the number as aforesaid shall not affect the then composition of the *gram panchayat* until the expiry of the term of office of the elected members then in office.

(2) Seats shall be reserved in a *gram panchayat*:

(a) for the Scheduled Castes: and

(b) for the Scheduled Tribes,

and the number of seats so reserved shall bear as nearly as may be, the same proportion to the total number of seats in the *gram panchayat* as the population of the Scheduled Caste in the *panchayat* area or of the Scheduled Tribes in the *panchayat* area bears to the total population of the Panchayat area:

Provided further that if no persons falling under Category 'A' is available, the seats reserved for that category shall also be filled by the persons falling under Category 'B' and vice versa

Section 44(2) of Karnataka Panchayat Raj Act, 1993 reads as follows:

44(2) Subject to the general or special order of the (State Election Commission), the Deputy Commissioner shall reserve-

(c) such number of Offices of *Adhyakshas* and *Upadhyakshas* of the *gram panchayats*, which shall as nearly as may be, one-third of the total number of offices of *Adhyaksha* and *Upadhyaksha* in the state for the persons belonging to the Backward Classes.

Held: "The Court in exercise of its power under Article 226 of the Constitution of India cannot take up the role of legislature and interpret the provisions by incorporating the provisions, which are not incorporated in the Act. Such interpretation cannot be made by this court as the legislature has expressly made it clear as to whom the Chairpersons are required to be reserved if that category of reserved members to fill up the offices of the aforesaid Chairpersons are not available. Therefore, the contention that in the absence of the candidate belonging to ST, SC women can be permitted to contest to the office of the *Adhyaksha* which is reserved to the ST category by the Deputy Commissioner, cannot be accepted.

"The reservation of the Chairpersons of the *grama panchayats* in a district is based on the consideration of the relevant materials such as the population of the respective reserved categories under the provisions of the Act to achieve the constitutional object under Article 243-D of the Constitution of India. Further the reservations of Chairpersons to the *gram panchayats* is an administrative function of the Deputy Commissioner and as such neither the petitioner has got the right to seek for a direction nor the Court can direct the Deputy Commissioner to allot the Office of *Adhyaksha* or *Upadhyaksha* for a particular reserved category by rotation as it would be contrary to the statutory provisions of the constitutional scheme as provided under Article 243-D of the Constitution of India.

The Court further held that the office of *Adhyaksha* of the *gram panchayat* cannot be kept vacant on the ground that no candidate belonging to Scheduled Tribe is available. That is contrary to the object of the local self-government as provided under the provisions of the Act. Therefore, the Deputy Commissioner was directed to take necessary steps to re-allot the post of *Adhyaksha* of the said *gram panchayat* after following the guidelines framed in this regard and see that the election is held to that office within eight weeks from the date of the court's order.

B. Geetamma versus Smt. Gulfom and Others (2003 (4) KL.J 401), decided on 4.6.2003

The petitioner contested the election held to the Shimoga *Taluk Panchayat* in May/June 2000, which was reserved for a Backward Classes woman, claiming that she belonged to the Kumbara caste. At the time of filing her nomination papers, the petitioner also produced the necessary caste certificate. Smt Geetamma secured the highest number of votes and was declared elected. After the results were declared one Smt. Gulfom who also contested the said election and had secured the second highest number of votes, complained to the *Tahsildar* that the petitioner did not belong to the *Kumbara* caste and sought withdrawal of the certificate issued to her. The order of the *Tahsildar* withdrawing the certificate was challenged by the petitioner in an appeal before the Assistant Commissioner. The Assistant Commissioner dismissed the appeal. Aggrieved against the said order, the petitioner filed a writ petition. The defeated candidate Smt. Gulfom also filed an election petition before the Principal Civil Judge under Section 132(1) of the Karnataka Panchayati Raj Act. In this petition also Smt. Gulfom succeeded, as the election of Geetamma was declared null and void. Thereafter Geetamma preferred an appeal before the Additional District Judge, Shimoga which was rejected. Aggrieved by this order Geetamma preferred another writ petition. These two writ petitions were heard together by the High Court.

The court noted that the core of the controversy was that the petitioner Geetamma was a Lingayat as indicated in her school transfer certificate and the certificate obtained from the *Tahsildar* stating that she belonged to the Kumbara caste was contrary to what is borne by the TC. The High Court held that where a subsequent entry relating to the caste of a person was different from the one from entries in earlier records such as school admission records, it is for that person concerned to show how this change was brought about. In the absence of a suitable explanation, the court would be justified in discarding the subsequent entries.

The Hon'ble Court also pointed out a major shortcoming in the Act. The shortcoming related to the omission in the Act to prescribe the competent authority for issuance of the caste certificate. There was not even a reference made in the statute to the effect that the certificate issued by the *Tahsildar* under the Karnataka Scheduled Caste, Scheduled Tribes and Backward Classes (Reservation of Appointments etc.) (Amendment) Act, 1990 would hold good for the purposes of the *Panchayat* Act. Therefore the court opined that there appeared to be a void in this regard, which required the attention of the legislature.

Kerala

In *C.R. Suresh versus State of Kerala (2000(3) KLT 159, decided on 14.6.2000)*, a question arose whether a ward newly created by combining parts of two other wards can be reserved in the process of rotation if the two wards from which the new ward was created are themselves reserved in the previous election. Under the Kerala

Panchayati Raj Act previously reserved wards should be excluded for the purposes of rotation. It was held that since the entire population in the newly created ward was covered by portions taken from three other wards previously reserved, the new ward has to be excluded from drawing of lots for the purpose of reservation.

Maharashtra

In a 1995 case *Kashi Nath Kodambarao Katake (1995(2) MLJ 714 decided on 17.8.1995*, the question discussed was whether in determining caste affiliation what would be the irrelevant, documentary evidence or oral evidence or both.

The election of a candidate who was elected as *Zilla Parishad* member in a reserved constituency was challenged by one of the contestants on the ground that the elected candidate did not belong to a Scheduled Caste. It was stated that on the basis of a caste certificate issued by the *Naib Tahsildar*, the said candidate contested from the reserved constituency but subsequently the certificate was cancelled by the District Collector and the order was confirmed by the Additional Commissioner in appeal. The elected candidate filed an application for permission to lead oral evidence before the trial court. The application was rejected on the ground that there was sufficient documentary evidence on record to prove the fact for which oral evidence was sought to be led in writ petition by the elected candidate challenging the said order.

Held, that as per Section 27(2) of the Maharashtra Zilla Parishads and Panchayat Samitis Act, the judge has to conduct an enquiry and for the purposes of the enquiry, powers of the civil court can be exercised. The question whether the petitioner belonged to a Scheduled Caste could not be decided on the basis of the certificate issued by the authority as such certificate could not be the conclusive proof of the fact. The controversy had to be decided on the basis of oral and documentary evidence. The oral evidence was a must. The order of the trial court was without jurisdiction. The trial court was directed to allow parties to lead oral and documentary evidence and decide the case in accordance with law.

In Maharashtra several *panchayat* or municipal constituencies are multi member constituencies. In such a case one of the seats is reserved for woman. In *Shobha Ashok Patil versus Mahananda Rajaram Nikam and others (1997(3) MLJ 353)*, the question arose whether candidates contesting for reserved seats could be considered for election to other seats in the same ward on the basis of votes obtained by them.

Elections were held to a *gram panchayat* wherein one ward was a multi seat ward. Three candidates were to be elected from the said ward out of which one seat was reserved for a woman. The Returning Officer declared the woman candidate who got 119 votes as elected to that reserved seat, she having secured the highest number of votes amongst the women candidates. Thereafter the candidate who had secured 134 votes was declared elected and for the third seat the candidate who had secured 115 votes was declared elected. An election petition was filed by a woman candidate who had secured 118 votes challenging the decision of the Returning Officer. The joint civil judge, Junior Division held that as the petitioner had contested an election for a reserved seat and as the candidate who had secured 119 votes had been declared elected to the reserved seat for women, the petitioner was disentitled to be considered for the general seat and therefore dismissed the election petition. In a writ petition the woman candidate who had secured 118 votes challenged the decision.

The court considered whether the reasoning adopted by the Returning Officer and the Civil Judge, holding that once a candidate is declared elected from a reserved seat whether other candidates who had contested the reserved seat are barred from being considered for the seat or seats which remain. The High Court referred to a decision of the Apex Court while interpreting a similar provision under the Representation of People's Act when the Double Member Constituency system was in vogue.

In the case of *V.V. Giri versus D. Suri Dora reported in AIR, 1959 C|SC1318*, it was held that in the case of Double Member Constituency wherein one seat is reserved for a Scheduled Caste if the candidate who secured the highest number of votes after the result of the Scheduled Caste candidate is declared is also a Scheduled Caste, then such candidate shall be declared to be elected. The argument that if a candidate has not opted to contest the general seat while giving the declaration for the reserved seat and is ineligible to contest the general seat, was also rejected. Accordingly in the present case the decision of the Civil Judge was set aside.

The matter thereafter has also arisen before another Division Bench of the court in the case of *Smt. Manjuli versus Civil Judge, Senior Division Wardha reported in 1969 MLJ 435 = AIR 1970 Bom.1*. In this case one seat was reserved for a woman. After the counting of results the woman securing the highest number of votes was declared elected. Thereafter from the other candidates another woman topped the list from amongst the remaining candidates and she was declared elected by the Returning Officer. This became the subject matter of an election petition. The election petition against the declaration of result by the Returning Officer was dismissed and the petition came before the High Court. A challenge was also made to Rule 34 of the Bombay Village Panchayat Election Rules. The Division Bench after considering the matter, dismissed the petition relying on another judgement in the Special Civil Application No.127 of 1963 dated 14th September, 1964 Mah. In this case one of the woman candidates had made an endorsement on a nomination paper that she was a candidate for a general seat. The question arose whether this would disqualify such a candidate from contesting the reserved seat.

The court pointed out "that the reservation of seats for women and of the Scheduled Castes and Scheduled Tribes is in the nature of a facility given to them or a concession made to a weaker section of the society in order to offer them reasonable opportunity of being represented in the administration as such. The plea, therefore, is to see that a minimum number of seats as contemplated by the legislature are filled in. There is no objection if more members from these weaker sections are elected to the village *panchayat* or other elected bodies. This result of guaranteeing minimum seats as required by the statue is properly carried out by the provisions of Rule 34. We might take up the instance of the present disputed Ward

No.2 and examine how Rule 34 is, in fact, beneficial and not obstructive to affording proper representation to women. This rule, according to us, fulfils two requirements. It ensures one seat from that ward being allotted to the woman candidate for which class a seat has been declared reserved in this ward. At the same time, it fulfils another important requirement of the democratic set up of the institution. Those candidates who are favoured by the electorate and in whose favour highest number of votes are cast must represent the constituency."

It held that what is contemplated by Rule 34 of the Bombay Village Panchayats Election Rules, 1959 is that in the first instance when there is a seat reserved for Scheduled Castes or Scheduled Tribes, the result therein shall be first declared. After that is declared, the result of the seat reserved for women should be declared and only thereafter the candidate securing the highest number of votes among the remaining candidates has to be declared elected for the remaining seat or seats. This in turn may possibly result in all seats being filled by candidates belonging to a particular category, say Scheduled Castes or Scheduled Tribes or women. Once a candidate is declared elected from a reserved seat, then other candidates who had contested the reserved seat are not barred from being considered for the seat or seats which are left. The order passed by the Civil Judge, in the election petition was quashed and the petitioner declared elected from ward no.3 in the place of the candidate who had secured 115 votes. The Returning Officer was also directed to make the necessary changes as required by the provisions of the Bombay Village Panchayats Act and the Bombay Village Panchayats Election Rules. AIR, 1959 SC 1318, ELR Vol. XV 187 and 1969.

In *Pushpa Prakash Kalpande versus Collector, Amravati and others,* the question arose whether a woman elected to a seat reserved for an OBC is entitled to contest the election for office of *Sarpanch* which in turn was reserved for a woman from the general category (1998(1) MLJ 325) decided on 10.12.1997.

It was held that the ratio of the judgement in Kasambhai's case, 1998(1) MLJ.1(SC) was applicable to the facts of the case. There is nothing in the provisions of the Bombay Village Panchayats Act,

1958 or the relevant rules of election to the post of *Sarpanch* or *Upsarpanch* to suggest that in order to be eligible to contest the election for the post of *Sarpanch* which had been reserved for women belonging to the general category, it was necessary for the candidate to have been elected only from a seat reserved for women belonging to the general category and that if a woman belonging to the OBC had been elected as a member of the *gram panchayat*, she would be ineligible to contest such an election. In absence of any such specific provision, the petitioner cannot prevent the third respondent from contesting the election to the post of *Sarpanch* reserved for a woman in the general category.

In cases relating to reservation it is seen that some confusion between the constitutional provisions regarding employment under the state tend to get mixed up with matters of reservation in electoral posts. In *Mahesh Mujlibhai Mistre Vs. State of Maharashtra 1999(3) MLJ 84)*, the issue was agitated whether reservation of the post of Chairperson in a municipal council can be equated with matters of service under a state and whether the equality of opportunity in matters of service provided for under Article 16(1) of the Constitution could be invoked. The decision of the Maharashtra High Court ion this regard is reproduced below:

"An elective post in a body like municipal council and a post in the service of a state can never be equated. Article 16(1) of the Constitution of India guarantees equality of opportunity in matters of service under the state. Reservations made in service matters will have to be weighed against this constitutional guarantee. A post of a Chairperson or any other elected post, created under the statute, stands on a different foundation. Electoral rights, such as, right to be a voter, right to vote from a particular constituency, right to contest, right to enjoy a term of office, if elected, are all statutory rights created by the statutes and they can be enjoyed only within the framework of the statue. Such a right is not a fundamental right; and is subject to the limitations imposed by the statute. Therefore, no Constitutional guarantee can be used as a touchstone to examine the reasonableness of a statutory provision in Election Law."

Suresh Balakrishna Pogale versus State of Maharashtra (2003(3) MLJ 782

In this case elections for the post of *Sarpanch* (Chairperson) and *Upsarpanch* (Vice-Chairperson) were held on 8.9.2000. The petitioner was elected as *Upsarpanch* but for the post of *Sarpanch,* two women members belonging to the general category were elected as members, neither of them were willing to contest for the post of *Sarpanch.* The person elected as *Upsarpanch* then sought to file a nomination for the post of *Sarpanch.* The Returning Officer for the election rejected the nomination as the post of *Sarpanch* was exclusively reserved for a woman in the general category. The Returning Officer's decisions were confirmed by the Additional Collector and thereafter by the Additional Commissioner, Nagpur. These orders were challenged in a petition before the High Court. It was held that if a woman candidate belonging to the general category is not available for the allotment of the office of the *Sarpanch,* it cannot be said that any other male candidate belonging to the general category, SC/ST or Backward Classes of citizens is entitled for such allotment. In fact the rules do not make any provision for such a contingency. Holding otherwise would mean de-reservation of the post which can only be done by the legislature. The orders keeping the post of *Sarpanch* vacant for the tenure for which it has reserved was therefore legal and valid. The petition was accordingly dismissed.

Uttar Pradesh

The High Court of Allahabad in *Ejaz Ahmad versus Assistant District Election Officer, Azamgarh and others (Civil Misc. Writ Petition No. 13726 of 1995) decided on 19.07.1995* pronounced a very crucial judgement. In this case a writ petition was filed as the petitioner's nomination for contesting election for the office of *Adhyaksha Zilla Panchayat,* had been rejected by the Assistant District Election Officer. It was stated that the petitioner did not belong to the backward class for which category the seat was reserved. However, the court observed that the impugned order was a well-reasoned order based on objective considerations and not subjective satisfaction. The court stated that when the basis of the election of the petitioner as

"Member" stood knocked out, his candidature for *'Adhyaksha'* (Chairman) was bound to tumble because it was only from out of members that one might be elected as *Adhyaksha*.

The question whether the notification issued by the government regarding declaration of a particular community, as backward class would have retrospective operation or not came for determination and consideration before the High Court of Allahabad in the case of Ragho Prasad *versus* Special Judge/Additional District Judge and others (Civil Misc. Writ Petition No. 13920 of 1999) and was decided on 5.7.1999. The court held that the amendment in the Schedule, which was appended to the original Act, shall take effect not prior to the date of the amendment unless it is intended by the legislature to give the amendment retrospective effect.

In *Neeraj Kamboj and Others versus State of U.P. and Others (C.M.W.P. No.40842 of 2000 decided on 12.7.2001)*, the petitioners sought quashing of the order of reservation of seats dated 18.5.2000. The election actually took place in the third week of June 2000 more than a month later. The court held that it was fully open to the petitioners to challenge the notification dated 18.2.2000 but this should be done before the election actually took place. The challenge of the petitioners was filed as late as 11.9.2000 and could not therefore be entertained. Furthermore, any challenge to the appointment of the Sub-Divisional Magistrate as prescribed authority for conducting the elections should have been made by an election petition without which the petitioner has no *locus standi*. Accordingly the petition was dismissed.

In the case of *Shamiuddin versus Additional District Judge (I), Mathura and others (CMWP No.13838 of 1997)* the High Court of Allahabad decided an important issue on 16.10.1997. The office of *Pradhan* of the *gram panchayat* concerned was reserved for a male candidate belonging to the backward class. The petitioner filed his nomination paper as a Muslim backward class candidate and won the election. The opposite party filed an election petition under Section 12C of the UP Panchayati Raj Act, 1947 for setting aside the election of the petitioner as he did not belong to the backward class. The prescribed authority allowed the election petition and declared the election of the petitioner to the office of *Pradhan* as invalid. It was held by the Hon'ble Court that "Sheikh" was a title of respect and this question had not been looked into either by the Prescribed Authority or the Revisional Court and the learned 1st Additional District Judge, Mathura proceeded to decide the controversy involved in the case on an assumption that 'Sheikh' denoted a caste in the Muslim Community. Therefore, the order suffered from manifest illegality and could not be sustained. Moreover the Hon'ble High Court also observed "mere cancellation of the caste certificate which was issued in favour of the petitioner would be no ground to hold that he does not belong to the backward class and therefore, it cannot be said that his nomination paper was improperly accepted."

In the case of *Baldev Singh versus Tahsildar and Others (CMWP No.30727 of 2000) decided on 25.08.2000,* the High Court of Allahabad held that the system of caste is not confined to Hindus relying upon the Entry 78 of the Uttar Pradesh Public Services Act, 1994. It is also applicable to other people like 'Jats', 'Sikhs' etc., and it does not confine itself to any particular religion. Therefore, the petitioner was entitled to be issued a certificate that he belonged to a backward class and was eligible to contest for the office of *Adhyaksha, Zilla Panchayat*, Rampur, which had been reserved for a person belonging to the said class.

West Bengal

The substance of the reservation provisions were discussed extensively in three cases in West Bengal as follows:

i. Vidhya Charan Sinha *versus* West Bengal/WP No.1401 of 2003.

ii. Mala Maji *versus* West Bengal/WP No.8805 of 2003.

iii. Nirmala Gorai *versus* West Bengal/WP No.9274 of 2003.

In considering these cases together, the Calcutta High Court (Amitabh Lala J) has held that reservation for the post of chairperson of a *panchayat* at any level is unconstitutional; that Article 243D of the Constitution cannot ride over 243C and that where there is a conflict between the "rule of majority" and the "rule of reservation", the rule of majority will have to prevail; appeal has been preferred to a Division Bench and outcome is awaited.

This judgement raises important issues of interpretation. The constitutional validity making reservation for the post of chairpersons as a group is also related to the issues raised in Krishna Kumar Mishra's case decided in the Patna High Court. As mentioned before an appeal against that decision has also been pending before the Supreme Court and is awaiting a full bench hearing.

Supreme Court

Given the complicated nature of the reservation provisions, it is natural that from time to time cases have come on appeal to the Apex Court. We may begin with an important case *Saraswati Devi versus Shanti Devi and others 1997 (1) SCC 122 decided on November 18, 1996*. This case involved the election of the President of the Loharu Municipal Committee in Haryana. Both the contesting parties and the respondent belonged to the Schedule Caste. The grievance of the appellant Saraswati Devi against the order of the High Court in favour of respondent Shanti Devi emerges from the relevant facts of the case presented below:

For the purpose of the election of members, the Loharu Municipal area is divided into 11 wards. Out of these, ward no. 5 was reserved for SC women, ward no. 2 was reserved for backward classes and ward no. 6, 10, and 11 were reserved for women in the general category. The appellant was elected from ward no.5 reserved for an SC woman while respondent 1 was elected from ward no.11 reserved for a general woman. After the said elections were over the question arose about the election of the President of the said Municipal Committee. As per Section 10, sub-section (5) of the Act the offices of the President in the municipalities shall be filled up from amongst the members belonging to the General Category, Scheduled Castes, Backward Classes and women by rotation and by lots in the manner prescribed. Rule 70 sub-rule (4) of the Haryana Municipal Election Rules, 1978 ('Election Rules' for short) prescribes the manner in which the election to the office of the President of municipality could be held. The Local Government Department of

Haryana vide its notification dated 20.1.1995 declared in terms of Rule 70(4) of the election rules that the seat of the President, Municipal Committee, Laharu, *inter alia,* shall be filled up from amongst the members belonging to the Scheduled Caste category. Respondent No.1 Shanti Devi contended that as she was also an elected member belonging to a Scheduled Caste, she was entitled to contest for the Presidentship. The Government of Haryana issued a clarification order dated 11.2.95 that where there is a single member in a Scheduled Category, elected from a ward reserved for such category, that single member shall be deemed to have been elected as President. This put the Respondent out of the contest who then filed an appeal.

A Division Bench of the High Court allowed the writ petition of Respondent 1 and set aside the impugned order dated 7.5.1996. According to the High Court as there were two candidates in the field belonging to the category of Schedules Caste women, election had to be held for the post of President and till that is done, the appellant Saraswati Devi may continue in the interim as the President of the Municipal Committee. This order of the High Court was brought in challenge by the appellant in the present appeal.

The Apex Court held as follows:

"The short question for our consideration is as to whether the government order taking the view that the appellant is the sole candidate for the post of President, municipal committee, Loharu and there is no question of any contest between the appellant and respondent 1 for the said post, is justified in law or not. The relevant statutory provisions in this connection are required to be noted. By the 73rd Amendment of the Constitution, Parliament declared municipalities to be institutions of self-government and at the same time provided for constitutional reservation in favour of Scheduled Castes, Scheduled Tribes and women vide Article 243-T of the Constitution of India.

"The very concept of rotation presupposes that for the contest of Presidentship, once by rotation a reservation is made for members elected for a particular category, only those members can contest.

"In the result this appeal succeeds and is allowed. The judgement and order of the High Court are quashed and set aside. The writ petition filed by the respondent 1 stands dismissed. The appellant will be entitled to continue as the President of the Loharu Municipal Committee for her full term of office."

One year later, this decision of the Supreme Court was overruled by a three Judge Bench in *Kasambhai F. Ghanchi versus Chandubhai D. Rajput and others (1998(1) SCC 285) decided on November 25, 1997.* The question which arose for consideration in this appeal was whether the appellant, who belonged to a Backward Class but had been elected to the Jambusar municipality from an unreserved seat, could stand for election for the post of President of the municipality which was reserved for a Backward Class candidate or whether the candidate for that post could only be a person who was elected to the municipality from a seat which was reserved for the Backward Class.

The appellant, Kasambhai Ghanchi though belonging to a Backward Class, had been elected to a ward which was in the general category in the general elections held on 28.12.1994. Respondent 1 Chandubhai Rajpur was elected in a by-election held on 25.8.1995 to one reserved seat for backward class category, which had fallen vacant. As per the roster a person belonging to a Backward Class was to hold the office of the President of the Municipality for the term beginning in 1997. Anticipating that Councillors belonging to the Backward Classes, who may have been elected from the seats meant for general category, like the appellant herein, were also likely to contest in the election for president, Respondent 1 filed a writ petition in the Gujarat High Court. The claim of the said Respondent 1 was that those Backward Class members of the municipalities who had not been elected as members from the seats reserved in favour of Backward Classes were not entitled to contest the election for the office of president. In other words according to the said respondent it is only those Backward Class candidates who had been elected from the wards which had been reserved for them also could stand for elections for the post of President reserved for a backward Class candidate as per the roster.

The writ petition filed by the said respondent was initially dismissed but then an application for review was filed on the basis that the decision of the single judge was contrary to the judgement of this court in the case of Saraswati Devi *versus* Shanti Devi. The review petition was allowed, the judgement dismissing the writ petition was recalled and thereafter the writ petition filed by Respondent 1 was allowed holding that the appellant Kasambhai, who in the meantime had been elected as President pursuant to the election which was held, could not have stood for election because he was a member of the municipality from a seat which was in the general category and not from a constituency reserved in favour of the Backward Class. Both the single judge as well as the Division Bench decided against the appellant in view of the aforesaid decision of this court in Saraswati Devi case.

The Apex Court held "by providing for the office of the President to be filled from different categories of persons by rotation the effect is that as per the roster point, the office of the President is required to be filled from a specified or particular class e.g. the Scheduled Caste, or Scheduled Tribe or Backward Class or women, then all other members of the municipality who do not fall under that category, are all excluded from contesting the election. The eligibility and the corresponding exclusion of others is determined on the basis of the candidate answering to the description of the category or caste for whom the post is reserved as per the roster and not the nature of constituency from which the persons are elected. For example, when as per the roster the candidate for the President's post has to be a Scheduled Caste then the Act and the rules do not provide that it is only those Scheduled Caste candidates who have been elected from the Schedule Caste ward who can stand for election and the other Scheduled Caste candidates are not eligible even though they were popular enough to get elected from unreserved wards.

"The idea of providing reservation for the benefit of the weaker sections of the society is not only to ensure their participation in the conduct of the affairs of the municipality but it is also an effort to improve their lot. The reservation ensures that the specified minimum number of persons belonging to that category become members of the municipality. If because of their popularity a larger number of Scheduled Castes, Scheduled Tribes, Backward Classes or women get elected to the municipality than the number of reserved seats, that would be welcome. "When the idea is to promote the weaker sections of the society and to improve their lot, it would be a contradiction in terms if members belonging to that section are debarred from standing to the office of the President because such a candidate is popular enough to get elected from a general constituency. It is a fundamental principle of democratic election that a person who is more popular is elected, popularity being measured by the number of votes which the person gets. The language of various legal provisions do not in any way suggest, expressly or by necessary implication, that even though a person who belongs to a reserved category and is popular enough to get elected from a general constituency should be barred from contesting the election of the President when that office is to be filled only by a reserved category person.

"In our opinion, therefore, the conclusion which was arrived at in the Saraswati Devi case did not flow from the language of the relevant provisions and, it is not consistent with the concept of reservation. With respect, it does not lay down the correct law.

"From the aforesaid discussion it follows that the appellant who belongs to the Backward Class was eligible to stand for the office of President even though he had been elected as a member of the municipality not from a reserved seat but from a general seat. As per the roster it is a Backward Class member who in the year 1997 is to be the President of the Jambusar municipality. The appellant, who admittedly belongs to a Backward Class could not be regarded as being ineligible merely because he had not been elected to a seat which had been reserved for a Backward Class candidate. Consequently his election as the President, on this ground, could not have been set aside.

"For the aforesaid reasons the judgement of the High Court under appeal is set aside. Consequently, the writ petition filed by respondent 1 stands dismissed.

Conclusion

In this chapter we have considered cases relating to reservation of seats and chairpersons adjudicated in different High Courts. As mentioned at the beginning of this chapter though the constitutional provisions relating to reservation for SCs/STs and women are straightforward, problems have arisen mainly due to rotation. The formula for such rotation has not been easy to determine. When additional categories of people for whom reservations are to be made such as backward classes, the complexities of devising a rational and broadly acceptable formula for rotation become even more difficult. The double dose of election required for a reserved post of President, that the candidate should belong to the reserved category and also be elected from a constituency reserved for the same category, as espoused in Saraswati Devi's case, subsequently overruled in Kasambhai's case shows that erroneous interpretations, even at the level of the Supreme Court, may occur. It further appears that in matters of affirmative action in general and reservation in particular, the jurisprudential experience in the country is derived mainly from legislation and case law relating to service matters and educational institutions which may not be fully relevant to disputes relating to elections.

Some basic issues regarding reservation therefore remain. Reference has already been made to Krishna Kumar Shukla's case in Bihar and Vidya Charan Sinha/Mala Maji/Nirmala Gorai of West Bengal. In both these instances, the Patna and West Bengal High Court's have held that reservation of chairpersons posts are prima facie unconstitutional on the ground that these are single posts and reservation would amount to one hundred per cent. The full bench to which Krishna Kumar Shukla's case has been referred is yet to meet and decide. The Calcutta High Court's judgement has raised a further point that there is a conflict between Articles 243C and 243D. Though Parliament and the state legislatures have indeed consciously decided in favour of reservation the harmonious interpretation of the constitutional provisions as well as relevant state laws is yet to emerge. In the meantime elections continue to be held notwithstanding the controversial and constitutional points of law. One can therefore expect more disputes being posed for adjudication in the years to come.

6

Removal of Elected Persons

In this chapter we shall consider cases of removal in four broad categories as follows:

- Removal by no confidence motion.
- Removal for failure to call meetings.
- Removal due to defection/violation of a party whip.
- Removal by designated authorities for non-performance irregularities etc.

For each category, the cases are considered High Court wise and then the Supreme Court as appropriate.

The state *panchayat* laws and municipal laws usually provide for motions of no confidence against the chairperson of a *panchayat*. Such laws and regulations usually provide for the frequency at which such motions can be made, the procedures to be followed in proposing and discussing such motions, the majority required for moving or passing them etc. Given the nature of the issues involved and the procedures to be followed, it is understandable that a large number of cases have been agitated before the courts.

In many states, the municipal and the *panchayat* acts also contain some provisions for removal of *panchayat* members or chairpersons at different levels. Usually the laws specify circumstances where removal is warranted. Financial irregularities, misappropriation of funds, failure to perform functions entrusted including the failure to convene meetings, grave misconduct etc. are some of the grounds for which removal is resorted. *Prima facie*, the removal of any elected representative by an appointed official is inconsistent with the spirit of the Constitution and in particular the self-government objectives of the 73rd and the 74th Amendments. Taking these provisions for removal as a reality, it is seen that a number of cases have been agitated alleging a failure to adhere to the substance or procedures specified in the law. Additionally in some states special laws have been enacted to prevent defection of an elected representative from one party to another. Such defection is then cited as a ground for disqualification. Anti defection laws operate in the Parliament and state legislatures. Whether such measures have strengthened coherence and consistency of membership in political parties merits a separate analytical study. The application of such laws in some of the states, *panchayats* and municipalities have resulted in several legal disputes.

No Confidence Motions

Cases adjudicated in different High Courts have been numerous. A sample of them are briefly described below pertaining to some important questions:

What are the disputes usually raised regarding counting of the votes? How is the majority decided in determining the outcome of the confidence motions? How are fractions dealt with?

Gayam Iswaramma (1998(6) ALT 308 decided 23.9.1998)

Section 245 of the Panchayat Act pertaining to the subject was interpreted by the Andhra High Court to mean that fraction, even if less than half, should be counted as one, because it strengthens the minimum needed for carrying a motion forward. In the instant case out of a total of eight members, five supported the motion. Two-thirds majority out of a total of eight will be 5.33. The explanation to Section 245 of the Andhra Panchayat Act states that any fraction below 0.5 should be ignored was in the view of the Court not legal. The Court held the motion of no confidence should be considered as failed.

Gogineni Kotiswara Rao (1999(3) ALT 496 decided 30.4.1999)

The Andhra PR Act stipulates a two-third majority for carrying a motion of no confidence. For this purpose total number of members would include a suspended member if any but not vacant seats. In the present case the total membership on the relevant date was 11and 2/3rd majority would be 7.33 but under the relevant rules fraction is to be regarded as one. Hence eight members have to carry the motion. Since only seven were present, the motion was considered not valid.

Nandan Goud (2004(2) ALT 336 decided 16.9.2003)

In this case, the President of a *mandal panchayat* was sought to be removed. Total membership was 14. The court held that according to the Act, fraction of less than half would be ignored. Accordingly, two-third majority for carrying motion of no confidence would be 9.33, but nine was considered sufficient. This judgement is contrary to the decisions in the Iswaramma cases cited *supra*. Since this is a latter judgement, it will prevail.

Jiten Sakya versus Assam (2004(2) GLT 233 decided on 10.12.2003)

Section 43(1) of the Assam Panchayat Act stipulates that the President or Vice President of Anchalik *panchayat* will be deemed to have vacated his office forthwith if a motion of no confidence is passed with two-thirds majority which provision is required to be followed strictly. Fraction of less than 0.5 should be read as one, since every small fraction represents corresponding opinion and cannot be ignored. It may be noted that this interpretation varies from those given in the AP cases.

Rambhai Joitaram Patel versus State of Gujarat (1997 AIHC 2762)

The court while interpreting "total number of members of the *panchayat*" observed, that different expressions are being used in case of motions of no confidence. In case of a *Sarpanch* of a *gram panchayat*, the expression used under sub-section (2) of Section 56, is the "total number of the members of the *Panchayat*" whereas under Section 70(2) and 84(2), the expression used is "total number of the then members of the *Panchayat*" for vote of no confidence against a

President or Vice-President of a *Taluka Panchayat* or District *Panchayat*. The use of two different expressions at different places in the same statute clearly indicates that they have different connotations. It must be presumed that the legislature has used the different expressions at different places with different intentions. The word, "the then" used in Section 70(2) and Section 84(2) is of significance. It refers to a particular point of time. The total number of "the then" members of the *panchayat* can only mean the total number of members entitled to sit and vote at the time of motion of no confidence. The legislature, presumably, with a view to give greater protection to a *Sarpanch* who is elected by direct election has not used the word "the then" and has only said the total number of members of the *panchayat*, which means the total members of the *panchayat* as constituted.

Manubhai F. Patel versus State of Gujarat (AIR, 2000 Gujarat 170)

In the instant case, wherein a no confidence motion was brought against an *Up-Sarpanch*, the High Court ruled that the expression "total number of members of the *Panchayat*" appearing in Section 56(2) of the above mentioned Act, cannot be construed to mean all of the members of the *panchayat*. The number of vacancies of members of the *panchayat* which are not filled up, cannot be taken into consideration while interpreting the expression "total number of members of the *panchayat*" occurring in Section 56(2) of the Act. Accordingly Section 56(2) of the above mentioned Act cannot be interpreted to mean two-thirds of the whole number of the members of the *panchayat* and resolution passed by the *panchayat* by 16 in favour out of 24 members of the *panchayat* cannot be termed as illegal.

K. Ambili versus Deputy Director (1996(2) KLT 486 decided 31.7.1996)

It was held in the case that in a *panchayat* with a strength of nine elected members the resolution has to be carried by more than half according to Section 159(12) of the Kerala PR Act. Since only 5 had voted, it was held the motion cannot be said to have been passed.

Jacob Abraham versus State (1999(1) KLT 25 decided 21.12.1998)

It transpired, on the date convened for consideration of a no confidence motion, there was obstruction created by supporters to the President of the *panchayat* as a result of which the petitioners were prevented from attending the meeting. The Deputy Director, *panchayat* who had convened the meeting dissolved the same for lack of quorum. The court held that the Kerala Panchayati Raj Act had taken much care to protect the freedom of the members to move a no confidence motion. Such a safeguard as part of the democratic system cannot be defeated by extraneous interference. Accordingly the court allowed the petition to consider the dissolved meeting as adjourned and directed a fresh meeting be convened.

Smt. Roop Kaur versus State of Punjab (1998) 2 PLR 179)

The Court held that the language used in Section 175(1) of the Punjab Panchayati Raj Act, 1994 (9 of 1994) is clear and unambiguous that a Chairman shall be deemed to have vacated his office, only if a resolution expressing want of confidence in him is passed by a two-third majority of the total number of elected members of the *Zila Parishad* including the *Panchayat Samitis* of the district. The requisite two-third majority has to be calculated with reference to the total number of existing members. The Court further justified its decision on the ground that if the intention was otherwise, the Legislature would have used the word 'existing' or 'actual' instead of the word 'total'.

Rasaiyya versus State of Tamil Nadu 2004(3) MLJ 230

A motion of no confidence was moved against the petitioner who was the President of a *Panchayat* Union Council in Virudhnagar District. The Council consisted of 13 members. Out of them only 8 members attended the no confidence motion and supported the same. However, this fell short of two-thirds of the sanctioned strength which would be 8.66. Ignoring the fraction, it would be nine. The impugned no confidence motion was accordingly quashed.

Smt. Meera Devi versus State of Uttar Pradesh and others (AIR 1998 Allahabad 157)

The court relying on the decision in Raj Singh Vs. District Panchayat Raj Adhikari, Muzaffarnagar, 1997 Rev Dec 429, observed that by virtue of sub-section (6) of Section 12 of the U.P. Panchayati Raj Act as it stands substituted by U.P. Act 9 of 1994, a *Pradhan* shall be deemed to be a member of the *gram panchayat* of which he/she happens to be the *Pradhan* and that being the position, the *Pradhan* is entitled to participate in the meeting convened for the purposes of discussion and voting on the motion of no-confidence brought against him/her under Section 14 of the Act read with rule 33-B of the Rules.

Basant Lal versus District Panchayat Raj Officer, Distt. Rae Bareli and others (2000 AIHC 3523)

The court held that where two-thirds majority of the members present and voting in the no-confidence meeting falls short by a fraction, in that eventuality, the motion would be deemed to have failed.

The case cited above indicates that in matters of counting votes, provisions in the state laws vary. Some stipulate a simple majority while some others specify two-thirds. Some refer to the total constituted strength of members while in others it is the total number of members present and voting. Even in counting fractions, there is no uniformity in including or ignoring fractions of more than or less than half of one. The interpretation of the courts have also not been uniform. It is not known whether the state legislatures in response to these judgements have made the necessary modifications in their laws and rules. Till they do, the legal disputes will persist.

Notice Period

How is the notice period described? What are the violations in this regard and how are they dealt with?

K. Sujata 2004(3) ALT 682 decided 2.4.2004

In Andhra High Court full Bench decision, it was held that the time spent in postage would be taken into consideration and not affect the notice which would be 15 days normally.

The Patna High Court have also given various judgements in regard to the notice period. In Smt. Phoolmanti Devi and others *versus* State of Bihar and others (2004) 3 BLJR 1829, it was held that seven days clear notice is mandatory for convening a meeting to discuss a no confidence motion.

In Anita Kumari and Another versus State of Bihar and Others (2004) 3 BLJR 2268)

It was further clarified that the margin of seven clear days between the date of the notice and the date of the meeting has to be maintained. In Smt. Rambha Sinha *versus* State of Bihar and others (2004) 2 BLJR 1408), it was reiterated that the day of the notice and the date of the meeting shall be excluded for this purpose The position was reiterated in Chinta Devi *versus* State of Bihar and others (2004) 2 BLJR 1456), in Sitaram Singh and another *versus* State of Bihar and others (2004)2 BLJR 1587) and in Mithelesh Pati Tiwari *versus* State of Bihar and others (2004) 1 BLJR 1032). In Gajendra Narayan Singh *versus* State of Bihar and others (2004) 3 BLJR 2127, the court held that the notice for the no confidence motion has to be directly served on the Pramukh against whom the motion is proposed.

C. Kuttaswamy versus Smt. Prema (WA No.2332/1991 decided on 24.2.1992)

A full bench of the Karnataka High Court held that the provision under Section 47(3) of the Karnataka Zilla Panchayat Samiti, Mandal Panchayat and Nyaya Panchayat Acts 1983 requiring the Assistant Commissioner to give the members of a *Mandal Panchayat* notice of a meeting for consideration of a motion of no confidence of not less than 15 clear days was mandatory. The notice period was reiterated in Smt. Sujaya Ramappa (2003(5) KLJ 76). Similarly, in Sangappa *versus* the Assistant Commissioner (WP No. 3990 of 2004 decided on 28.1.2004), it was held that without 15 days clear notice, the notice to discuss a motion of no confidence was liable to be quashed.

Muniappa and Another versus State of Karnataka and Others (1999(4) KLJ 42)

The court held that while the requirement of a 15 days notice for the proposed motion was essential, the requirement of holding a meeting within 30 days cannot be said to be mandatory, because the consequences of failure to abide by the requirement are not stipulated and the rule does not suggest that a motion duly moved by two-third of the members of the *panchayat* would lose its efficacy if a meeting is not convened within 30 days. The purpose is not affected or defeated if the meeting is conducted within a reasonable period by the authority concerned.

Joseph Verghese versus BDO Remany (OP 37440 of 2002 decided 11.12.2002)

The Kerala High Court held that it would be adequate if between despatch of notice and the meeting seven clear days are available. This view was also held by the Calcutta High Court in Menaka Haldar *versus* State (99 CWN 427, decided on 7.9.1994).

Dabir Mondal versus State of West Bengal (2000(2) CHN 696)

The Calcutta High Court held that the purpose for which the special meeting is to be called, i.e. whether it is to consider a motion of no-confidence or for removal of the *Pradhan* has to be specified. The notice by the members should clearly specify their intention and the same specifically has to be reflected in the notice given by the *Pradhan* in convening the meeting.

Can a motion of no confidence once introduced be withdrawn?
What should be the frequency of such motions?
What is the effect of postponed meetings?

The Andhra High Court's decisions indicate that motions of no confidence cannot be moved more than once, against the same person during his tenure of office, vide section 245 of the AP PR Act. (Tiparti Chandramouli (1998 (10 ALT 574 decided on 11.12.1997). The High Court also held, once members have supported a motion of no confidence, there was no scope for changing their mind. The discussion on the motion has to take place and be decided (D Ramachandraiah (2000(1) ALT 772 decided 16.11.1999).

The Assam High Court has held similar views. In Mybeyaima Devi (2000(2) GLT 421 decided on 15.3.2000), the court held once a *panchayat* member has given support to a motion of no confidence, it cannot be withdrawn. Motion has to be discussed and decided. The Court also held in Kanika Chandra Vs Assam 2004(2) GLT 417 decided 26.3.2004) that as per Section15 of the Assam *Panchayat* Act, a second no confidence motion cannot be moved within six months even if the first had either failed or was bad in law.

A slightly different decision was given by the Karnataka High Court in V Manjunath *versus* Assistant Commissioner Bangalore, North (1997 (2) KLJ 456 dated 21.12.1995). Section 54 of the Karnataka Act provides that a resolution of no confidence shall not be moved or cancelled within six months except by another resolution passed by not less than half of the total number of members of the *panchayat*.

The pursuit of sport came in the way of a no confidence debate in G. Narendran *versus* State of Kerala (OP 4113 of 1992 decided 26.3.1992). A notice to consider a motion of no confidence was convened by the District *Panchayat* Officer as provided for the rules. However, the day of the meeting was declared a public holiday by the Government to celebrate the success of the Kerala Football team in the Santosh Trophy tournament. The meeting was then adjourned. A fresh meeting for consideration of motion was scheduled. The petitioner challenged this fresh meeting on the ground that a no confidence motion cannot be considered for six months if the earlier one had failed. It was held that the earlier meeting having been adjourned due to unavoidable contingencies, the bar of six months did not apply.

The frequency of meetings to consider no confidence motions has come up for adjudication in some other High Courts as well.

Nimai Charan Mohanty versus State of Orissa (79(1995) CLT 123

Sections 46 B (2) (a), s. 46 B (3) of the Orissa *Panchayat Samitis* Act, 1959.

Fifteen members of a *Panchayat Samiti* had sent a requisition to the District Sub-Collector asking him to convene a special meeting to consider a motion of no-confidence against the Chairman of the *Panchayat Samiti* in the district. This was rejected by the Sub-collector on grounds that it was not in accordance with the mandate of S.46 B(2) (a) which says that 1/3rd of the members of the *Panchayat Samiti* with a right to vote should have signed on the requisition. Subsequently another petition was given to the sub-collector within two months of the rejection of the first requisition, this time signed by 30 signatories of whom only 13 had a right to vote. The total number of members of the *Panchayat Samiti* with a right to vote was 24.

S.46 B (3) (as amended by a 1994 ordinance) insists that there be a gap of one year between the meeting convened to consider one no-confidence motion and a subsequent motion against the same individual. The petitioners contended that the second requisition, given within one year of having given the first was hence statutorily barred. The court negated this contention by saying that the statute puts a bar on considering a requisition within one year of convening a meeting to consider a no-confidence motion. In this case no such meeting was held as the requisition was rejected by the sub-collector. Hence, there was no statutory bar in considering such a requisition.

Ramashraya and etc. versus District Panchayat Raj Officer, Gorakhpur and Another (AIR 1998 Allahabad 87)

The Allahabad High Court relying on Mohan Lal Tripathi *versus* District Magistrate, (AIR, 1993 SC 2042) upheld the *vires* of Section 14 of the U.P. Panchayati Raj Act and Rule 33-B framed thereunder.

It is further held that:

1) *Pradhan* of *Gram Panchayat* can be removed by a 2/3rd majority in a special meeting of which at least 15 days prior notice should be given. According to Section 14 and Rule 33-B, the period is to be computed from the date of the issue of the notice and not from the date of service.
2) Only if a motion is taken up in the meeting and for want of quorum or for lack of requisite majority it fails, no subsequent

meeting for the removal of the same *Pradhan* would be convened within a year from the date of the previous meeting. This ratio was also observed in Banshoo *versus* District Panchayat Raj Officer, Jaunpur, 1986 (UPLBEC 429).

Dilip Bhattacharya versus State of West Bengal (1996(II) CHN 142)

In the instant case a meeting was called for the removal of *Pradhan* and *up-Pradhan* of a *grama panchayat*. But the meeting could not be convened due to a bandh being called on the same day. As per Proviso iii to Section 16 of the WBPA (which was amended in 1995), it is said that if at a meeting convened under s.12, no meeting is held or no resolution removing an office bearer is adopted, no other meeting shall be convened for the purpose of removal of the same office bearer within six months from the date appointed for such meeting.

The court said that in order to give a harmonious construction to the said amendment with s.12, it must be held that it could not have been the intention of the legislature to include meetings, which could not be held due to circumstances beyond the control of the concerned parties.

Ram Chandra Oraon versus State of West Bengal and Others (2001 (2) CHN 83)

In this case the issue was whether a second notice for a no-confidence motion can be moved within six months from a date which was fixed for an earlier motion to remove the same *Pradhan*. Earlier, a Division Bench of the High Court, in Muktasin Hossain *versus* State of West Bengal, 1998 (2) CLR 28 had held that this proviso does not call for strict observance. In the present case, the High Court held that while interpreting a statute the intention of the legislature had to be kept in mind. The legislature while drafting the proviso, intended the six month embargo as a restraint in main motions of no confidence. To this extent the decision in Muktasin Hossain was "*per incuriam*" as it ignored a well established principle of statutory interpretation and was contrary to the provision in law.

Should notice for no confidence motions specify the reasons for which the motion is sought to be moved?

In *Samala Jayaramaiah (AIR, 1998/AP 205 decided 23.1.1998)*, the Andhra High Court held that holding the post of a chairperson is neither a statutory nor a fundamental right. Motions of no confidence are part of the democratic process and deal only with political rights. In the present case, initially a single judge gave a Stay Order on discussing the motion, because reasons were not adduced while proposing the motion of no confidence and the judge considered this should be done as part of an inherent scheme of things under Article 14 and 18. However, this initial stay was vacated. The appeal was preferred against the stay being vacated. It was decided that under the AP PR Act, reasons need not be given for moving a no confidence motion. Accordingly the appeal was rejected.

However, this decision may be contrasted with another decision of the Patna High Court. In Uday Shankar Singh *versus* State of Bihar and others (2003 A.I.H.C. 1348), the court held that the motion of no confidence must rest on a cause and allegations against the person sought to be removed has to be intimated to him and an opportunity for him to defend himself is to be given before passing the motion.

Nimba Rajaram Mali versus the Collector, Jalgaon (AIR 1999 Bombay 335)

Though the grounds of a no-confidence motion are required to be incorporated in the notice or giving details of reasons, this is not a pre-requisite of a no-confidence motion. So the alleged vagueness in the reasons given in the notice of a No Confidence Motion does not invalidate the notice or the motion passed on such a notice. In the instant case, the minutes of the meeting held, showed that each and every ground was discussed by the members present and thereafter the no-confidence motion was put to vote which was passed with a majority of seven against four members during the said special meeting. So, it was full compliance under Rule 2 (i) of the above stated Rules, i.e. process of notice.

The decision in this case reiterates the decision taken in an earlier case in Bandopant Mallewar (1997-10) MLJ 52 that existence of a ground is not the prerequisite in a motion of no confidence. The substance of these decisions was again reiterated in Raju Kisan Awale 2000(4) MLJ 592 decided on 20.9.2000. In moving a motion of no confidence, the grounds need not be specified. The motion of no confidence is neither an administrative nor a quasi-judicial action but a democratic action and is within an exclusive domain of the House.

Natha Singh versus State of Punjab and Others (1997) 3 PLR 791

The court held that the *Sarpanch* against whom a no-confidence motion has been moved must have knowledge of the allegations that have been made against him, failing which a discussion on the motion would be meaningless. Hence, the court observed that seven days notice to the defaulting *Sarpanch* is mandatory for the purpose of discussion and taking a decision on the no-confidence motion against him. It was further opined that the issuance of notice to the defaulting Sarpanch would be even more obligatory where all the members of the *gram sabha* constitute the body, which is to take a decision on the no-confidence motion.

Smt. Brij Rani Singh versus State of UP and Others (2000 AIHC 4083)

The court held that the principle of moving a no-confidence motion cannot be equated with a criminal trial or the disciplinary proceedings and it is only the mandate of the people which has to be respected particularly in the democratic set up. There is no reason to hold that the notice of no-confidence motion without reasons is not a notice moved in accordance with the provisions of Section 14 or Rule 3-B of the rules framed under the Act.

It will be seen from the above cases that High Court decisions have differed. Some have held that motions of no confidence are a democratic exercise and the grounds need not be mentioned in the notice for such a motion: some others have held a different view.

Are there restrictions about nominated members voting in motions of no confidence? What is the position regarding MLAs and MPs who may be members of a municipal body?

Vijay Kumar Manmouji versus State of Bihar and Others (2005) 1 BLJR 303 (Pat)

In considering whether the nominated members of a *Panchayat Samiti*, can requisition a meeting of no confidence and have a right to vote in such a meeting, the court held that they do not have such a right. This position was reiterated in Hiralal Mandal Vs State of Bihar (2005) 1 BLJR 763 (Pat), and in Bindu Devi and another *versus* State of Bihar and others (2005) BLJR 2004 (Pat). The court also clarified that a meeting for the removal of a *Pradhan* or *Up-pradhan* of the *Panchayat Samiti* should be requisitioned by a majority of total number of elected members. This would be with respect to the total number and not the total of those who are attending the special meeting.

Lakshmappa Balaganur and Another versus State of Karnataka and Others (1994(4) Kar.L.J. 603)

The substantial question that arose for consideration was with regard to the constitutional validity of sub-section (2) of Section 159 and sub-section (3) of Section 179 of the Karnataka Panchayati Raj Act, 1993, in so far as they do not permit the non-elected members of *Zilla Panchayats* to participate and vote in the meeting convened for the purpose of considering the 'no-confidence motion' moved against the *Adhyaksha* and *Upadhyaksha*. The Court held that in the absence of a specific provision in the law it would not be appropriate for the court to exclude the nominated members from voting in a *Zilla Parishad* meeting.

M.V. Shantha Kumari versus Jabalpur Taluk Panchayat (2001(4) Kar L.J. 541)

Under Section 120(2) there is a specific bar on nominated members from voting in a no-confidence motion so far as a *Taluk Panchayat* is concerned. The court said that this makes it amply clear that while considering the total strength it is enough to look at the total number of elected members excluding the nominated members.

Kishore Chandra Sahoo versus State of Orissa (90 (2000) CLT 279)

Section 16(1) of the Orissa Panchayat Samiti Act, 1959 enumerates the constitution of the *Panchayat Samitis*. S.16 (3) further says that all the members specified in S.16 (3) have a right to vote in the meetings of the *Samiti*. S.46-B is the provision, which deals with the vote of no-confidence against the Chairman and Vice-Chairman of the *Samiti*. Sub clause 3 of the above provision the Sub-Divisional Officer on receipt of a requisition from 1/3rd of the members of the *Samiti*, shall convene a special meeting and give a notice of the same to all the members with a right to vote. The contention here was that only elected members had a right to vote. But the court said this was a misconception from the plain reading of the provision.

This important matter about voting rights of nominated members such as MLAs came up for consideration before the Supreme Court in 2004. In Ramesh Mehta *versus* Sanwalchand Singhvi (2004 (5) SCC 409 decided on 20.4.2004), the question considered was about, the meaning of the words the 'whole number of members of a municipal board, in terms of Rule 3(9) of the Rajasthan Municipalities Motion of No Confidence against Chairman or Vice Chairman Rules 1974'. The question was whether votes of the nominated members are to be taken into consideration. A single judge of the Rajasthan High Court, Jodhpur held that these votes have also to be taken into account. A Division Bench, however held that such nominated members would be excluded. The matter then went on further appeal to the Apex Court. After a careful review of the Rajasthan state laws regarding elections and removal of chairperson as well as the stipulations of the Constitution after the 73rd and 74th Amendments, the Apex Court held the view that the expression 'whole number' or 'total number of members connote 'total number of elected members'. Accordingly the Supreme Court held that only elected members could participate and vote in motions of no confidence. This particular decision of the Supreme Court settles the law.

What are the powers of the state government in regard to matters of no confidence? Do the governments have revisional powers?

Geetaben L. Rathwa versus State of Gujarat (2005 AIHC 3083)

In this case, a no-confidence motion was brought against President of Devgadh Baria Taluk Panchayat, and the motion was carried by a majority of the two-third members of *Panchayat*.

The court while interpreting Section 259 of the Act observed that the power of the state government under Section 259 of the Act cannot be attracted when it is a matter pertaining to carrying of the motion of no confidence or otherwise. When the legislature itself provides for express language and giving effect to the carrying of the motion of no-confidence and the contingencies thereupon, the state government will not have the revisional jurisdiction over the decision of the elected representatives in the matter of considering the motion of no-confidence or otherwise. As such, Section 70 of the Act provides for a complete mechanism of its own for reflecting the will of the elected representatives regarding the President and Vice-President of the *panchayat*.

Valsalam versus State of Kerala (233 (1) KLT 858)

Once a no confidence motion has been discussed and decided there is no provision for the State to interfere with the result of voting and to reverse or set aside the same.

Can those directly elected by the people as Chairperson of a Panchayat or Municipality be removed by a no confidence motion?

Jagdish Prasad versus State of MP (AIR 1997 MP 184)

This important issue of constitutional *vires* was raised in Jagdish Prasad *versus* State of MP (AIR 1997 MP 184). In this case, the petitioner challenged the validity of Section 21 of the Act of 1994 on the ground that it is unreasonable and violative of Article 14 of the Constitution. The main contention of the petitioner is that the *Sarpanch*, who is directly elected by the voters in a village cannot be removed by *Panchas* or members of the *Panchayat* by passing a no-confidence motion. This is arbitrary and is also in violation of Article 243 of the Constitution.

The Court observed that by virtue of Article 243-C(5), the States have the power to provide for the method of election and passing of 'no-confidence motion'. Such provisions cannot be held arbitrary merely because a better method of removal could have been provided by the legislature.

The court also observed that Section 21, wherein the state Legislature has provided for removal of a *Sarpanch* by *Panchas,* who are also elected by the voters in a village cannot be said to be anti-democratic and violative of Article 14.

Later that year this issue of interpretation came up before the Apex Court in Ram Beti *versus* District *Panchayati Raj Adhikari* and others (AIR, 1998 SC 1222 decided on 17.12.1997). The appellant contended that as he was elected as *Pradhan* of the *gram sabha* by the electorate of the village as a whole the *gram panchayat* as such did not have the right to move a motion of no confidence and seek to remove him. The said contention was however rejected by the learned single judge of the Allahabad High Court as well as the Division Bench. These judgements were under challenge before the Apex Court. Some of the *Pradhans* of *gram sabha,* who were sought to be removed in similar manner had also filed writ petitions.

In the impugned judgement the High Court had placed reliance on the decision in Mohanlal Tripathi *versus* District Magistrate, Rai Bareilly and others where the court was dealing with the provision contained in sub-section (2) of Section 87-A of the U P Municipalities Act, 1916 which empowered the members of a municipal board to remove the President even though he was directly elected by the electorate by moving a motion of no-confidence. The validity of the said provision was challenged before the court on the ground that it was violative of the democratic concept since it provided for removal or recall of an elected representative by a smaller and different body than the one which elected him. The contention was, however, rejected by the Apex Court which observed:

> Democracy is a concept, a political philosophy, an ideal practised by many nations culturally advanced and politically mature by resorting to governance by representatives of the people elected directly or indirectly. But electing representatives to govern is neither a

'fundamental right' nor a 'common right' but a special right created by the statutes, or a 'political right' or 'privilege' and not a 'natural', 'absolute' or 'vested right.' Concepts familiar to common law and equity must remain strangers to election law unless statutorily embodied. Right to remove an elected representative, must stem out of the statute as in the absence of a constitutional restriction it is within the power of a legislature to enact a law for the recall of officers. Its existence or validity can be decided only on the provision of the Act and not as a matter of policy.

An elected representative is accountable to its electorate. That is the inherent philosophy in the policy of recall. For the President his electorate, to exercise this right, is the board as it comprises representatives of the same constituency from which the President is elected. Purpose of Section 87-A of the Act is, to remove an elected representative who has lost confidence of the body which elected him. It may be by people themselves or they may entrust their power through legislation to their representatives. In the Act it is the latter. Members of the board are elected from smaller constituencies. They represent the entire electorate as they are representatives of the people although smaller in body. A President who is elected by the entire electorate when removed by such members of the board who have also been elected by the people is in fact removed by the electorate itself. Such provision neither violates the spirit nor purpose of recall of an elected representative. Rather it ensures removal by a reasonable body. It cannot be criticised either as irrational or arbitrary or violative of any democratic norm.

The board is thus visualised as a body entrusted with responsibility, to keep a watch on the President whether elected by it or the electorate. Any arbitrary functioning by the President or disregard of provision of the statute or acting contrary to the interest of the electorate could be known to the board only. Therefore it was not only proper but necessary to empower the board to take action, if necessary.

After citing the observations of the Apex Court as above, in the instant case, the court considered the applicability of the decision in Mohanlal Tripathi (*supra*). The court could not agree that the said case was decided in the context of the office of the President of a municipal board who is elected by a larger body of electorate and has no application to case of removal of a *Pradhan* of a *gram sabha* who is elected by a much smaller body of the electorate. The Court observed, the considerations which weighed with this court for upholding the validity of sub-section (2) of Section 87-A of the U P Municipalities Act, 1916 relating to the removal of the President of a municipal board in Mohanlal Tripathi (*supra*) are also applicable to the removal of the *Pradhan* of a *gram sabha*. Although under Section 14 of the Act the power of removal of a *Pradhan* is conferred on the members of the *gram panchayat*, which is a smaller body than the *gram sabha*, but the members of the *gram panchayat*, having been elected by the members of the *gram sabha*, represent the same electorate which has elected the *Pradhan*. The removal of a *Pradhan* by two-thirds members of the *gram panchayat* who are also elected representatives of the members of the *gram sabha* is, in fact, removal by the members of the *gram sabha* through their representatives. *Just as the municipal board is visualised as a body entrusted with the responsibility to keep a watch on the President, whether elected by it or by the electorate, so also the gram panchayat is visualised as a body entrusted with the responsibility to keep a watch on the Pradhan who is not elected by it and is elected by the members of the gram sabha. An arbitrary functioning of a Pradhan in disregard to the statute or his acting contrary to the interests of the electorate could be known to the members of the gram panchayat only. In the circumstances, it is but proper that the members of the gram panchayat are empowered to take action for removal of the Pradhan, if necessary.* (emphasis supplied)

The court accordingly decided, for the reasons aforementioned "we are unable to hold that Section 14 of the Act, in so far as it empowers the members of the *Gram Panchayat* to remove the *Pradhan* of a *Gram Sabha* by moving a motion of no confidence, is unconstitutional and void being violative of the concept of democracy or is arbitrary and unreasonable so as to be hit by Article 14 of the Constitution."

Failure to Call Meetings as a Cause of Removal

Regular meetings of the *panchayats* at various levels, especially at the *gram panchayat* level have been considered very important for the proper functioning of the *panchayat* system. In several states, the laws specify the periodicity and enjoins the Chairperson to call for the meetings and also provide that failure to do so will entail removal. Where such removals have taken place, some have been contested. We may consider some cases in this regard.

In Karnataka, in Jayamulya (2002(6)/KLJ 2005), it was held that absence in three consecutive meetings would act as a disqualification. However, valid reasons for non-attendance would be an appropriate defence against disqualification and must be taken into account. (see Aruna Reddy (2002(3)/KLJ 509)

In Kerala it was held in Lissy Valsalan *versus* SEC (2003(03)/ KLT 1185), while failure to convene meetings would be held as a disqualification by the State Election Commission which was vested with powers of removal, such action should be preceded by a valid show cause notice. Since this was not done in the present case the impugned order of SEC was struck down.

Similarly in an Orissa case, in Meena Rani Kar (AIR, 1994/Orissa 218), it was held that while failure to convene meetings and non-attendance at meetings would act as a disqualification but the same will have to be established by proper procedure before disqualification.

In Tamil Nadu, in Velu *versus* State of Tamil Nadu (WP 33703 of 2002, decided on 21.8.2002) and others, it was held that absence from meetings of the *Panchayat* Union Council for three consecutive months would normally entail disqualification. However, this did not apply to a person in detention.

Removal Due to Defection or Disobeying Party Whip

In some of the states, laws have been enacted seeking to disqualify elected members of a local authority such as a municipal corporation, municipal council, *Zilla Parishad* or *Panchayat Samiti* if such members defect from the political group to which they belonged and on the basis of which they were elected to the local body concerned. Andhra Pradesh, Kerala, Maharashtra and West Bengal are some examples. Usually the laws and regulations provide for registration of parties or political groups, maintaining a register of members with designated officials of the government, identification of persons authorised to issue a party whip or other instructions to members, circumstances in which disqualification is incurred, procedure for removal etc. The Maharashtra Local

Authority Members' Disqualification Act, 1986 (Act No.20 of 1987) is one such Act. Rules under the Act have also been formulated. The procedure envisages the formation of a political group, Front, or *Aghadi* in local language prior to the election, the adherence of the members of such a group to the commonly accepted programme of the Front or *Aghadi* and voting in the meetings of the local body, consistent with any whip which may be issued by. Defection by members of such an *Aghadi* or Front and voting in violation of the whip results in disqualification. Other states applying defection processes prescribe similar procedures. We may review briefly some of the cases adjudicated in some of the states.

Andhra

The High Court of A.P. in *Mohan Rao and others versus Revenue Divisional Officer (RDO), Ranga Reddy (1995(5) ALT 323) decided on 31.7.1998)* held that the provision for disqualification for disobeying party whip can be made only by a law and not by rules. Later, an ordinance was passed and various provisions were laid down including disobedience to party whip as a disqualification. It was held by the court that in applying such provisions, the rules of natural justice such as opportunity to be heard should be followed.

This judgement of the High Court of A.P in Mohan Rao's case cited above was upheld in *Satyanarayana Reddy versus Revenue Divisional Officer (R.D.O, Kurnool (1999 ALT 389)* decided later on 30.12.1998. In this case during the vote of no-confidence six members voted in favour of the motion and three against but out of the first six, three had voted in disobedience of a party whip. The RDO-Kurnool presiding over the meeting as required by law had disqualified these three and held the motion of no confidence had failed to carry the requisite two-third majority. A single judge upheld this order but on appeal the Division Bench found the disqualification was not according to the process of natural justice. It was held that since six numbers had voted in favour of the motion of no confidence in a house of nine, the required majority was available. Accordingly the single judge verdict was reversed.

In *Akulu Gangaraja versus Presiding Officer, Yeleswaram Mandal Parishad* a similar situation arose. Under the relevant Act, a member ceases to hold office if he violates the whip. The dispute was whether the whip was properly issued. The High Court held that it is settled law that refusal of a notice is proof of service. There was evidence to show that the whip was actually read out prior to the election meeting.

Kerala

In *Nasirabibi versus State Election Commission decided on 9.3.2004,* defying a party whip was regarded as a disqualification. However, Kerala Local Authority Prohibition of Defection Act was repealed in the meantime. Hence it was held that the disqualification would not apply.

Maharashtra/Supreme Court

We may now consider a case in the Bombay High Court which went on appeal to the Apex Court. *Sadashiv Patil versus Vithal D. Teke and others before the Apex Court (AIR, 2000 SC 3044) decided on 31.8.2000* may be taken as an illustration.

Under the Maharashtra Local Authority Members Disqualification Act, voting or abstaining from voting in any meeting of the Municipal Council may entail disqualification, if: (1) such voting or abstention is contrary to any direction issued by (a) the political party or *Aghadi* or Front to which he belongs, or (b) by any person or authority authorised by the political party or *Aghadi* or Front in this behalf; (2) such voting or abstention is not accompanied by a prior permission of such political party or *Aghadi* condoned subsequently within 15 days from the date of such voting or abstention. Condoning is not permissible if such voting or abstention is not preceded by prior permission and is relatable to election of any office, authority or committee under the relevant Municipal Law. Thus, the power to issue a direction, popularly called a whip, in order to attract the penalty of disqualification had to be issued either by the political party or by the *Aghadi* or front, to which the Councillor belongs.

In the instant case a meeting of the *Janata Aghadi* Councillors of Vita Municipal Council was convened on 16.12.1997 and the appellant Sadashiv Patil was elected as 'Party Spokesman'. It was decided at that meeting that one Nandkumar Patil shall be the official candidate for the post of President of the Municipal Council and Sadashiv Patil as a substitute candidate. Inspite of this resolution another member of the Front, Vithal Teke filed his own nomination for the post of President of the Municipal Council and eventually was declared elected. As this was in defiance of the whip of the *Janata Aghadi,* in a meeting held subsequent to the election it was decided not to condone the defiance and accordingly Shri Vithal Teke and others who defied the whip were considered disqualified.

In keeping with the provisions of the Maharashtra Local Authority Members' Disqualification Act, the Collector declared these persons as disqualified. The High Court allowed writ petitions challenging the order of the Collector and eventually these orders were quashed. The appeal to the Apex Court arose therefrom. The Apex Court held that under the Disqualification Act, a mere resolution would not suffice but to incur disqualification there must be a specific direction contained in the whip issued by either party or persons authorised in this behalf. In the circumstances, the Apex Court upheld the decision of the High Court.

In another SLP, which was considered by the Apex Court around the same time, elections for constituting the Municipal Council of Karad were held on 1.12.1996. Eleven persons belonging to a Front known as Nagar Vikas Aghadi were elected and their names were duly registered by the Collector as required by the Maharashtra Local Authority Members' Disqualification Act. Here again election for the post of the President of a municipal council became necessary. The front decided on one of the councillors as official candidate for the post of President. But eventually one Smt. Balutai contested the election in opposition to Shri Shinde, the official candidate of the *Aghadi*. Another meeting of the Council was held on 15.12.1997 wherein certain important resolutions were to be tabled. Prior to this a meeting of the *Aghadi* was convened giving directions in regard to the pattern of voting to be followed by the councillors belonging to the *Aghadi*. The four appellants in this case who had earlier voted against the official candidate of the party defied the whip once again and voted to the contrary. In this case the Apex Court found that the whip did not suffer from any deficiency. The Apex Court accordingly held that the appellants could not avoid disqualification as a sequence of defying the whip and therefore their appeals were dismissed.

The application of anti defection laws to *panchayat* and municipal bodies is a recent phenomenon. The case cited including the ones from Mumbai which went up to the Supreme Court illustrate how complicated the procedures for dealing with defection cases become. Given the position of party and caste politics in the country, it is possible that the procedures to prevent defection and the use of the party whip are emerging as an over dominant phenomenon in vexatious litigations and causing discontinuity in the functioning of local bodies. There is a need to re-examine the issue and suggest what laws would be appropriate and least liable for misuse to destabilise these bodies. In the meantime, the valid application of the existing laws will depend on the procedures prescribed in each state.

Removal of Elected Persons by Designated Officials

The suspension and removal of elected members of *panchayats* and municipal bodies used to be a part of the bureaucratic system previously. Under the 73rd and 74th Amendments to the Constitution all these local bodies are envisaged as institutions of self-government. Their democratic composition is also provided for in the Constitution itself. While the provisions in regard to no-confidence motion is a part of the democratic process in many states, the laws also contain provisions allowing officials like Sub-Divisional Officers, Collectors or Departmental Heads to suspend and if necessary remove elected representatives. The existence of such measures runs counter to the principles of democracy but the competence of the state legislatures to enact such laws has not been challenged because the right to be elected as a member of a chairperson of a *panchayat* or a *nagarpalika* is considered only as a statutory right and therefore subject to statutory conditions. As can be expected a number of cases have been agitated in different High Courts arising from such orders of suspension or removal. Generally, the Courts have held that the power vested in an official to remove an elected representative is an power and the principles of natural justice and the required procedure should be followed. The courts have also held that in matters relating to misconduct, it should be established that such misconduct was willful.

We may now consider some of the cases adjudicated in different High Courts pertaining to this category.

Andhra

Kamasundaram Kotiswara Rao (AIR, 1993 AP 248 decided 26.3.1993)

In this case which arose out of removal of a *Sarpanch* by a Collector for misappropriation of funds, it was held that removal of a person from elective office is an extraordinary power. A willful omission of duties and responsibilities has to be established before such action is taken.

V. Parasuramaiah versus *Government of AP*
(1995AIHC 1469 decided 3.2.1993)

The *Sarpanch* was sought to be removed by the Collector under the provisions of the AP Gram Panchayat Act for misappropriation of *panchayat* funds and other irregularities. Among charges levelled against the *Sarpanch* were failure to obtain the permission of the Superintending Engineer before giving private tap connections, disposal of wind fallen trees without putting them into public auction, construction of a cattle ramp without estimates, failure to collect sale proceeds from sale of green grass etc. The High Court held that the removal of a person from elective office is an extraordinary power and has to be exercised not upon mere omission. "In the absence of venality, willfulness, or contumacy in alleged charges, the *Sarpanch* cannot be removed for technical lapses."

M.S. Rukhmini (1999 (40) ALT 897) decided on 28.6.1999

In removing a *Sarpanch*, the Collector has to apply his mind, failing which an order of removal would not be valid. Accordingly the order was suspended till disposal of the statutory appeal before the Commissioner.

Chava Rosaiah versus Chinthala Ventakateswarlu (2004(1) ALT 3287 DB, decided on 21.11.2003. In this case the Commissioner of *Panchayati Raj* directed the District *Panchayat* Officer to conduct an enquiry against the Petitioner *Sarpanch* on charges of misappropriating funds and thereafter passed an order observing that the petitioner should de disqualified. A single judge dismissed the writ petition against this order. In the present writ appeal, the Division Bench held that unless there is a decision on the allegations against the *Sarpanch* by an adjudicatory authority (District Judge) such allegations cannot be used against the *Sarpanch* who will then continue to hold office.

Bihar

Kaushal Kishore Verma versus State of Bihar and Others (2004) 3 BLJR 2269) Section 18(5) of the Bihar Panchayati Raj Act, 1993. The court observed that the legislature in its wisdom has not conferred any right upon the Collector to take an action against *Mukhiya* under sub-section (5) of Section 18 of the Act or has not reserved any right unto itself to suspend the authority of the *Mukhiya* during the pendency of the proceedings initiated under sub-section (5) of Section 18. Hence, the Collector cannot assume jurisdiction nor can the Collector or the State have authority to suspend the authority of the elected *Mukhiya*. Therefore, in absence of the basic jurisdiction or discretion, the doctrine of necessity could not confer any jurisdiction on the Collector to suspend the authority of the elected *Mukhiya*.

Gujarat

Kalaji Hathji Thakore versus State of Gujarat (AIR 2000 Gujarat 289), Gujarat Panchayat Act (18 of 1993), Section 57 (Removal of Up-Sarpanch)

In the instant case, the *Upsarpanch* was removed on the ground of disgraceful conduct. The High Court in appeal while confirming the order of removal held that encroachment on *panchayat* land by the *Upsarpanch* clearly constitutes disgraceful conduct and his removal is fully justified even though he was not a member of panchayat at the time of committing unauthorised encroachment itself constitutes disgraceful conduct. Accordingly, removal was held as legal and proper.

Haribhai Galbabhai Patel versus Parmabhai Kanjibhai Parmar (AIR 2001 Gujarat 127), Gujarat Panchayats Act (18 of 1993), Section 57

In the instant case, the High Court ruled that for removal of a *Sarpanch* or a member of a *panchayat* under section 57 of the Act, mere initiation of criminal prosecution is not sufficient. An action of removal can be taken only after a finding as required by section 57 of the Act against the *Sarpanch* or Member, as the case may be.

Nasirkhan Nivaskhan Pathan versus District Development Officer, Bharuch (AIR 2002 Gujarat 143)

In the instant case, the High Court ruled that the order of suspension by the competent authority like the District Development Officer, against the *Sarpanch* or *Upsarpanch* cannot be passed on the ground of any criminal proceeding if such proceedings came to be initiated prior to election. So, suspension cannot be resorted to against the holder of public office on ground of any pre-election criminal proceedings if the same was not a disqualification under the Act for being elected to that office.

Kanakbhai Narsangbhai Padhar versus State of Gujarat (2003 AIHC 1081).

In this case the order of removal of a *Sarpanch,* on the charges of negligence and failure to discharge duties such as non-passing of the budget before 31st March was challenged. The High Court held that such provision is not mandatory and set aside the order of removal as the said order of removal was passed without considering the plea of the petitioner. The plea of the petitioner was that as a no confidence motion was moved against him, he was not sure which meeting he should call first and therefore sought directions of the concerned authorities. In this situation persistent default in discharge of duties by the petitioner has to be established.

V.L. Roy versus Mona Khadhar (2005 (3) GLH 64)

In the instant case wherein the President of *Gariadhar Taluka Panchayat* was removed from the post on the basis of certain materials which were not disclosed to the petitioner, the High Court held that such order would suffer from violation of principles of natural justice and liable to be set aside. The High Court observed that there has been grave injustice and prejudice caused to the petitioner when the Authority passed the impugned order relying upon certain materials without disclosing the same to the petitioner and without supplying copies thereof to the petitioner at any stage of the inquiry proceedings.

Madhya Pradesh

Hari Shankar Patel versus State of Madhya Pradesh (1999 (1) JCJ 253), Section 39, 39(1) (b), and 40 of 1993

Writ petition was filed to seek relief for setting aside the show cause notice and the order of suspension on the ground that the requirement of law has not been followed.

S-39 (1) (b) says that a notice for removal has to be given along with a charge sheet to show cause. The court opined that notice to show cause accompanied with articles of charges U/S 39 (1) (b) is a combined document and hence substantial compliance of the provisions of 39(1) (b) of the Adhiniyam Act was required.

Kailash Kumar versus State of Madhya Pradesh (1999 (2) JCJ 280)

The Sub-Divisional Officer (SDO) passed an order of removal of *Sarpanch* from the office. Aggrieved by this, appeal was filed before the Additional Collector on the ground of not providing an opportunity of hearing before passing the order of suspension, but it was rejected. Revision before the Commissioner was also rejected. The *Sarpanch* thereafter approached the state government under section 40 by virtue of delegation. The state government set aside the order of suspension. Hence, the writ was filed by the opposite party on the ground that the revision can be entertained only on a point of law.

The court held that removal of an elected *Sarpanch* is a serious matter as he is further disqualified for six years to be elected under the Act. So mere show cause notice and consideration of reply is not sufficient. The words in the provision of S-40 (1) "after such enquiry as it may deem fit to make" and words "unless he has been given an opportunity to show cause why he should not be removed from his office" are of crucial importance.

Removal of a *panchayat* office bearer U/S 40 is not less injurious and stigmatic than removal of a civil servant under U/A 311 of the Constitution. Hence the court said that principles of natural justice should be applied and since this was not done in the instant case struck down the order of removal.

Kamal Kishore versus Janpad Panchayat (1999 (2) JLJ 370)

The court said that if at all any action is to be taken in view of the provisions of Section 40 of the Act for the purpose of removal of office bearers of a *panchayat,* the prescribed authority will have to hold first an enquiry for purpose of finding out whether the delinquent happens to be guilty of things described U/S 40 (a), (b) or the proviso to S.40(1). Further the prescribed authority will have to point out that the conduct of the delinquent is falling under the category of 'Misconduct' as indicated by the explanation provided in S.40(1) of the *Adhiniyam*. In the present case, the court said that the opponents did not have any ground to show that the petitioner's conduct was in any way coming under the category prescribed by the word 'Misconduct.'

Orissa

Subhash Chandra Jaina versus State (1994LCT 662 decided 29.7.1994)

It was held Section 115 of the Orissa Gram Panchayat Act does not permit suspension or removal of the *Sarpanch* by the Collector for any prejudicial act or omission done in the past prior to his election.

Baikunthannath Mohanty versus State of Orissa
(AIR, 1998 Orissa 150 decided 24.8.1998)

This case related to the suspension of a *panchayat* President for certain irregularities. The court held that the Collector cannot suspend the *Sarpanch* unless he is satisfied that the alleged delinquency is willful and not accidental or negligent. The use of the word 'willful' in Section 115 (1) of the Orissa Panchayat Act implies that the action should be deliberate, calculated, intentional and conscious. The charges in this case related to retaining excess cash in hand, disobeying orders of the SDO in canceling a lease, failure to realise security deposit from the Gram Panchayat Secretary etc.

Sukanta Bhoi versus State (OJC 6959 of 1999 decided on 10.8.1999)

For removal of a *Sarpanch* on grounds of irregularities and violations, the mere use of the word 'willful' in the suspension or other order will not be adequate. That the delinquency was indeed willful should be established.

Kanakalata Mallik versus Collector, Kendrapara (AIR, 2001 Orissa 161)

Ratio in the case supra was followed and the court held that circumstances should exist for the Collector to form a clear opinion that the *Sarpanch* willfully omitted or violated the provisions of the *Panchayat* Acts or rules.

Punjab

Dev Singh versus State of Punjab and others (1996 AIHC 4368)
Section 20(3) of the Punjab Panchayati Raj Act (9 of 1994)

The court upheld the suspension of the *Sarpanch* as he was charge-sheeted for a criminal offence of murder involving moral turpitude. In the instant case criminal appellate authority had also found him prima facie responsible for alleged offence and therefore had rightly debarred him from performing the function of *Sarpanch.*

Satnam Singh Kala versus State of Punjab and Others (2003) 3 PLR 522)
Section 20, 113 and 208 of the Punjab Panchayati Raj Act, 1994 (9 of 1994)

The court held that on reading of Section 113 of the 1994 Act it is evident that the power regarding suspension and removal is limited with the government, as compared to the powers available for suspension and removal of *Sarpanches* and *Panches* under Section

20 of the 1994 Act. It further stated that the conditions on the basis of which the persons shall be disqualified for being chosen as and for being a member of a *panchayat* are enumerated under Section 28 of the Act. Therefore, a mere pendency of an FIR against a member of a *Panchayati Samiti*, cannot be made a ground for his suspension/ removal.

Chand s/o Piara Singh versus Special Secretary to Govt. of Punjab, Chandigarh and Others 2004 AIHC 4557. Section 20(3) of the Punjab Panchayati Raj Act (9 of 1994)

The court held that any order which causes civil consequences cannot be passed, unless the person against whom it is passed, has been given an adequate opportunity to rebut the allegations/charges made against him. The court further held that a duly elected *Sarpanch* has a legitimate expectation to continue as such for the entire term of five years. If the period is to be cut short, it is expected that the authorities would comply with rules of natural justice, before any order is passed adversely affecting the tenure of the *Sarpanch*. Similar view was held in Mange Ram, *Sarpanch, Gram Panchayat versus* Financial Commissioner and Secretary to Government, 1997 (1) Pun. L J 437: (AIR 1997 P & H 252) and Kashmiri Lal *versus* Deputy Commissioner, Sonepat, 1980 Pun LJ 222: (AIR 1980 P & H 209).

Rajasthan

Anant Ram Sharma versus State of Rajasthan (1998 AIHC 2809) Section 17(4) of the old Act

In this case, order of removal of *Sarpanch* by the state government was set aside on the ground that the person removed was not afforded reasonable opportunity to defend himself and also the order was passed without application of mind.

Chaganlal Solanki versus State of Rajasthan (2003 AIHC 984) Section 38 of the Act

The court observed that suspension under Section 38(4) could be ordered only when an inquiry has been initiated against the person. It is a condition precedent before passing the suspension order. Mere recording of statement in suspension order that enquiry was under contemplation would not comply with such condition. Suspension order made, in this case, was held invalid.

Jagdish Chandra versus State of Rajasthan
(2004 AIHC 3081) Section 38(4) of the Act, 1994

Under this section, the state government may suspend a *Sarpanch*, if any criminal proceedings in regard to an offence involving moral turpitude, is 'pending trial' in a court of law. In this case, the *Sarpanch* was suspended on the ground that criminal proceedings were pending against him in the court of law. At that point of time charges had not been framed against him.

The Court observed that 'pending trial' implies the stage after the framing of charges in the case. Till the charges are framed, the trial does not commence. In this case, no charges were framed and thus the order suspending the *Sarpanch* was quashed and set aside.

Uttar Pradesh

Chunmun versus District Magistrate, Sonbhadra and Another
(AIR, 1999 Allahabad 88). Section 95(1) (G) of the U.P. Panchayat Raj Act (26 of 1947). Rules 4(2) and 85 of U.P. Panchayat Raj (Removal of Pradhans, Up-Pradhans and Members) Enquiry Rules (1997)

The court held that the expression 'prima facie found' read with expression 'in an enquiry held by such person and in such manner as may be prescribed' used by the legislature in the first proviso to Section 95(1) (g) of the Act unequivocally suggests that the requisite prima facie finding must be arrived at on consideration of the preliminary enquiry report submitted by the District Panchayati Raj Officer under Rule 4(2) or the report submitted by the Enquiry officer under Rule 8 of the Enquiry Rules. Therefore any other view of the matter would be tantamount to over reaching the first proviso to Section 95 (12) (g) of the Act. It further observed that though the District Magistrate may order a formal enquiry to be held on the basis of reports received 'otherwise' in that event no action could be taken under the first proviso to Section 95(1) (g) of the Act until receipt of the report prepared by the Enquiry Officer under Rule 7 of the Enquiry Rules.

Chandrajit Rai Bihar versus District Magistrate, Pilibhit and Others (2002 AIHC 1290). Section 95(1)(G) of U.P. Panchayat Raj Act (26 of 1947). Rules 29 (c), 4 and 5 of the U.P. Panchayat Raj (Removal of Pradhans, Up-Pradhans and Members) Enquiries Rules 1997)

The court held that a *Pradhan* or *Up-Pradhan* cannot be deprived of his financial and administrative powers and functions in a perfunctory manner against the mandatory provisions envisaged under Section 95(1) (g) of the Act of 1947 and statutory rules of 1997, unless preliminary enquiry is held by the District Panchayati Raj Officer and in that enquiry he is *prima facie* found to have committed financial and other irregularities. It further held that the *Pradhans* or *Up-Pradhans* before being deprived of the authority to perform their financial and administrative powers and functions, are also entitled to show cause to the preliminary enquiry wherein prima facie they are found to have committed financial or other irregularities. In the preliminary enquiry report from the District Panchayati Raj Officer, if a *Pradhan* or *Up-Pradhan* is *prima facie* found to have committed financial or other irregularities, a copy of a preliminary enquiry is to be made available to such delinquent *Pradhan* or *Up-Pradhan* asking his explanation. But if in the preliminary enquiry conducted by the District *Panchayat Raj* Officer nothing is found against him the question of depriving of financial and administrative powers and functions does not arise. In the instant case, the order passed by the District Magistrate depriving the *Pradhan* of his financial and administrative powers and functions was based on a report submitted by the Assistant Engineer, which was, 'per se' illegal within the meaning of Rule 2(c). No reasonable opportunity of showing cause was given to the *Pradhan* before passing the impugned order as envisaged under the second proviso of Section 95(1) (g) of the Act of 1947.

An overview of the cases presented above relating to removal indicates that the courts have clearly upheld the principle that in a democracy an incumbent, once elected to an office, is entitled to hold the office for the term elected for, unless his election is set aside by a prescribed procedure known to law. This valuable statutory right is available not only to the returned candidate but also to his constituency. The adherence to democratic provisions and procedures are essential whatever be the reasons for removal, whether motion of no confidence, failure to call meetings, defection of non-performance or misconduct. One important message which runs through all these decisions is that in cases alleging misconduct, proper application of mind is essential. Perfunctory and peremptory orders of removal are not acceptable in law.

The Apex Court has strongly condemned removal of elected representatives by designated officials. In *Tarlochan Dev Sharma versus State of Punjab (AIR 2001 SC 25)*, the facts of the case are stated in some detail as they illustrate how far the powers of removal case be misused. The appellant was elected as President of the Rajpura Municipality in April 1998. He had held the office hardly for a period of four months when he was served with a notice by the Principal Secretary, Local Government Department, Punjab requiring him to show cause why he should not be removed from the post. Another charge was that as President he instructed the Executive Officer for not making payment for the purchase of a fogging machine. He was then charged for obstructing municipal work as a result. The President's response was that the machine was found to be defective. In a hearing before the Principal Secretary, Local Government, the Municipal President also detailed the reasons for not making the payment and also indicated that the real reason for seeking his removal was political. Nevertheless, the Principal Secretary, issued orders for removal. The appellant filed a writ petition thereafter but a Division Bench of Punjab and Haryana formed an opinion that it cannot test the validity of the impugned order. The matter then went in appeal to the Supreme Court. A Bench of three Judges headed by the Chief Justice allowed the appeal and set aside the judgement of the High Court. The Apex Court further observed "the manner in which the power under Section 22 of the Punjab Municipal Act has been exercised by the competent authority is suggestive of betrayal of the confidence which the state government reposed in the Principal Secretary in conferring upon him the exercise of drastic powers like removal of a President of a municipality. To say the least what has been done is not what is expected to be done by a senior official."

State of Punjab and Others versus Bhajan Singh (2001 (3) Supreme 179 decided 27.2.1001)

In this case Bhajan Singh the first respondent was elected as President of the Municipal Council of Samrala on 6.4.1998. Despite the election, the notification in terms of Section 24 of the Punjab Municipal Act was not issued by the government. Aggrieved by this inaction, the respondent filed a writ petition on 15.5.1998. On 1.7.1998 a show cause notice was issued to the respondent proposing to take action against him for interfering in the working of the municipal council and for misuse of powers. Though a reply was filed by the respondent, he was removed from office. This order of removal was quashed by the High Court. The state government then went in appeal to the Supreme Court.

"The appeal which is bereft of any merit is liable to be dismissed. We are at pain to note that by his acts of omission and commission the said Secretary has consistently and persistently deprived the respondent No.1 of the duty to assume and discharge his duties as member and President of the municipal council, despite his election from 2.1.1998 till date. The term of the Municipality is a fixed term out of which three years of the respondent No.1 have been wasted in uncalled for and forced litigation upon him. No law can compensate the loss of opportunity provided to the respondent No.1 for serving the people after his election as Member and President of the municipality. We find it a fit case to award exemplary costs and are of the firm view that such costs should not be burdened upon the state exchequer. The said Secretary who is responsible for the violation of the statutory provisions and weakening the concept of rule of law, is, therefore, personally liable to pay the costs from his own pockets. While dismissing this appeal we direct the said Secretary to personally pay the costs of Rs.25,000to the respondent No.1 within a period of two months."

Does Limiting Tenure Amount to Removal?

Though directly not related to the subject of removal, before leaving this chapter we may consider an important issue about the term of office of the Mayor of a corporation as compared to the tenure of the corporation itself. This issue was raised in Bihar Mayors Council vs. Union of India and others (2003(3) BLJR2012. The question was whether the term of the office of the Patna Municipal corporation should be limited by statute to only one year and election of a new mayor organised every year when the term of the corporation itself as also the Chief Executive Officer who is an official appointed by the state government is five years. A Division Bench of the Patna High Court found that there was an area of conflict in so far as the Mayor's office was limited to one year whereas the term of the municipal corporation itself was five years. In reaching a decision the Division Bench of the High Court observed as follows:

> The tenure of an elected representative to an institution of self-government, the third tier of government today, whether municipality or *panchayat* has been provided by the Constitution to be five years. It is the tenure of elected representatives collectively returned to office as a result of an election. The pattern is the same whether it is the Parliament, the legislatures or institutions of self-government; all will have a tenure of five years. Can a Mayor have a lesser tenure? The Constitution of India does not seem to suggest it. The Constitution clearly shows the perspective that the tenure of an elected member to any tier of government whether Parliament, legislature, municipality or *panchayat* will be five years. The tenure of a Mayor in the spirit of the Constitution, is co-terminus with the tenure of the municipality or corporation.
>
> Merely because the state legislature of Bihar forgot to define the Mayor in the very Act which constitutes the Patna Municipal Corporation as an incorporated corporation, it cannot belittle the position of a Mayor. While the Act does not even recognise the Mayor and define his office, the Constitution overrides to eclipse the Act.
>
> Some states of the nation have taken notice of the changes in the Constitution and have made the tenure of a Mayor co-terminus with the tenure of the corporation or the elected body. The state of Punjab apparently has taken notice of the constitutional provisions and has clearly stipulated in the enactment that the term of office of a Mayor

shall be co-terminus with the duration of the municipal corporation Section 24 of the Punjab Municipal Corporation Act, 1976. Tamil Nadu, in Madras City Municipal Act, 1919 has made an amendment, after the Constitution of India was amended, so as to give the Mayor a term of office of five years. So has the Uttar Pradesh *Nagarmahapalika Adhiniyam*, 1959 and West Bengal.

While this judgement of the Patna High Court is of far reaching significance and the amendments directed by the High Court would bring the Patna Municipal Corporation Act on par with the provisions of similar laws in Punjab, Kerala, Andhra Pradesh, West Bengal and Uttar Pradesh, the fact also remains that in some other states the term of the Mayor or the Deputy Mayor is not co-terminus with the term of the municipality or the corporation. For instance in Maharashtra, Karnataka and Delhi among other states, the term continues to be less than five years. Challenges to the Patna High Court's judgement in the instant case have not come to notice so far.

Conclusions

In this chapter we have considered numerous cases relating to the broad subject of removal of elected persons, be they members, or chairpersons or vice-chairpersons of local bodies.

(a) In regard to no confidence motion we have seen that the courts have clearly recognised this to be an important aspect of the democratic system to ensure accountability. Cases have varied depending on the relevant state laws but courts have generally insisted on adherence to the statutory provisions and procedures as well as adherence to principles of natural justice.

(b) Some judgements have varied between different courts as well as in the same court in regard to counting of votes, particularly how fractions are to be dealt with in deciding whether the requisite majority of votes has been obtained. Since these are essentially a matter of arithmetics it is expected state governments would take note of the judgements and make appropriate changes in the laws and regulations rather than allow needless confusion to remain, requiring judicial interpretation.

(c) In asserting the total strength of a house some doubts persist about whether vacant seats should be taken into account or not. The case law does not point to a clear conclusion.

(d) The voting rights of the nominated members in motions of confidence appear to have been settled in Ramesh Mehta's case by the Supreme Court. As per this judgement such nominated members are not to participate or vote on motions of no confidence.

(e) However, if the ratio in this judgement is pursued it can well be argued that the power to remove an elected person should vest only in those who are themselves elected members of houses concerned. In the parliamentary system, positions such as Prime Minister, or Chief Minister are filled by members of the legislature and persons holding these positions are clearly answerable to the Parliament or the state legislature. The position of a directly elected *Pradhan*, a Municipal Chairman or a Mayor is a departure from the Parliamentary system. Though some High Courts have held that these positions are statutory in nature and therefore subject to statutory restriction, it remains to be seen whether challenges including removal by elected representatives of a chairperson who is directly elected by people, will continue to be mounted notwithstanding the Apex Court's decisions in Ram Beti's case.

(f) The case law in regard to removal due to defection from a political party or for disobeying party whip indicates a rather complicated and tenuous system vulnerable to political pressure.

(g) The same situation applies to removal for non-performance of elected persons by designated officials. Besides, the grounds for removal are widely varied, from financial irregularities which are matters of fact to grave misconduct which is a matter of subjective judgement. Kerala is one of the states where an Ombudsman established as a quasi judicial entity, enquires into allegations of this nature against elected representatives. While the power of removal still rests with the government, an enquiry by the Ombudsman and its advice are a prerequisite. This issue of removal of elected persons by appointed officials is only partly legal in nature. It pertains more to adherence to the spirit and substance of the Constitutional Amendments.

The functional domain of the *panchayats* and municipalities and the case law on the subject will be considered in the next chapter.

7

Functional Domain of *Panchayats* and Municipalities

Introduction

The functional domain of the *panchayats* and municipalities is the most crucial element in the entire system of decentralisation sought to be achieved through the 73rd and the 74th Amendments. These two amendments are without doubt the largest additions to the Constitution of our country. It is important to recount briefly the history of these amendments. The government led by late Shri Rajiv Gandhi decided on the decentralisation programme as an important plank of its mandate and in the words of the Prime Minister "maximum devolution with maximum power to the people" was the objective. It was also considered that for a country of India's size and diversity, there was a compelling need to widen the representative structure. The sum total of members in the Parliament and the state legislatures put together did not exceed 6000. It was felt that the funnel of representation should therefore be significantly enlarged. An elaborate structure based on democratic elections with reservation for weaker sections of the society such as women, scheduled castes and scheduled tribes was considered essential. To begin with the 64th Amendment Bill was introduced in the Lok Sabha in May 1989 pertaining to *panchayats*. Later on another bill, the 65th Amendment was introduced in August 1989 dealing with municipalities. The introduction of these bills was preceded, accompanied and followed by an extensive range of consultations, held country wide, with elected representatives and officials of urban and rural local bodies, state government leaders and officials, other officials of the central government etc. The passage of these bills in the Lok Sabha by an overwhelming majority and their defeat in the Rajya Sabha have been described in the Introductory chapter.

After the 10th Lok Sabha was formed and the government headed by the late Shri Narasimha Rao took office, the 64th and the 65th Constitution Amendment Bills were suitably redrafted and introduced in the Lok Sabha in September 1991. For both Bills, the statement of objects and reasons were couched in very similar language. Both statements referred to the problem of local bodies having become weak and ineffective on account of a variety of reasons including failure to hold regular elections, prolonged supercession and inadequate devolution of powers and functions. The intention to make these bodies perform effectively as vibrant democratic units of self-government was explicit. It was further stated that the amendment bills sought to put on a firmer footing the relationship between the state government and the local bodies with respect to functions, taxation powers, revenue sharing, regular conduct of elections and adequate representation for weaker sections like SCs, STs and women. Extracts from the statement of objects and reasons in respect of both these Constitutional Amendment Bills are contained as annexures A-7.1 and A-7.2 to this chapter.

After introduction, both the bills were referred to two separate joint committees of the Parliament. Both the joint committees devoted considerable time to a discussion of the draft bills and made several recommendations. The Joint Committee on the 73rd Amendment Bill, as it was then called, relating to municipalities also recommended addition of two articles providing for a committee for district planning and another committee for metropolitan planning. Extracts of the reports of the two joint committees are also presented as annexures A-7.3 and A-7.4 to this chapter. A reading of these two committee reports are essential for a proper understanding of the intent, and substance of the Constitutional Amendments.

The Provisions Regarding Functional Domain

The language of Articles 243G on powers, authority and responsibilities of *panchayats* and Article 243W relating to municipalities are almost identical. Both articles are explicit in stating that the purpose is to "endow the *panchayats* and municipalities with such powers and authority as may be necessary to enable them to function as institutions of self-government." If the intention was only to make the *panchayats* and municipalities as agencies of the state government for carrying out some functions on their behalf or for implementing certain schemes, the question of making them institutions of self-government would not have arisen. This language was also not alien to the Constitution. Article 40 in Part IV of the Constitution on Directive Principles of State Policy contains a stipulation that the state "shall take steps to organise village *panchayats* and endow them with such powers and authority as may be necessary to enable them to function as units of self-government." The Amendments therefore were only to carry forward this directive principle towards the establishment of such units of self government. The language used in Articles 243G and 243W are in part, a reiteration of Article 40. Both Articles 243G and 243W also prescribe the manner in which powers and authority are to be devolved. The constitutional language itself is adequate to explain the important components of these two articles and how they are to be acted upon.

Firstly the purpose is "to endow the *panchayats* with such powers and authority as necessary to enable them to function as institutions of self-government." **Secondly** the process of such *endowment should be by law.* The rationale for this is what is endowed by law, can be amended or withdrawn only by law. **Thirdly** the law is to contain "provisions for the devolution of powers and responsibilities upon *panchayats,* at the appropriate level." In other words, the Constitution requires that the law itself should assign the functions and specify the levels of the *panchayats* concerned where such functions would be performed. **Fourthly** such a law may include conditions "as may be specified therein", i.e. as may be specified in the law itself. It is a principle of natural justice that the conditions should not be so onerous or restrictive as to render the devolved task impossible to perform or render what is devolved as meaningless. **Fifthly** the powers and responsibilities to be devolved will relate to "the preparation of plans for economic development" and "the implementation of schemes for this purpose including those in relation to the matters listed in the 11th Schedule."

These five ingredients of the constitutional stipulations are common to both *panchayats* and municipalities. It is important to recognise that the 11th and 12th Schedules are not an exhaustive compilation. There could be other subjects or tasks which are also related to schemes for economic development and social justice. However, the intent of the Constitutional provision is that the matters listed in the 11th and the 12th Schedules would, in the normal course, fall within the purview of the *panchayats* and the municipalities which would mainly be responsible for their implementation.

However, some confusion persists about the position of Schedules 11 and 12. Schedule 11 contains 29 items and Schedule 12 contains 18 items. All these items are subjects and not specific tasks or activities. While a reference to the Schedules are contained in Articles 243G and 243W adherence to these provisions are not entirely contingent on these Schedules. As stated before, the principal direction in both these articles is that a state, by law, should endow the *panchayats*/municipalities with such powers and authority as maybe necessary to enable them to function as institutions of self-government. This point needs to be stressed again and again. Additionally both the Articles contain a mandate for the *panchayats* and municipalities to prepare 'plans for economic development and social justice.' It is only in the subsequent part of the two Articles that a reference is made to the implementation of schemes including those in relation to matters listed in the 11th and 12th Schedules.

A plain reading of the Schedules makes it clear that they are lists of subjects. Subjects as such, cannot be devolved. Tasks and functions have to be defined and then devolved on the *panchayats* and municipalities by law which requires a conscious application of mind on the part of the state legislatures. The subjects listed are also not exhaustive. In other words they do not represent the entire gamut of functions, which may be undertaken by a *panchayat* or a municipality. The subjects listed are also not exclusive. For that matter entry 5 in the State List in the 7th Schedule of the Constitution vide Article 246 is also not exhaustive or exclusive. It is well established that the scope of every subject contained in the Union, State and Concurrent lists are co-extensive with legislative, executive and financial functions related to each of them. The clear intent of the Constitutional Amendment is that the state legislature will, by law, devolve various functions and tasks upon the *panchayats* and municipalities in such a manner that the exercise of the executive and legislative tasks including regulatory and financial tasks in this regard are harmonised with the domain of the state. To ensure that the necessary application of mind does take place in the wake of the Amendments and that the relevant laws are harmonised, the Constitutional Amendments also specifically provided in Articles 243N and 243ZF that the existing laws obtaining in any state relating to *panchayats* and municipalities shall be amended or repealed if they are found inconsistent with the provisions of part IX and IXA of the Constitution. A time limit of one year from the date on which the Amendments come into force, has also been stipulated. It is not the intention of the Constitution makers that the powers of the state as contained in the 7th Schedule shall be 'removed' or 'stand denuded' in so far as they relate to the subjects in the 11th and the 12th Schedules. On the contrary the plenary powers of the state shall have to be 'adjusted and modified' in keeping with the constitutional provisions.

The failure to understand this position has led several of the state governments to apprehend that Schedules 11 and 12 are a subtraction from the state's plenary powers. To a large extent this apprehension has been fed and reinforced by various authorities, special purpose agencies or departments of the state government which over a period of time were created and which took over some of the key functions performed earlier by *panchayats* or municipalities such as drinking water supply, drainage, sanitation, land use planning, development of land etc.

It is appropriate to dwell briefly on the pre-amendment scene. In several states such as Karnataka, Maharashtra or Rajasthan, *panchayats* whether at the village or district levels were given significant responsibilities in regard to these functions. In the case of municipalities the relevant state laws, which were broadly similar across the country, specified a broad division of core or obligatory functions on the one hand and discretionary functions on the other. For instance, water supply, sanitation, roads, control of building operations, public health etc., invariably formed part of the core functions, while education, libraries, hospitals etc., were considered discretionary. During the 60s and 70s, special purpose agencies were created in many states to take over these core functions from the municipalities like the Jal Nigam in Uttar Pradesh, the Water Supply and Sewerage Board in Maharashtra, the Public Health Engineering Department in Kerala or the Water Supply and Drainage Board in Tamil Nadu. In course of time other functions like acquisition and development of land for extension of urban areas, formation of residential colonies, disposal of developed plots, housing construction etc., came to be entrusted to development authorities. Prior to independence City Improvement Trusts were created in Kolkata, Mumbai, Chennai etc., but it was recognised that these Improvement Trusts were performing in essence municipal functions and therefore the composition of these trusts included representatives from the municipalities or the city corporations. Additionally, the corporations were also expected to contribute to the funds of these Improvement Trusts and take over the areas developed by the Trusts for maintenance and administering municipal taxation. The development authorities which came after independence were much more ambitious in their mandate and jurisdiction. Apart from acquisition and development of land, these authorities became real estate developers and empires of public works. Access to financial resources gave them significant clout. Additionally these bodies were also entrusted by the state governments with land use planning powers, though this was a patent conflict of interest, since the same organisation became responsible for planning land use and also developing, selling and profiting from land development schemes sanctioned as part of the plan. Today in all the large cities or agglomerations in the country which have more than one million population such development authorities exist. Together these authorities and other special purpose agencies have been successfully resisting the devolution of tasks to municipalities.

In the case of *panchayats,* though in the pre-amendment phase, conscious efforts were made in some states to carve out an independent functional domain for them, in the wake of the Constitutional Amendment, legislative actions have been retrograde. For instance, in the case of Tamil Nadu, under the Panchayats Act, 1958, the *panchayat* Unions were administering various schemes relating to elementary education, public health, maternity centres, dispensaries etc., in addition to agricultural extension, vetenary relief, cottage and village industries etc. The Act also provided for all water sources, reservoirs, tanks, wells, standpipe, water works etc., to vest in the *panchayat* and be subject to its control. However, in 1994, this important provision was omitted and control of all water sources was vested in the State Water and Drainage Board. In several other states, the Panchayat Acts which came into force after the Constitutional Amendment and which were intended to bring the state laws in conformity, in fact reduced their functional domain.

The Case Law

We may now consider the cases adjudicated in different High Courts pertaining to the subject. Compared to cases on election, reservation or removal matters, disputes about the functional domain have not been many. Where they have arisen, questioning the basis and extent of the powers and responsibilities of the *panchayats* at different levels and municipalities, the courts have generally held in favour of a specific jurisdiction to be exercised by these bodies but have also examined whether in the exercise of that jurisdiction the principles and procedures of natural justice as well as public interest have been maintained. In many of the cases, the issue has also been raised whether the functional domain of the *panchayats* and municipalities is limited by other laws and if so whether such laws are consistent with the constitutional provisions. The courts have also recognised that *panchayats* and municipalities being local authorities are expected to understand local needs and circumstances better. We may consider the cases in two broad categories namely those relating to licensing and regulatory powers of the local bodies and thereafter, cases on the exercise of planning powers, in particular spatial and land use planning.

Andhra

As early as 1997, in *Velpur Gram Panchayat versus Assistant Collector Marketing (AIR 98, AP 142, decided 7.8.1997,* the High Court held that the Panchayati Raj bodies have not merely a statutory position but a constitutional status as well and the holding of weekly bazaars has been a historical function of the *panchayats*. Though the AP Agricultural Produce Marketing Act assigned such a function to market committees, the court held that AP Market Act or the AP Agricultural Produce Act cannot override the jurisdiction of the *gram panchayat* provided for in the Constitution itself. Furthermore the PR Act being the more recent Act it would override the earlier APAP Act.

In several other cases which followed, the AP High Court examined the functional domain of the *gram panchayats*.

In *Satyanarayana versus Akiveedu Gram Panchayat (1998(3)/ALT 175 decided 4.3.1998),* the High Court held that the *gram panchayat* has planning powers which included grant or denial of planning and building permission. In *Doddigunta Fishermen Cooperative Society versus AP (1998(4)/ALT 595 decided on 21.7.1998),* the issue was about the auction price payable for a fishery. Though the case arose out of the quantum of the price, the right of the *panchayat* to make the levy was upheld. The subject came up for examination again in *Vaddavalli Fishermen Cooperative Society (2000(4)/ALT 1 decided 21.7.1998).* The court held that fishery rights including the right to levy taxes or fees on fishing in respect of those water bodies and tanks vested in the *gram panchayat* and that there powers were available specifically to the *panchayats*. In a similar case, *Ipur gram panchayat, Guntur District versus AP (2000(4)/ALT 678 decided 21.7.2000)*, the High Court clarified that while such fishery rights may not be available to the *gram panchayats* in regard to major irrigation tanks, so far as minor irrigation tanks are concerned, the fishing and other rights including the usufruct belong to the GP.

Goa

A very important case arose in Goa in the *panchayat* area of Querim when a multinational company Du Pont decided to set up a chemical plant in the area to manufacture Nylon among other things. While the Goa Panchayati Raj Act 1993 conferred some planning and licensing powers on the *panchayats* such powers were not available previously and the Panchayats were dealing only with limited activities. The Du Pont Company started work in 1990 with the construction of a compound wall for which permission of the *panchayat* was not taken. Later on, the company also undertook some blasting operations at its site which caused some damage to several houses in the village. The *panchayat* accordingly issued a show cause notice to the Du Pont company as to why its operations should not be stopped and the construction of the wall without authorisation be demolished. The company then preferred an appeal before the Director of *panchayats*. The Director upheld Du Pont's contention that powers relating to demolition of unauthorised constructions were conferred only on the *panchayat* as a corporate body and not on the *Sarpanch*. However, the Director rejected Du Pont's claim about deemed permission under the Village Panchayat Regulations of 1962, since these provisions were repealed when the 1993 Act came into effect. The company was directed to submit appropriate applications for permission. The Goa Foundation and some other environmental groups then moved the Bombay High Court with writ petitions. The High Court in its judgement of 21st November 1994 directed the company to submit necessary plans and required documents to the Querim *panchayat* and to seek its permission. In January 1995, the *panchayat* resolved not to allow the setting up of the factory as it apprehended damage to the surrounding areas and other environmental problems. The Du Pont company then petitioned the High Court seeking to quash the resolution of the *panchayat*. The Company argued that the *panchayat's* resolution against the setting up of the factory was prompted by extraneous considerations such as opposition to nylon manufacture. The *panchayat* argued that its own responsibility for the development of the village included the right to grant or reject applications for any development. The High Court while accepting the *panchayat's* argument regarding deemed permission not being applicable, issued nevertheless a writ of *Mandamus* to the *panchayat* to grant permission to the company for a compound wall. The High Court however, recorded that the permission to construct a compound wall did not imply that the company was automatically authorised to use the land for any industrial project.

Litigation in the court was accompanied by public protests from time to time. The partly raised compound wall was also demolished during one such protest. In January 1995, a bus load of visitors including foreigners were brought to the site by the company. A crowd of irate villagers blocked the road. Matters took a violent turn, police opened fire and one person was killed. The Du Pont company decided to withdraw from the area and did not pursue the project. Here was a case when a legal interpretation of a *panchayat* licensing powers was sought but the dispute was resolved by extra legal measures.

Himachal Pradesh

Another major case of a similar nature arose in this state. In *Baldev Singh and Others versus State of Himachal Pradesh and Others (CWP No.490 of 2004 decided on 27.7.2006)*, Ranbaxy Laboratories, India's largest pharmaceutical company and one of the top ranking pharmaceutical manufacturers in the world had established a bulk drugs manufacturing plant near the town of Paonta Sahib in Himachal Pradesh. In February 2004, the company sought permission from the Himachal State Environment and Pollution Control Board to expand the capacity of its fermentation plant in Ganguwala and a formulation unit in the neighbouring Batamandi village. Apprehending large scale pollution, in July 2004, Baldev Singh and three other villagers including the Vice President of one of the *gram panchayats* in the area filed a public interest litigation in the HP High Court. During proceedings, it transpired that the rapid environmental impact assessment submitted by the Ranbaxy Company had several shortcomings. Under the High Court's decision a committee was set up with representatives of the government, the Ranbaxy Company as well as experts which went into various environmental aspects of the proposal. The emissions resulting from the proposed expansion of the plant, the toxicity of the effluents to be discharged, possible contamination of the ground water, conformity with the development plan of the area, conformity with the land laws, disposal of sold wastes etc., were some of the aspects, which were considered. The High Court after due consideration of the report decided that the proposed expansion should be put on hold, pending a comprehensive environmental impact assessment. The court observed "in our considered view, keeping in mind the toxicity of the gases being emitted and their highly adverse effect on all living beings, we feel that the proposal for expansion of the fermentation plant needs to be reviewed. In our considered opinion, it would not be proper to set up a plant of such huge capacity after making a huge investment and after some years order the plant to be closed down because it does not comply with emission norms."

The High Court also found that there were various violations relating to the Development Plan, the Land Laws, the Town and Country Planning Act, Factories Act etc. Accordingly the court directed that further construction or expansion of the fermentation plant in Ganguwala shall not be resumed until a Comprehensive Environment Impact Assessment and Environment Management Programme is prepared and the same is taken into consideration by the various authorities before granting requisite permissions. The Court however, held that the formulation plant at Batamandi can be taken up subject to various specific directions.

Though this case does not directly pertain to the functional domain of the *panchayats*, the fact remains that it is the initiative of the village residents and some *gram panchayat* leaders, which had brought the matter to the High Court's attention. This is also one of the few instances where the state government authorities, the company and the experts joined their efforts through a committee set up by the High Court to reach a resolution acceptable to various stakeholders including the villagers. While the setting up of a major manufacturing facility with possible adverse environmental consequences has been halted, pending a detailed review, it now remains to be seen to what extent the manufacturer will undertake such a comprehensive review, how transparent the process of Environmental Impact Assessment will be and how far the *gram panchayats* and other local bodies will be involved or consulted.

Karnataka

Taluk Panchayat versus State of Karnataka/AIR, 2000, Karnataka 220, decided on 2.2.2000. In this case it was held that under the Karnataka PR Act, women and child development activities pertain to the *Taluk panchayat* and as such *Zilla Panchayat* cannot have jurisdiction.

Akirampura Gram Panchayat versus Karnataka (2000(4) KAR LI 226)

Under the Karnataka Agricultural Produce Marketing Act 1996, local authorities cannot operate as market functionaries in areas under the state APMC Act. In keeping with the provision of the Act the High Court held the *panchayat* had no right to levy fees in respect of the market. This decision may be contrasted with the Velpur case, in Andhra, cited *supra*. The Karnataka Act appears *prima facie* repugnant to the provisions of the Constitution indicating further a conflict between this Act and the Karnataka PR Act.

The clash of jurisdictions between state authorities and *panchayats* also figured in *Falma Laboratories versus State of Karnataka, AIR, 1997 Kar 321 decided on 20.3.1997*. In this case the decision of the Karnataka Industrial Area Development Board to collect entry tax was challenged. It was held that since the layout of the industrial area fell within the jurisdiction of a *gram panchayat*, it was permissible to levy a tax on goods entering the *panchayat* area.

Orissa

In this case the petitioner challenged a provision in the Orissa Gram Panchayat Act which stipulated that if a Market Committee established under the Orissa Agricultural Produce Markets Act, 1956 calls upon a *panchayat* to transfer a building or land used as a market for agricultural produce, the *gram panchayat* shall make the transfer, only if the requisition from the market committee is accompanied by a written permission of the Collector of the district for the purpose. There was also a provision that within 90 days it is open to the state government to review the permission granted by the Collector and if the state government is satisfied that such permission is not in the interests of the village *panchayat* it can cancel the same. The petitioner's contention was that this requirement of permission from the Collector was unnecessary and the Market Committee was in the best position to protect the interests of the agriculturists without exploitation of middlemen. The High Court held that written permission from the Collector would definitely operate as a check on the arbitrary and whimsical desire of a market committee to get the land or building in possession of a village *panchayat* and appropriate to itself the income derived from such land or building. The power of the state government to review the Collector's decision if it is found prejudicial to the interests of the *gram panchayat* was an additional safeguard. Accordingly the court dismissed the petition.

Prima facie this case revolved around the issue of the jurisdiction between a Market Committee under the APM Act, 1956 and the Gram Panchayat PR Act. It is however not clear whether the listing of market and fares as an activity exclusively or predominantly within a *panchayat* functional domain vide item 22 of the 11th Schedule of the Constitution was specifically raised during the adjudication.

One other case of jurisdiction conflicting with *panchayat* domain relating to markets went upto the Apex Court. In *Talcher Municipality versus Talcher Regulatory Marketing Committee (2004(6) SC 65 decided on 28.7.2004)* the Supreme Court held that even if a market is owned and operated by a municipality or a *panchayat*, if a requisition is made by a Marketing Committee under the Orissa Agricultural Produce Marketing Act 1956, the municipality or the *gram panchayat* is obliged to transfer the same. It may be noted in this regard that in the examination of the case, the arguments adduced on behalf of the municipality do not appear to have stressed the functional domain of municipalities and local bodies subsequent to the constitutional amendment. It was also not urged that (a) the Orissa Municipal Act having been amended after the 74th Amendment is the latter Act passed by the Legislature with knowledge of laws already existing (b) that the Municipal Act should, therefore prevail over the earlier Orissa APM Act and that (c) under Article 243N, the provision to take over a municipal market would be repugnant to the Constitution.

Supreme Court

The functional domain of the *panchayat* as a statutory authority and its position and duty in safeguarding public interest has come up before the Apex Court from time to time. In Secretary, Sarvodaya Education Society *versus* Ginjala Panasaiah and others (2002 (10) SEC 691 decided on 13.3.2000), the *gram panchayat's* decision in transferring two acres of land to a society for setting up a school was challenged. The High Court held that lands vested with *Panchayat* could be alienated only by public auction. In appeal the Supreme Court held that the paramount consideration should be the general benefit to the people of the *gram panchayat*. Furthermore, the rules framed under the Panchayat Act did not permit land vested in the state to be transferred through a public auction. The High Court's orders were accordingly reversed.

In the case of the *Action Council Poovathode versus Benny Abraham 2001(2) KLT 690 decided on 2.7.2001*, the Kerala Panchayat (Licensing of Dangerous and Offensive Trade and Factories) Rules, 1996 and the authority of the *panchayat* derived from the Kerala Panchayati Raj Act 1994 came up for examination. The *panchayat* had refused to give licence for installing a metal crusher machine for specific reasons of public interest. The order was considered arbitrary and the High Court exercising jurisdiction under Article 226 directed the *panchayat* to issue the licence. The judgement of the High Court reflects the contention usually advanced on how far a local body acting in public interest can exercise regulatory jurisdiction and to what extent this can be denied or reduced because such local body does not possess technical expertise.

To quote: "A combined reading of the relevant provisions would indicate that an industry which is notified as likely to be offensive or dangerous to human life or health or property can function in a Panchayat but with the licence issued by the *panchayat*. The *panchayat* is also entitled to specify in the licence, necessary conditions to be followed. R.6 of the Rules as issued in 1996 empowers the President of the *panchayat* to refuse licence in the interest of the public. When the Act provides for industrial use of a place in the *panchayat* with licence and subject to conditions imposed in the licence with a view to protecting human life or health or property, is it open to the *panchayat* or its President to arbitrarily refuse to grant permission/licence by merely stating that it would be against the interest of the public? We are of the clear view that they are certainly not clothed with unbridled powers under the Act and Rules. Once it is possible to protect the interest of the public, meaning thereby protecting the human life or health or property by specifying appropriate conditions in the licence, it will not be open to deny permission/licence to an industry; unless of course there is a valid industrial policy decision taken by the *panchayat* regarding ban on certain types of industry, industrial zoning etc. There arises the question as to who is to assess the likelihood of offence or danger to human life or health or property and suggest preventive measures? Those are areas requiring expert opinion. Kerala State Pollution Control Board, District Medical Officer and authorities in the concerned field like factories inspector, explosives director, geologist, fire officer, etc., are the some of such experts. It has to be seen that those experts and other statutory agencies also discharge their duties in clearing a project in the interest of the public only. Protection of human life or health or property are certainly to be given prime consideration by those agencies. But once on such consideration the clearance is given, then the *panchayat*/President shall not, except for policy decisions as indicated above deny permission/licence to an industry. After all an industry in a *panchayat* is also in the interest of the public. And in any case, once permission having been granted to install machinery and all the safeguards directed by the *panchayat* having been provided, the *panchayat*/President will not be justified at all in taking an unreasonable stand that it has decided in public interest not to grant any licence."

In the appeal before the Supreme Court, the Apex Court set aside the High Court's judgement and held as follows:

> The short question that arises in this appeal is whether the High Court in exercise of its power under Article 226 of the Constitution of India was justified in interfering with the order of the *panchayat* concerned refusing to grant licence for installing a metal crusher machine within the *panchayat* in exercise of powers under Rules 6 and 12 of the Kerala panchayat (Licensing of Dangerous and Offensive Trade and Factories) Rules, 1996, hereinafter referred to as "the Rules."
>
> It is no doubt true that the entrepreneur had obtained the necessary "no-objection certificate" from the environmental authorities. But the *panchayat*, on consideration of the matter, was of the opinion that the decision not to grant permission to install the metal crusher machine would be in the interest of the public and it ascribed four reasons as to why the *panchayat* comes to the conclusion that it would not be in the public interest to grant such licence. All those reasons, to our mind, are germane to the issue and cannot be held to be arbitrary or fictitious.
>
> Having regard to the parameters prescribed by this court in the exercise of power under Article 226 of the Constitution of India against an order of a statutory authority, we have no hesitation to come to the conclusion that the High Court seriously erred in law in issuing the impugned direction. In our view, in the facts and circumstances of the present case, the *panchayat* was fully justified in refusing to grant licence to the entrepreneur.
>
> In the aforesaid premises, the impugned judgement of the High Court is set aside and appeal allowed accordingly.

The Apex Court's verdict clearly indicates that the regulatory or licensing jurisdiction of a local body, be it a *panchayat* or a municipality, cannot be denied or restricted on the ground that it does not possess within itself the technical expertise relating to a project. The local body has a prominent role as guardian of local public interest and if for valid reasons, it refuses a licence, another body or even the High Court cannot invoke Article 226 to override the local body's decision.

In *M.C. Mehta versus Union of India (2004-5 SCALE 405)*, the Supreme Court held that the municipalities have constitutional responsibilities of town planning and that such responsibility covers matters enumerated in the 12th Schedule such as regulation of land use, public health, sanitation, conservancy, solid wastes etc. The Apex Court also drew attention to Section 235 of the Municipal Corporation of Delhi Act and Section 416 which stipulates that no person shall, without previous permission of the MCD, establish any factory, workshop or trade premises. The Apex Court upheld the power of the MCD to seal premises in violation of these provisions. The shifting of polluting industries was within the ambit of the municipal domain.

Perumatty Gram Panchayat versus State of Kerala, KLT 731, currently on appeal before the Supreme Court invokes the same issues in regard to the regulatory or licensing jurisdiction of *panchayats*. As mentioned earlier Kerala is one of the few states where functions and activities have been specifically identified and devolved on *panchayats* at various levels. Chapter 20 of the Kerala Panchayati Raj Act, 1994 deals with public safety, convenience and health. Under Section 218 of the Act all water courses and water works within its territory vests in the *panchayat*. Drinking water supply is also an important item listed in Schedule 11. Under Article 243G of the Constitution, ensuring pure drinking water, clean environment and safeguarding the residents from health hazards is an important responsibility of the *panchayat*. Section 233 of the Panchayati Act stipulates that no person shall construct or establish any factory or install in any premises any machinery or manufacturing plant without the permission of the *panchayat*. The power to grant licence is thus vested in the *panchayat* and Section 233A also provides for abatement of nuisance caused by factory, workshop etc. The facts of the case may be elaborated.

In the year 2000, the respondent company Hindustan Coca-Cola Beverages Pvt Ltd was granted a licence by the *panchayat* to set up a plant in Plachimada in the Perumatty *panchayat* area to manufacture, store, distribute and sell aerated and carbonated non-alcoholic beverages, soft drinks and packaged drinking water. The licence was renewable on an annual basis. The company set up six bore wells and two dug wells for extracting ground water for manufacture of its products and according to its on assessment about 5 lakhs litres of ground water was extracted per day by the company.

During 2001-02 acute shortage of drinking water as a result of drying up of wells and ponds was experienced in the *panchayat* area. The *panchayat* was deluded with representations and requests from individuals, leaders of political parties and organisations to take remedial steps urgently. The *panchayat* taking into account the fundamental rights of its residents under Article 21 of the Constitution decided to cancel the licence granted to the Company. The Company filed a writ petition challenging this cancellation. The petition was disposed off by a direction to the Company to avail the statutory appeal available under Section 276 of the Panchayat Act. This appeal filed before the Local Self-Government Department, Government of Kerala was disposed off with a direction to the *panchayat* to appoint an Expert Committee to consider the question of ground water depletion, environmental and health hazards by a scientific study. The *panchayat* filed a writ petition before the High Court challenging this order of the Local Self-Government Department as in its view such committees served no useful purpose. By its judgement dated 16.12.2003 the High Court disposed off this writ petition with the following directions:

- The company shall stop drawing ground water. The *panchayat* and the state shall ensure this.
- The *panchayat* shall renew the licence and shall not interfere with the function of the company provided it is not extracting ground water and is depending on other sources.

- The *panchayat* with the assistance of the ground water department will assess the quantity of water that a land owner with 35 acres of land, which was the area of the Coca-Cola Company, would normally extract for his domestic and agricultural purposes.
- The company shall be permitted only to draw that much quantity of water as ascertained in this manner.

Against the above judgement of the learned single judge, the company filed a writ appeal before a Division Bench. The *panchayat* also filed a writ appeal aggrieved by certain portions of the judgement. In the meantime, the term of the licence granted to the company by the *panchayat* expired and the company filed an application before the *panchayat* for renewal for a period of five years. Around the same time the Expert Committee set up at the instance of the state government filed its interim report indicating that there is excessive extraction of ground water by the company and depletion of ground water in the entire locality. Certain health hazards and environmental pollutants were also found to be caused by the Company's manufacture. Thereafter the expert committee submitted its final report which found that depletion of ground water and drought like conditions faced by the residents of the locality were due to insufficient rainfall.

This final report was accepted in its entirety by the High Court's Division Bench which then directed the *panchayat* to renew the licence in favour of the company. The impugned judgement held that the *panchayat* has no legal authority to cancel the licence provided the required licences are obtained under the Factories Act and the required clearances are received from the State Pollution Control Board. The *panchayat* felt that this judgement denudes the regulatory and licensing powers of the *panchayat* which is derived from Article 243 of the Constitution of India and the Kerala Panchayat Act. The *panchayat* has, therefore, preferred an appeal (SLP 15680/2005) against the impugned judgement by the Division Bench before the Supreme Court. The Government of Kerala have also joined this appeal seeking in its prayers to the Apex Court to uphold the regulatory jurisdiction of the *panchayat* in matters affecting local public interest. The matter awaits hearing by the Apex Court.

Around the same time as the Perumatty case, another dispute was being agitated in the nearby *panchayat* Pudussery. Here the factory involved was Pepsi Cola and the issues raised by the *Panchayat* were broadly similar such as overdrawal of ground water, depletion of water sources in the *panchayat* area, environmental adversity etc. However in this case the *Panchayat* had participated in the 'single window clearance' system set up by the State Government under which all regulating and licensing bodies were required to consider the merits or demerits of a prospective industry at the proposal stage itself. Besides the factory was located in an industrial area set up for the purpose. Once the participants in the process had given their concurrence to the proposed project they were not to oppose or withhold sanction or renewal of license thereafter. In this case also, the matter went up to the Supreme Court which held that since the *Panchayat* had given its consent earlier it could not withhold it at a later stage.

However, several important issues await resolution. Some pertain to the use of ground water and whether extraction from an aquifer whose spread and depth are not dependant on land boundaries can be determined on the basis of ownership right on the surface land. For our purposes, equally important is the extent of the regulatory and licensing jurisdiction of a *panchayat* or a municipality and whether such jurisdiction can be denied or curtailed on the ground that these bodies do not have the technical expertise themselves and have to perforce depend on the so-called technical bodies and expert committees.

The Supreme Court has indeed provided a pointer by its interpretation in the Poovathode Action Council case that the judgement of a *panchayat* or a municipality on what is best in public interest has to be respected and not substituted. The Perumatty case provides an additional opportunity to clarify the limits of self government in the exercise of the licensing and regulatory domain.

Annexure A 7.1

The 72nd Constitution Amendment Bill (Panchayats)
This Bill later became the 73rd Constitution Amendment

Statement of Objects and Reasons

Though the Panchayati Raj Institutions have been in existence for a long time, it has been observed that these institutions have not been able to acquire the status and dignity of viable and responsive people's bodies due to a number of reasons including absence of regular elections, prolonged suppressions, insufficient representation of weaker sections like Scheduled Castes, Scheduled Tribes and women, inadequate devolution of powers and lack of financial resources.

2. Article 40 of the Constitution which enshrines one of the Directive Principles of State Policy lays down that the State shall take steps to organise village *panchayats* and endow them with such powers and authority as may be necessary to enable them to function as units of self-government. In the light of the experience in the last forty years and in view of the short comings which have been observed. It is considered that there is an imperative need to enshrine in the Constitution certain basic and essential features of Panchayati Raj Institutions to impart certainty, continuity and strength to them.

3. Accordingly, it is proposed to add a new part relating to *panchayats* in the Constitution to provide for, among other things. *Gram sabha* in a village or group of villages; constitution of *panchayats* at village and other level or levels; direct elections to all seats in *panchayats* at the village and intermediate level, if any, and to the offices of Chairpersons of *panchayats* at such levels; reservation of seats for the Scheduled Castes and Scheduled Tribes in proportion to their population for membership of *panchayats* and office of Chairpersons in *panchayats* at each level; reservation of not less than one-third of the seats for women; fixing tenure of 5 years for *panchayats* and holding elections within a period of six months in the event of supercession of any *panchayat*; disqualifications for membership of *panchayats*; devolution by the state legislature of powers and responsibilities upon the *panchayats* with respect to the preparation of plans for economic development and social justice and for the implementation of development schemes; sound finance of the panchayats by securing authorisation from state legislatures for grants-in-aid to the *panchayats* from the Consolidated Fund of the state, as also assignment to, or appropriation by the *panchayats* of the revenues of designated taxes, duties tolls and fees; setting up of a Finance Commission within one year of the proposed amendment and thereafter every 5 years to review the financial position of *panchayats*; auditing of

accounts of the *panchayats*; powers of state legislatures to make provisions with respect to elections to *panchayats* under the superintendence, direction and control of the chief electoral officer of the state; application of the provisions of the said part to Union Territories; excluding certain states and areas from the application of the provisions of the said part; continuance of existing laws and *panchayats* until one year from the commencement of the proposed amendment and barring interference by courts in electoral matters relating to *panchayats*.

The Bill seeks to achieve the aforesaid objectives.

G. Venkat Swamy
(then Minister of State
for Rural Development)

New Delhi,
10th September, 1991

Annexure A 7.2

The 73rd Constitution Amendment Bill (Municipalities)
This Bill later became the 74th Constitution Amendment)

(Statement of Objects and Reasons (Extracts)

In many states local bodies have become weak and ineffective on account of a variety of reasons, including the failure to hold regular elections, prolonged supercessions and inadequate devolution of powers and functions. As a result, Urban Local Bodies are not able to perform effectively as vibrant democratic units of self-government.

2. Having regard to these inadequacies, it is considered necessary that provisions relating to Urban Local Bodies are incorporated in the Constitution particularly for-

- (i) Putting on a firmer footing the relationship between the state government and the urban local bodies with respect to:
  - (a) the functions and taxation powers; and
  - (b) arrangements for revenue sharing;
- (ii) ensuring regular conduct of elections;
- (iii) ensuring timely elections in the case of supercession; and
- (iv) providing adequate representation for the weaker sections like Scheduled Castes, Scheduled Tribes and women.

3. Accordingly, it is proposed to add a new part relating to Urban Local Bodies in the Constitution to provide for-

- (a) constitution of three types of municipalities;
  - (i) *Nagar Panchayats* for areas in transition from a rural area to urban area;
  - (ii) Municipal Councils for smaller urban areas;
  - (iii) Municipal Corporations for larger urban areas.

The Broad criteria for specifying the said areas is being provided in the proposed Article 243-O

- (b) composition of municipalities
- (c) reservation of seats in every municipality
- (d) For Scheduled Castes and Scheduled Tribes
  - (i) in favour of backward class of citizens if so provided by the legislature of the state;
  - (ii) for Schedule Castes, Scheduled Tribes and women in the office of Chairpersons as may be specified in the state law;

(iii) fixed tenure of 5 years for the municipality and re-election within six months of end of tenure if a municipality is dissolved before expiration of its duration, elections to be held within a period of six months of its dissolution.

(iv) devolution by the state legislature of powers and responsibilities upon the municipalities with respect to preparation of plans for economic development and social justice; and for the implementation of development schemes as may be required to enable them to function as institutions of self-government;

(v) levy of taxes and duties by municipalities, assigning of such taxes and duties to municipalities by state governments and for making grants-in-aid by the state to the municipalities as may be provided in the state law;

....

The Bill seeks to achieve the aforesaid objectives.

Sheila Kaul

New Delhi, (then Union Minister

11th September, 1991 for Urban Development)

Annexure A 7.3

Report of the Joint Committee on the Constitution (Seventy-Second Amendment Bill, 1992.

This bill later became the 73rd Constitution Amendment) (Extracts)

1. I, the Chairman of the Joint Committee to which the Bill further to amend the Constitution of India viz., the Constitution (Seventy-Second Amendment) Bill, 1991 (insertion of new part IX and addition of XIth Schedule) was referred, having been authorised to submit the Report on their behalf, present this Report.

2. The Bill was introduced in the Lok Sabha on 16 September, 1991. The motion for reference of the Bill to a Joint Committee of both Houses of Parliament was moved in the Lok Sabha by Shri G Venkataswamy, Minister of State Ministry of Rural Development on 20 December, 1991 and was adopted (Appendix I).

3. The Rajya Sabha concurred in the said motion on 21 December, 1991 (Appendix II)

4. The message from the Rajya Sabha was published in Lok Sabha Bulletin Part II on 24 December, 1991.

5. The Committee held 13 settings in all.

15. The Committee considered and adopted the Report at their sitting held on 30 June, 1992.

16. The observations of the Committee with regard to principal changes proposed in the Bill are detailed in the succeeding paragraphs.

17. Article 243 – The Committee feel that the definition of the expression *'Gram Sabha'* as included in Article 243 (2) should be included in Article 243, since all other expressions have been defined in Article 243.

A new clause (b) relating to definition of *'Gram Sabha'* has been added accordingly in Article 243 and existing clauses (b) to (f) have been renumbered as clauses (c) to (g) of that Article.

18. Article 243A – The committee feel that the *'Gram Sabha'* cannot exercise any powers and that at best it can perform certain functions. The details of such functions can be laid down by the legislature of a state.

Article 243A has been revised accordingly. Clause (2) of this Article has been omitted as definition of *'Gram Sabha'* has been included in Article 243.

19. Article 243B – the Committee find that there is wide diversity in the number of tiers of *panchayats* existing in different states. The Committee note that the majority of the bigger states have a three-tier system. Even where there is a three-tier system, there are structural differences in states

like Karnataka, Tamil Nadu and Assam. However, there are States like Haryana, Manipur, Kerala and Sikkim and the Union Territory of Lakshadweep with only two-tier system adopted by them. Still there are some states like Goa, Jammu & Kashmir and Tripura and the Union Territories like Andaman and Nicobar Islands and Dadra & Nagar Haveli etc., which follow only a one-tier system. The Committee are of the opinion that a common and uniform three-tier system of *panchas* may be adopted throughout the country.

Article 243B has been amended accordingly.

20. Article 243C- The Committee note that the issue relating to direct or indirect elections in Panchayati Raj Institutions is very vital. Directly elected persons have an inherent strength of having been elected by the people. Moreover, indirect elections have led to various manipulative practices. The Committee, therefore, are of the opinion that in order to strengthen the democracy at the grass-root level, all seats in a *panchayat* at any level should be filled by direct elections. The Committee also agree that as provided in the Bill it may be left to the legislature of a state to make provisions relating to representation of Chairpersons of *panchayats* in the *panchayats* at the next higher level i.e., the Chairpersons of the *panchayat* at the village level may be represented at the intermediate level and Chairperson of the *panchayat* at the intermediate level may be represented at the district level.

The Committee are also of the opinion that the Legislature of a state may also make necessary provisions regarding the representation of members of the Rajya Sabha and Members of the Legislative Council of a State, where they are registered as electors in the *panchayat* area at the intermediate level, in the *panchayats* at the intermediate level and where they are registered as electors in a *panchayat* are at the district level, in such *panchayat* at the district level.

Clauses (2) and (4) of Article 243C have been amended accordingly and clause (3) has been omitted as all seats in *panchayats* will be filled by direct election.

The bill provides that only the Chairperson and directly elected members of a *panchayat* have the right to vote in the meetings of the *panchayat*. The Committee are of the opinion that all members of a *panchayat* irrespective of the fact whether or not chosen by direct elections should be given the right to vote in the meetings of the *panchayat* for their smooth functioning.

The provisions of clauses (5) and (6) of Article 243C have been clubbed accordingly and incorporated in the revised clause (4).

The Committee further feel that the Chairperson of a *panchayat* at the village level only should be chosen by direct election and that the

Chairperson of a *panchayat* at the intermediate level or district level should be chosen by indirect election. Where the Chairperson of a *panchayat* at the village level has been chosen by direct election, he shall not be removed from that office unless the *panchayat* has made a recommendation to the *Gram Sabha* to that effect after adopting a motion by a majority of the total number of the elected members of the *panchayat* and by a majority of not less than two-thirds of the members present and voting and the *Gram Sabha* at the specially convened meeting after a notice of not less than fifteen days has passed a resolution for such removal by a majority of its members present and voting, so however, that not less than fifty per cent of the members are present at such meeting. If the meeting cannot be held for want of quorum, the *Panchayat's* motion shall lapse and no further motion for removal of the Chairperson shall be brought within one year of the date of adoption of the previous motion. Similarly, where the Chairperson of a *panchayat* has been chosen by indirect election he shall not be removed from that office unless the *panchayat* has passed a resolution to that effect by a majority of the total number of the elected members of the *panchayat* and by a majority of not less than two-thirds of such members present and voting.

Clause (7) of Article 243C has been amended accordingly and renumbered as clause (5). New clauses (6) and (7) have also been inserted to give effect to the above recommendations.

21. Article 243D - It has been represented before the Committee that in some States seats reserved for Scheduled Castes are filled in by Scheduled Tribes either due to non-availability of such candidates or owing to some other reasons.

Clause (1) of this Article has, therefore, been slightly amended to make it clear that the seats will be reserved for Scheduled Castes and Scheduled Tribes separately.

22. Article 243E – The Committee find that in order to ensure durability of, and building up confidence in, Panchayati Raj Institutions, it is provided that every *panchayat* should have a duration of five years. However, keeping in view the fact that *panchayats* at any level can be superseded for indefinite periods or they can be dissolved, and in certain cases elections of the institutions have not been held for long periods, the Committee recommend that the elections to these bodies must be completed before the expiration of their duration of five years. Similarly, in case a *panchayat* is dissolved before the expiration of its duration, election to constitute a new *panchayat* must be completed before the expiry of a period of six months from the date on which it was dissolved. The Committee also feel that no amendment of any state law should have the effect of causing dissolution of *panchayats*

which are functioning immediately before such amendment, before the expiration of their duration of five years.

Existing clause (2) has been amended accordingly and re-numbered as clause (3) and a new clause (2) has been inserted in this Article. Certain consequential amendments have also been made in clause (1).

23. Article 243F – The Committee note that in order to prevent undesirable persons from becoming members in the *panchayats*, certain provisions for disqualification have been included in the bill. These are based on similar provisions with respect to disqualification for Members of Parliament and State Legislatures.

The Committee feel that the existing sub-clause (a) to (d) of clause (1) are covered by the provisions of sub-clause (c) and they are also of the opinion that with the advent of electronic media and rise in standards of general education, the level of awareness amongst people in small towns and cities has gone up. Now, a person of the age of twenty-one years is responsible enough to hold a public office. The Committee are, therefore, of the opinion that all persons who have attained the age of twenty-one years should be eligible to stand for election in the Panchayati Raj Institutions. The Committee further feel that the disputes relating to disqualification instead of being referred for the decision of the Governor should be referred for the decision of such authority and in such manner as the legislature of a State may, by law, provide.

Sub-clauses (a) to (d) have been omitted and sub-clause (c) of clause (1) and clause (2) of Article 243F have been amended accordingly.

24. Article 243I – The amendment made in clause (1) of Article 243I is of a formal nature.

25. Article 243K – The Committee note that the elections in Panchayati Raj Institutions are to be conducted under the superintendence, direction and control of the Chief Electoral Officer of a State who is accountable to and a functionary of the Chief Election Commissioner so far as conducting of elections are concerned. The Committee feel that it should be left to the legislature of a State to provide for a separate authority for conducting the said elections.

Article 243K has been amended accordingly.

Article 243L – The Committee feel that the enabling power of the President not to apply the provisions of part IX to any Union Territory should be omitted. The President should only have the power to apply the said provisions to any Union Territory or part thereof subject to such exception and modifications as he may specify by public notification.

Article 243L has been modified accordingly.

26. Article 243N- The Committee feel that all the existing state laws relating to *panchayats* which are inconsistent with the provisions of part IX proposed to be inserted by this Bill, shall continue to be in force until amended or repealed by a competent legislature or other competent authority or until the expiration of one year from the commencement of this Legislation, whichever is earlier. The Committee note that the duration of the existing *panchayats* shall not be affected by it in view of the stipulation in proviso to this Article.

Article 243N has been amended accordingly:

27. Clause (1) and Enacting Formula – The amendments made in clause (1) and the enacting formula are of a formal nature.

28. The Joint Committee recommend that the Bill, as amended be passed.

New Delhi,
30 June, 1992

Nathuram Mirdha
Chairman
Joint Committee

Annexure A 7.4

Report of the Joint Parliament Committee on the 73rd Constitution Amendment Bill (Extracts)

Articles 243S – Constitution and composition of committees at ward level or other levels

1.1 I, the Chairman of the Joint Committee to which the Bill further to amend the Constitution of India viz. the Constitution (Seventy-third Amendment) Bill, 1991 (insertion of new part IXA and addition of XII Schedule) was referred, having been authorised to submit the Report on their behalf, present this Report.

1.2 The bill was introduced in the Lok Sabha on 16 September, 1991. The motion for reference of the bill to a Joint Committee of both Houses of Parliament was moved in Lok Sabha by Smt. Sheila Kaul, Cabinet Minister in the Ministry of Urban Development on 20 December, 1991 and was adopted (Appendix-I).

1.3 The Rajya Sabha concurred in the said motion on 21 December, 1991 (Appendix-II)

1.15 The Committee considered and adopted the Report at their sitting held on 3 July, 1992

1.16 The observations of the Committee with regard to the principal changes proposed in the Bill are detailed in the succeeding paragraphs.

1.20 There is a growing feeling that in the larger municipal bodies the citizens do not have easy access to the elected representatives since the ward sizes become very large. The Committee therefore are of the view that within the territorial area of municipalities having population of three lakhs or more wards committees should be constituted. The details relating to the composition and the territorial area of the Wards Committees and the manner of filling seats in such committees can be left to the state legislatures. Further, the Committee feel that a member representing a ward in a municipality should be a member of the Wards Committee. The Committee are also of the opinion that where a wards committee consists of one ward, the member representing that ward in the municipality should be the Chairperson of the Wards Committee. However, where a wards committee consists of two or more wards, one of the members representing such wards in the municipality should be elected by the members of the wards committee to be its Chairperson. The Article 243S has been amended accordingly.

1.21 The Committee also feel that nothing contained in the provisions of this article should prevent the legislature of a state from making any provision for the constitution of committees in addition to the wards committees. A provision has been made in Article 243S accordingly.

Article 243U—Duration of Municipalities etc.

1.24 The Committee feel that an election to constitute a municipality should be completed before the expiry of its duration of five years and if dissolved earlier within six months of its dissolution. However, if the legislature of a state passes a resolution that due to drought, flood, earthquake or any other natural calamity or emergency, the election cannot be held within the said period of six months, the election can be postponed but must be held within a period of one year from the date of dissolution of the municipality. The Committee also feels that an enabling provision may be made for the state legislature to provide by law for suspension or dissolution of a municipality and where a municipality is suspended or dissolved, it shall be given a reasonable opportunity of being heard by an authority to be constituted by such law. In case a municipality is suspended, such suspension should not affect the continuation of the wards and other Committees constituted under Article 243S. Article 243E of part IX has accordingly been incorporated as Article 243U with suitable amendments to cover the above aspects.

Article 243V—Disqualifications for Membership

1.25 The Committee feel that existing sub-clauses (a) to (d) of clause (1) are covered by the provisions of sub-clause (e) which relates to disqualifications for elections to the legislature of the state. Further, the Committee feels that with the advent of education, the level of awareness amongst people in small towns and cities has gone up and a person of the age of twenty-one years is responsible enough to hold a public office. The Committee are, therefore, of the opinion that all persons who have attained the age of twenty-one years should be eligible for election to the municipalities. The Committee are also of the view that the disputes relating to disqualification should be referred for the decision of such authority and in such manner as the legislature of a state may by law, provide. Article 243F of part IX has accordingly been incorporated as Article 243V after omitting sub-clauses (a) to (d) of clause (1) and re-lettering the existing sub-clauses (e) and (f) as sub-clauses (a) and (h). Other modifications have also been made to cover the above mentioned aspects.

Article 243ZD—Committee for District Planning

1.33 The planning and allocation of resources at the district level for the Panchayati Raj institutions are normally to be decided at the *Zilla Parishad*. In regard to urban areas, the municipal bodies discharge certain defined functions within their respective areas. However, some important questions may arise which concern the urban-rural interface. There is a need to take an overall view in regard to development of the district as whole and decide on allocation or investment between rural and urban institutions. The Committee therefore, feel that there should be a provision for constitution of a District Planning Committee in every state at the district level with a view to consolidating the plans prepared by the *panchayats* and the municipalities in the district as a whole. In order to impart a democratic character to such committees, not less than four-fifths of the total number of members of these committees should be elected members of the *panchayat* at the district level ad of the municipalities in the district in proportion to the ratio between the population of the rural areas and of the urban areas in the district. The other details relating to composition of the said committees the manner of filling the seats therein, the functions relating to district planning to be assigned to such committees and the manner in which the chairpersons of such committees shall be chosen may be left to the state legislatures keeping in view the local conditions. The District Planning Committee, in preparing the draft development plan, should have regard to matters of common interest between the *panchayats* and the municipalities including spatial planning, sharing of water and physical and natural resources, the integrated development of infrastructure and environmental conservation; the extent and type of available resources whether financial or otherwise. While preparing such a draft development plan, the said committee should also consult such institutions and organisations as the state governments may specify. The Draft Development Plan so prepared shall be forwarded to the state government concerned by the Chairperson of the Committee. Article 243ZD has been inserted accordingly.

Article 243ZE—Committee for Metropolitan Planning

1.34 There are 23 metropolitan cities in the country where the metropolitan area would encompass not only the main city corporation but also a number of other local bodies, both urban and rural surrounding the main city corporation. By the end of the century, this number may be about 45. These metropolitan areas influence the life and economy of the surrounding areas in several ways. To ensure that there is an orderly development of the fringe area, proper plans for these areas need to be drawn up in association with the plan of the main city. Considerable investments in these cities are also undertaken by Central and state government agencies. It is necessary to coordinate these investment plans with the developmental plans and requirements of the metropolitan city.

1.35 There is, therefore, need for a suitable planning mechanism which would take care of the interaction between the various local bodies, both rural and urban in such metropolitan areas. At present, the system that is adopted in many metropolises is the creation of a metropolitan development authority. The functions assigned to the metropolitan development authority differ from case to case. In some cases, they are only planning bodies while in some cases they take on executive functions particularly of major schemes. Further, at present, these bodies are not democratic institutions. They are nominated by the government. While care is taken that there are some representatives on the body from different urban local bodies in the area, the forum is still not a democratic one wherein the opinions of the local bodies in the region can be articulated.

1.36 The Committee therefore feel that there should be a provision for constitution of a metropolitan Planning Committee to prepare a draft development plan for the Metropolitan area as a whole. In order to impart democratic character to the said committees not less than two-thirds of the members of such committees should be elected by and from amongst, the elected members of the municipalities and Chairpersons of the *panchayats* in the metropolitan area in proportion to the ratio between the population of the municipalities and of the *panchayats* in that area. The other details relating to composition of the said committees, the manner of filling the seats therein, the representation in such committees of the Government of India and the government of the state and other organisations and institutions, the functions relating to planning and coordination for the metropolitan area to be assigned to such committees and the manner in which the chairpersons of such committees shall be chosen may be left to the state legislatures. The Metropolitan Planning Committee should, in preparing the draft development plan, have regard to the plans prepared by the municipalities and the *panchayats* in the metropolitan area, matters of common interest between the municipalities and the *panchayats* including coordinated spatial planning of the area, sharing of water and other physical and natural resources, the integrated development of infrastructure and environmental conservation, overall objectives and priorities set by the Government of India and the government of the State; the extent and nature of investment likely to be made in the metropolitan area by agencies of the government and other available resources whether financial or otherwise. The said committee should also consult such institutions and organisations as the state government may specify. The draft development plan so prepared shall be forward to the state government concerned by the chairperson of the said committee. Article 243ZE has been inserted accordingly.

Article 243ZF: Continuance of Existing Laws and Municipalities

1.37 Article 243N of Part IX has been incorporated here as Article 243ZF with slight modifications so as to change the reference to the "Constitution (Seventy-Second Amendment) Act, 1992" to "Constitution (Seventy-Third Amendment) Act, 1992" to "Constitution (Seventy-Third Amendment) Act, 1992."

Article 243ZG: Bar to Interference by Courts in Electoral Matters

1.38 Article 243-O of Part IX has been incorporated here as Article 243ZG with slight modifications to change the reference to Article "243K" to Article "243 ZA."

Clause 3

1.39 The Committee feel that amendment should be made in Article 280 relating to constitution of the Central Finance Commission so that the said Commission should make recommendations to the President as to the measures needed to augment the Consolidated Fund of a State to supplement the resources of the municipalities in the state on the basis of the recommendations made by the Finance Commission of the State. Clause 3 accordingly has been inserted in the bill. The need for this amendment has been explained further in detail in Chapter II of this Report.

Clause 4

1.40 The existing clause 3 has been renumbered as Clause 4. The Committee feel that the Twelfth Schedule proposed to be inserted by clause 4 should also cover subjects relating to protection of the environment; public amenities including street lighting, parking lots, bus stops and public conveniences; regulation of slaughter houses and tanneries. Item 8 of the Twelfth Schedule has been amended accordingly and new items 17 and 18 have been inserted in the said schedule.

(Chapter 2 relating to Municipal Finance is as follows)

2.31 The Joint Committee recommend that the Bill, as amended be passed

K P Singh Deo
Chairman
Joint Committee

New Delhi,
July 1992

8

The Planning Domain of *Panchayats* and Municipalities

Introduction

Over the past five decades an elaborate structure for planning has been established in the country. At the national level there is the Planning Commission set up by an executive order of the Union Government. Most of the states have a State Planning Board as well. Additionally there are several organisations at the national and the state levels, each claiming a mandate for sectoral planning in one field or another be it, agriculture, irrigation, land use, environment or various social services and utilities. Inspite of this elaborate structure, or possibly because of it, the very meaning of the word 'planning' has been confounded. The planning for economic development of the country which have been presented successively in one Five-Year Plan after another, is regarded by many as merely a discourse on economic philosopy or at best a collection in quantitative terms of sectoral expenditures and targets.

In public parlance, planning has invariably meant a plan for developing a piece of land or a plan for the development of a city space. The spatial connotation of planning has been a strong feature of public perception. However, in these five decades land use or spatial planning has come to be regarded as a municipal level exercise, often titled as a land use master plan. These master plans are also regarded as static and unresponsive to the dynamics of change in most cities. Furthermore, various aspects of spatial planning, its interpretation and enforcement have been taken away from the corporations and municipalities and vested in development authorities and other special agencies established by the state governments. As urbanisation spread and spilled over previously established municipal boundaries and as the shift in economic activities from agriculture to other activities prompted urbanisation, it became necessary to deal with town and country planning in an integrated manner.

The legal backing for town and country planning was inspired largely by the experience and laws in the UK. During the 1960s such town and country planning laws were enacted in many of the States in India. Town Planning Laws in this country are thus a derivation from the U.K. Laws. These Acts usually provided for the delineation of planning areas and the creation of planning authorities who will be responsible for planning the land use, setting the norms for development of land and for the control of building operations. Usually city corporations or municipalities were designated as planning authorities within their respective jurisdictions but for other areas which were yet to acquire a patently urban character separate planning authorities were created.

In course of time, conflicts of jurisdiction arose. In multi municipal metropolitan areas this was sought to be resolved by vesting land use planning powers in a special purpose metropolitan or other development authorities. In some other states such as Punjab, Haryana, UP or MP state wide special development authorities were created to exercise planning jurisdiction over the entire state or all its urban areas (e.g., HUDA, PUDA). Eventually, the municipalities and the city corporations became less important to the process of planning and were left dealing mainly with passing of individual building plans. Inspite of these centralising trends the demand for decentralised planning or 'planning from the bottom up' to use popular parlance continued. In rural areas planning was perceived more as the process of assembling various schemes and projects, the determination of priorities among them, getting them implemented and monitoring their progress. Economic and social diversity were additional factors to be taken into consideration. Concern for economically weaker sections as well as socially disadvantaged sections like women, SCs/STs, Backward Classes etc became another important direction.

When the initiative to amend the Constitution to confer a constitutionally recognised status and domain for the *panchayats* and municipalities was initiated, the locus of the planning functions became an important issue. The numerous debates which preceded the amendment initiative, brought out some sharp differences of opinion. The range of discussions and outcome of these have been documented elsewhere in several publications. It is not therefore necessary to dwell about them in detail for our present purposes. However, it is important to note that both Articles 243G and 243W specifically refer to "the preparation of plans for economic development and social justice." Items listed in the 11th or the 12th Schedule also pertain to the broad purposes of economic development. Item 3 in the 12th Schedule repeats the words "planning for economic and social development." Part IX A of the Constitution goes even further in stipulating that District Planning Committees and Metropolitan Planning Committees have to be set up to prepare development plans for each district and metropolitan area. Their terms of reference specifically include spatial development. It should also be noted that item 20 in list III in the 7th Schedule identifies 'economic and social planning' as a concurrent subject.

Since 'justice, social, economic and political' is part of the preamble to the Constitution of India and the objectives expressed in the preamble have been regarded as the basic structure of the Constitution, it is expected that these objectives will infuse the exercise of all powers and responsibilities of the different organs of the state be it at the Union, state or sub-state levels. Admittedly it was neither feasible nor necessary to elaborate on what aspects of socio-economic or development planning are to be exercised at which levels and to demarcate a clear cut division among the levels. Nevertheless it was expected that in implementing the 73rd and the 74th Amendments to the Constitution, the state legislatures would apply their mind and seek to provide as far as possible, a harmonious set of laws. As a further reminder the Amendments also contain Articles 243N and 243ZF calling upon the states to identify inconsistencies in the regime of laws and either amend or repeal what is inconsistent. Unfortunately, with the exception of a few states, this opportunity was not utilised. On the other hand attempts have been more towards protecting the powers of the state government *vis-à-vis* those to be exercised by the *panchayats* and the municipalities. The well recognised principle of subsidiarity has been overlooked in many cases. Inspite of decentralisation being a central purpose of the constitutional amendments the so-called conformity legislations enacted by many states have been minimal or cursory, merely repeating the language of the Constitution itself and in some cases retrograde by subtracting from even the previously existing functional domain. Instances of this non-conformity can be found in laws relating to urban planning or town planning.

Urban Planning in the Municipal Domain

We may consider the situation as it evolved before and after the Constitutional Amendment in two important states namely Maharashtra and Karnataka. Maharashtra being one of the first states in moving towards industrialisation and urbanisation enacted the Maharashtra Regional and Town Planning Act, 1966. The enactment was preceded by deliberations of expert groups and wide consultations in the state. Contemporary planning practices elsewhere in the world were also studied. In terms of its comprehensive coverage, structure and depth of detail, this Act was path breaking and has indeed been a model, which some other states have followed subsequently. The enactment recognised that urbanisation in Maharashtra would not be confined only to a few cities like Bombay, Pune and Nagpur but would be spreading to different parts of the state. The Act was probably the first to recognise the need for regional planning. The preamble to the Act reads as follows:

> Whereas, it is expedient to make provision for planning the development and use of land in regions established for that purpose and for the Constitution of Regional Planning Boards therefor; to make better provision for the preparation of development plans with a view to ensuring that town planning schemes are made in a proper manner and their execution is made effective; to provide for the

> creation of new towns by means of Development Authorities; to make provision for the compulsory acquisition of land required for public purposes in respect of the plans; and for purposes connected with the matters aforesaid; It is hereby enacted in the Seventeenth Year of the Republic of India....

Section 2 (15) of the Act defines "local authority" to mean the Bombay Municipal Corporation, the Nagpur Municipal Corporation or any Municipal Corporation constituted under the Bombay Provincial Municipal Corporations Act, 1949, a Municipal Council constituted under the Maharashtra Municipalities Act, 1965 and a *Zilla Parishad* constituted under Maharashtra Zilla Parishads and Panchayat Samitis Act, 1961. Sub-section 19 states a 'planning authority' means a 'local authority.' The Act also prescribes an elaborate procedure for preparation, submission and sanction of development plans and enjoins every planning authority to prepare and publish a draft development plan. The contents of such a plan are described in Section 22 of the Act. The Maharashtra Act, even three decades before the Constitutional Amendment, clearly recognised the planning domain of municipal councils, corporations, *panchayat samitis* and *zilla parishads* within their respective jurisdictions. The Act also contained specific provisions for delineation of regions, the constitution of regional planning boards, the preparation of regional plans and how plans prepared by the local authorities will be integrated with the regional plans.

The Bombay Municipal Corporation has had a long history and experience in matters of town planning. In fact, the Bombay Town Planning Act of 1915 was one of the very early laws on the subject in the country. This Act was replaced by the Bombay Town Planning Act 1954 which was also applied to other towns in the state till the Maharashtra Regional and Town Planning Act 1966 was enacted. The Development plan for the city was prepared by the Bombay Municipal Corporation in keeping with the provisions of the Maharashtra Regional and Town Planning Act, duly approved and notified in 1981. Section 159 of the MRTP Act empowers a Regional Planning Board, a Planning Authority, or a Development Authority to formulate regulations to carry out the purpose of the Act. The Development Control Rules of 1967 were formulated by the

Corporation accordingly. Several years later the Maharashtra Government amended S.159 of the MRTP Act and provided for itself the power to make similar Development Control Regulations for the purpose of executing a special township scheme. In common usage a special township would mean a new settlement to be located in some area outside municipal limits. However S.18, amended again, conferred on the state government the power to approve any request for such a development as a special township scheme. In 1991 under the amended S.159, a new set of Development Control Regulations (DCR for short) for Greater Bombay were formulated replacing the Development Control Rules of 1967. These regulations are regarded as a part of the development plan for Mumbai and are intended to control all development within the BMC's jurisdiction. The DCRs determine the uses to which any land within the BMC maybe put. The Municipal Corporation cannot grant permission for development or re-development of any land except for the uses permitted.

The Textile Mills Case

One of the regulations i.e. DCR 58 of 1991 provided for development or redevelopment of lands belonging to cotton textile mills in order to raise resources by sale of surplus lands and applying the funds for modernisation of the mills or shifting them elsewhere. A special provision under DCR 58 stipulated in 1996 that one third of the land comprised in a textile mill would be made available as open space for the public, one third for public housing and Mill workers housing and the remaining one third for residential, commercial or other industrial use by the owner of the mill land. For nearly a decade various attempts were made to apply this formula. During discussions between mill owners, financing institutions and the government, various proposals were made for modifying the formula. The provision for keeping one third of the mill land as open space became a critical issue. The city, woefully short of open space with no more than 0.03 acres of such open space per 1000 population badly needed the additional space to be freed from the textile mills. The mill owner's view was that releasing one third to the Municipal Corporation for maintaining it as public open space would not be financially viable. The definition of the words "open lands" became the issue. The 1996-DCR 58 stated "open lands" and lands after demolition of existing structures. In 2001, the Government modified this to read "open lands and balance FSI" (floor space index) as follows:

"(1) lands of sick and/or closed cotton textile mills—With the previous approval of the Commissioner to a layout prepared for development or redevelopment of the entire open land built-up area of the premises of a sick and/or closed cotton textile mill, and on such conditions deemed appropriate and specified by him, and as a part of a package of measures recommended by the Financial Instuitions and Commissionerate of Industries for the revival/ rehabilitation of a potentially viable sick and/or closed mill, the Commissioner may allow;

(a) The existing built-up areas to be utilised:

(i) for the same cotton textile or related user subject to observance of all other regulations;

(ii) for diversified industrial users in accordance with the industrial location policy, with office space only ancillary to and required for such users, subject to and observance of all other regulations';

(iii) for commercial purposes, as permitted under these regulations;

(b) Open lands and balance FSI shall be used as in the Table below:

No.	*Extent of Land (in ha.)*	*Percentage to be earmarked for recreation Ground/ Garden, Play Ground or any other open user as specified by the Commissioner.*	*Percentage to be earmarked and handed over for development by MHADA for public housing/(for mill workers' housing as per guidelines approved by Government to be shared equally.*	*Percentage to be earmarked and marked and to be developed for residential or commercial user to be developed (including users permissible in residential or commercial zone as per these Regulations) or diversified industrial users as per Industrial Location Policy to be developed by the owner.*
(1)	(2)	(3)	(4)	(5)
1.	Upto and inclusive of 5 Ha.	33	27	40
2.	Between 5 Ha. and upto 10 Ha.	33	34	33
3.	Over 10 Ha.	33	37	30

(iv) Where FSI is in balance but open land is not available, for the purposes of column (3) and (4) of the above Table, land will be made open by demolishing the existing structures to the extent necessary and made available accordingly."

Amendment Goes to Court

In PIL, WP No.482 of 2001 Bombay Environmental Action Group *versus* State of Maharashtra and 31 other parties as respondents, the issues relating to interpretation of DCR 58 became the crucial issue. In this highly contested case in which apart from the Maharashtra government, the Municipal Corporation and the Maharashtra Housing and Area Development Authority, several textile mills were also cited as respondents, the contention was whether in identifying the extent of open lands to be made available to the BMC for recreation and community purposes, the land that would become available upon demolition of the previously existing structures should be taken into account or not. The ground reality behind this contentious question was that if lands which would become open upon demolition of the existing structures were included about 200 acres would become available for public recreational use whereas if 'open lands' were excluded, land covered by the previously existing structures and the land to be surrendered to the Municipal Corporation would be a mere 32 acres.

Amendment of DCR 58 was possible because of a previous amendment to Section 37 of the Maharashtra Regional Town and Country Planning Act which contained a provision and a specific procedure to be followed by the planning authority, if any modification is to be made to a final development plan. Section 37 (1AA) was inserted in 2001 which reads as follows:

> 37(1AA) Notwithstanding anything contained in sub-sections (1), (1A) and (2), where the state government is satisfied that in the public interest it is necessary to carry out urgently a modification of any part of, or any proposal made in, a final development plan of such a nature that it will not change the character of such development plan, the state government may, on its own, publish a notice in the Official Gazette, and in such other manner as may be determined by it, inviting objections and suggestions from any person with respect to the proposed modification not later than one month from the date of

such notice, and shall also serve notice on all persons affected by the proposed modifications and the Planning Authority.

Prior to this amendment, it was the Planning Authority, in other words, the Municipal Corporation which had the main responsibility for initiating a change in the final development plan. Section 37 also stipulated that the proposed modification should be of such a nature that it will not change the character of the development plan itself. The Section also contained a provision for the state government to issue the notice in case a Planning Authority fails to do so but the procedure for carrying out the change would be the same.

What 37 (1AA) did was to enable the state government to initiate a change in the final development plan on its own. In other words the state government took over an important function and responsibility which hitherto remained with the Municipal Corporation. The stipulation about not changing the character of a development plan remained. The questions to be considered by the court were therefore, (a) whether this amendment to the MRTP was valid and (b) whether the changes made in DCR 58 would be altering the character of the final development plan. There was also the question of a clarification sought by the Bombay Municipal Corporation in August 2001 to which a response was given 18 months later as a 'purported clarification' to amend the DCR 58. The said clarification was never published or notified. The state government clarified that lands which became open upon demolition of existing structures were not to be taken into account for sharing between the Municipal Corporation, the MHADA and the owner. This was considered a radical departure from the initial understanding and interpretation of the term "open lands." The Court was required to pronounce its verdict of this clarification as well. Finally a Division Bench of the Bombay High Court in its decisions dated 17.10.2005 held as follows:

260. Having regard to the above, we are clearly of the view that the words 'open lands' occurring in amended DCR 58(1)(b) would also include the lands after demolition of structures.

261. The above interpretation is in consonance with the constitutional provisions under Article 21 and 48A of the Constitution of India.

262. In view of our aforesaid interpretation of DCR 58(1)(b), with regard to 'open lands', the clarification dated 28th March 2003 will clearly amount to an amendment of DCR 58, and not a clarification under DCR 62(3). Hence it cannot be sustained.

263. The above clarification is contrary to the mandatory procedures contemplated under Section 37 of the MRTP Act i.e. inviting objections etc. and considering them.

264. The above clarification is clearly violative of Article 21 of the Constitution of India.

The matter went on appeal to the Supreme Court (SLP 23040 of 2005 and other SLPs: decided 7.3.06). The Supreme Court made an extensive analysis of the legal basis and case law in regard to interpretation of statutes, subordinate legislation and clarifications by the executive. Reversing the decisions of the High Court, the Apex Court by its judgement dated 07.3.2006 held as follows:

(a) Interpretation of DCR 58 :DCR 58 was made in a special situation. In any other situation probably this court might have interpreted a similar provision differently. But DCR 58 seeks to strike a balance between different public interests. The state has its own limitations. DCR 58 cannot be struck down solely on the ground that the interest of the common citizen (from the ecological point of view) has been affected, unless its actions are considered to be unfair.

The state in making the regulation intended to solve a longstanding problem wherewith it was beset. The state while framing the aforementioned regulation had to deal with various objectives in mind. It might have taken recourse to the trial and error method. It started with an experiment in the year 1991 but having failed therein it introduced a new policy. The state considered the same to be fair on its part.

We must take notice of the fact that the 1991 Regulation failed to achieve the desired objective forcing the state to take a conscious policy decision, which according to it, would satisfy everybody's need. All players may not feel happy as evidently a group of workers and the writ petitioners are not. Even the Bombay Municipal Corporation and MHADA has shown its reservation by the same by itself would not resist us in any manner in arriving at a correct interpretation. In Forward Construction Co. and others *versus* Prabhat Mandal (Regd), Andheri and others (1986) 1 SCC 100, it was clearly recognised that in a given case there can be more than one public interest and these

> interests can be in conflict with each other. The law maker has to make his choice and preferring one to the other is inevitable.
>
> A substantive law as also delegated legislation raises a presumption of constitutionality. Attempt is, thus, required to be made for upholding the same. Sale of lands belonging to mills which are absolutely unviable and/or those which are lying closed for one reason or the other as also those who intend to modernise their mills and/or shifting the same and/or part of it must be kept for consideration in the matter of interpretation of DCR 58.

Shanti Patel Case

While the Textile Mills Lands case focused specifically on the interpretation of the development control regulations, there was another case being adjudicated in the Bombay High Court around the same time in WP 1980 of 2005 Shanti Patel and others v/s State of Maharashtra and others. The issues raised related to the procedure to be adopted in making modifications of the final development plan, the powers of the state government and the Bombay Municipal Corporation respectively in the context of the 74th Amendment to the Constitution, the failure to set up a Metropolitan Planning Committee as stipulated in Article 243ZE etc. The question posed for determination was whether some parts of Section 37 of the Maharashtra Regional and Town Planning Act were *ultra vires* part IX A of the Constitution and more particularly Article 243W. The petitioners, who included among others a former Mayor of Mumbai as well as two former Municipal Commissioners contended that after the 74th Amendment came into effect the authority for preparing a development plan including modification to the same was available only to the local government namely the Bombay Municipal Corporation and the Metropolitan Planning Committee under Article 243ZE which the state government had failed to set up. The petitioner's case was that the amended sub-section 37(1AA) was a patent interference with the working of the local government and therefore contrary to the constitutional mandate. The learned Advocate General argued that Section 37 (1AA) or for that matter the Maharashtra Regional and Town Planning Act operated in an area separate from part IXA of the Constitution and therefore the question of the provisions of the MRTP Act overriding the constitutional provisions did not arise. Furthermore, the learned Advocate General also submitted that the state government were taking all necessary steps to constitute a Metropolitan Planning Committee and that it would be able to complete the elections to this committee by April 2006.

The same Division Bench of the Court which dealt with the mill lands case gave its decisions in their case as well on the same date i.e. 17.10.2005 held as follows:

> A perusal of the relevant provisions of the MRTP Act as also Maharashtra Metropolitan Planning Committee Act leaves us in no manner of doubt that if the wider constitutional challenge is to be adjudicated upon, then merely challenge to Section 37 (1AA) of the MRTP Act would not be enough. The petitioners will have to lay a proper foundation in the pleadings as to how merely challenging this provision would suffice, when power to issue directions is also conferred by other provisions of the MRTP Act and the Planning Committees Act. Municipal administration is not without control and supervision of the state government. The state government in the scheme of municipal laws as well, has been conferred with power to issue directions and exercise control over municipalities/municipal corporations. Therefore, it is not as if elected bodies at local level are not subject to any supervision and control of the State Government.

Nevertheless, the Court recognised that there could be some issues of validity or conflict meriting further scrutiny.

> ...Section 37(1) read properly and as a whole confers an independent power on the state government to issue directions to the planning authority to set in motion the procedure for effecting modification of any part of, or any proposal made in the final development plan, provided, of course it is of such a nature that it will not change the character of the development plan. Section 37(1AA) although opening with a *non obstante* clause clearly postulates that if the state government is satisfied that in public interest it is necessary to urgently carry out a modification of any part of, or any proposal made in a final development plan, then it can on its own publish a notice in the Official Gazette and in such other manners as may be determined by it to invite objections and suggestions from any person with respect to the proposed modification. Such notice would be served on the planning authority in addition to persons affected by the proposed modification. It is only to enable the government to issue

> a notice for inviting objections and suggestions that the government thought it fit to refer to and take recourse to the amended provisions....

The High Court therefore directed *inter alia* that the challenge to Section 37 (1AA) of the Maharashtra Regional and Town Planning Act, 1966 is kept open for consideration in an appropriate case.

Instead of making a fresh challenge as indicated, the petitioner's then chose to move an SLP No. 63 of 2006 before the Supreme Court. In its orders dated 31.1.2006, the Supreme Court noted that the High Court had refused to enter into the question of the constitutional validity of 37 (1AA) in the absence of a comprehensive challenge by laying proper foundation therefore in the pleadings. The Apex court further added that the 12th Schedule of the Constitution referable to Article 243W provides for urban planning including town planning, regulation of land use and construction of buildings. Article 243W contains merely an enabling provision and it does not mean that the state is obligated to provide for such a statute." In the court's view the existing laws in the field would continue to operate unless another statute is enacted by the state Legislature in terms of Article 243W. The court added "even if we agree with the contention of the petitioners hereunder that the writ petition should have been entertained, the High Court or this court could only issue a direction upon the state to draft a legislation in terms of the provisions of Article 243W and the 12th Schedule of the Constitution of India within a time frame. By no stretch of imagination the existing laws could have been struck down only on that premise unless an appropriate case is made out for issuing such a direction. *Prima facie* the provisions of the Act as well as the rules and regulations under the MRTP Act have not become otiose." In the event, the SLP was dismissed.

Some Pending Questions

It is respectfully submitted that this judgement of the Apex Court still leaves a few crucial questions in regard to the planning domain of the *panchayats* and the municipalities created under the 73rd and 74th Amendment. One is if existing laws *prima facie* do not conform to the provisions of Articles 243G and 243W read with

Schedules 11 and 12 whether such non conformity would attract the provisions of Articles 243 and 243ZF and would cease to operate after the expiry of one year from the commencement of these amendments or will continue to be in force until specifically repealed or amended. In other words, Articles 243N and 243ZF contain implicitly the doctrine of implied repeal. The second unanswered question is whether laws such as the Maharashtra Regional Town Planning Act can be held to be operating in a field 'unrelated' to *panchayats* and municipalities. A plain reading of the Maharashtra Regional and Town Planning Act clearly shows that the provisions defining the contents of a development plan and the functioning of planning or development authorities in exercising the relevant powers are almost in entirety, pertain to matters falling within items listed in the 11th and the 12th Schedules. Nevertheless if the contention that such law operates in a different field is upheld, it will result in Parts IX and IXA of the Constitution being rendered superfluous. Later in this chapter we shall consider whether such a view of constitutional provisions becoming 'surplus' is maintainable at all. But before that we may consider an important case from Karnataka where again the decision of a single judge of the Karnataka High Court was reversed by a Division Bench and the matter is now before the Apex Court.

Karnataka and Arkavathi Layout Case

Karnataka in general and Bangalore in particular has not been lacking in laws relating to spatial development. In fact there is a profusion of them. There are more than 25 different laws dealing with planning and development of Bangalore and there are nearly that many organisations. The municipality of Bangalore was established in 1862 but the Bangalore Cantonment had a different set up. These two were brought together in 1949 as the Bangalore City Corporation. The City Improvement Trust had also come into existence in 1945. The main mandate of the Improvement Trust was to formulate specific improvement schemes, acquire lands, develop the same and also levy a betterment fee on lands, which were not acquired but whose values increased as a result of the execution of any scheme by the Trust. The Karnataka Town and Country

Planning Act, 1961, was enacted for the purpose of regulating land use and development and for making the execution of town planning schemes in the state as a whole. The Statement of Objects and Reasons of the T&CP Act specifically mentioned that "physical planning has to precede economic planning otherwise cities, towns and villages of our country will grow to unmanageable sizes without proper planning. Physical planning with co-coordinated planning on a large scale is necessary if the people are to live in a better, healthier and happier environment." The preamble to the Karnataka T&CP Act was also comprehensive and amply reflected this vision. To quote "whereas it is necessary and expedient:

(i) to create conditions favourable for planning and replanning of the urban and rural areas in the state of Karnataka, with a view to providing full civic and social amenities for the people in the state,

(ii) to stop uncontrolled development of land due to land speculation and profiteering in land,

(iii) to preserve and improve existing recreational facilities and other amenities contributing towards balanced use of land; and

(iv) to direct the future growth of populated areas in the state, with a view to ensuring desirable standards of environmental health and hygiene, and creating facilities for the orderly growth of industry and commerce, thereby promoting general standards of living in the state;

"And whereas, in order to ensure that town planning schemes are made in a proper manner and their execution is made effective, it is necessary to provide that a local authority shall prepare a development plan for the entire area within its jurisdiction;

"And whereas, it is necessary and expedient to consolidate and amend the law relating to town planning for the aforesaid and other purposes hereinafter appearing;

"Be it enacted by the Karnataka State Legislature in the Twelfth Year of the Republic of India."

Under Section 2 of the Act "local authority" was defined to mean a municipal corporation, municipal council, town *panchayat* or *gram panchayat*. The planning domain of a municipality was thus placed on a clear footing. However, the good start was not to last long. In 1976, the Bangalore Development Authority was created. A change was made in the Karnataka T&CP Act. Under sub-section 7, "planning authority" was defined to mean the Bangalore Development Authority in the case of Bangalore City. The jurisdiction of the Bangalore Development Authority was defined to mean the Bangalore Metropolitan Area comprising the City of Bangalore Municipal Corporation, the area where the Bangalore City Improvement Act, 1945 was in force and such other areas adjacent to the aforesaid as the government may from time to time specify. The use of the word Bangalore Metropolitan Area for defining the jurisdiction of the Bangalore Development Authority indicated the recognition of the city's expansion but at the same time left that definition open to accommodate future needs.

The BDA's range of functions were broadly similar to the Improvement Trust in regard to the formulation and execution of development schemes. Additionally, the BDA was also designated as a 'planning authority' under the provisions of the Town and Country Planning Act. In other words the BDA had a double jurisdiction of a development body preparing and executing development schemes and a planning body formulating and regulating land use planning. The contents of the plan and the procedure for their preparation and approval were specified in Sections 12 and 13 of the Act. Section 14 dealt with enforcement of the Master Plan and the regulations to be followed in this regard. Section 26 of the Act also dealt with the contents and procedure for preparing and implementing town-planning schemes. It is worth noting at this stage itself that many of the items listed as contents of the Master Plan under Section 12 and a town planning scheme under Section 26 or items such as zoning of land, reservation of areas for parks, playgrounds, public buildings or institutions complete street pattern, drainage including sewerage, lighting, water supply etc., were usually considered as municipal responsibilities under the City Corporation Act of 1949. Thus the process of diversion and diminution of the municipal domain began.

That there would be a conflict between the double jurisdictions of the BDA i.e., as a developer of land for sale and the planner and regulator of land use, came to notice before the Karnataka High Court in A.V. Laxman *versus* State of Karnataka, 1995 (6) KLJ 620B. It was held that the BDA derived its powers from two separate statues namely the BDA Act and the Karnataka T&CP Act. The Court held "it is clear that the Planning Authority in order to exercise its power to perform its functions and to discharge its duties under the provisions of the Planning Act, cannot invoke Section 32(5)(A) of the Bangalore Development Authority Act. It is needless to say that where a statutory body is empowered to exercise its power, perform its functions and discharge its duties under two different enactments in two different capacities, the exercise of power, performance of function and discharge of duties under one statute shall not be extended in respect of its powers, functions and duties under another statute. The powers, functions and duties of the authority are compartmentalised differently for the purpose of different statutes. The power under one Act cannot be exercised for the purpose of the other Act. The Planning Authority under the provisions of the Planning Act is not empowered to invoke the provisions of the Bangalore Development Authority Act for the purpose of the Planning Act."

Several years later, this conflict of jurisdiction also came to be commented upon by the Committee on Urban management of Bangalore City set up by the State Government of Karnataka in its report of November 1997.

Within a few years after the creation of BDA the Karnataka government found it necessary to bring about another institution into existence. The Bangalore Water Supply and Sewerage Board was created to take over the water supply distribution system previously under the control of the Bangalore Municipal Corporation and set up a body which would be responsible for a wider range of functions from water source to water distribution including drainage and sewerage. Here again the area of jurisdiction was defined as the Bangalore Metropolitan area in the same manner as the definitions obtaining previously in the BDA Act.

Even after this the Karnataka government found it necessary to set up yet another body in 1985 called the Bangalore Metropolitan Region Development Authority Act. The Statement of Objects and Reasons of the relevant Act was stated as follows:

> There is no proper coordination among the local bodies like Bangalore Development Authority, Bangalore Water Supply and Sewerage Board, Karnataka State Road Transport Corporation, Karnataka Electricity Board, Karnataka Slum Clearance Board, Bangalore City Corporation etc., in the Bangalore Metropolitan Area. It is necessary to coordinate the activities of these bodies by constituting an authority. There is also an urgent need to step up the authority in view of the growing problems of unplanned development, housing water supply and transport etc. Hence the bill.

In 1992, the 73rd and 74th Amendments to the Constitution became effective. In keeping with the Constitution's stipulation to enact conformity legislation, Section 503 of the Karnataka Municipal Corporations Act 1976 was amended by inserting a new Section 503B to enable the setting up of a Metropolitan Planning Committee for the Bangalore Metropolitan Area. However, under Sub-section 4 of 503B, the Commissioner of the Bangalore Development Authority was designated as the Secretary of the Committee.

The same amendment also provided for the abolition of the Bangalore Metropolitan Region Development Authority. Though the BMRDA authority for all intents and purposes was closer to the objectives for which a provision for a Metropolitan Planning Committee was made under Article 243ZE of the Constitution, this aspect does not appear to have been considered. On the contrary an organisation like the BDA, which by then had become a significant real estate developer in Bangalore was preferred to provide metropolitan planning. Accordingly provisions were made in the Amendment for the repeal of the Bangalore Metropolitan Region Development Authority Act, 1985 and its consequent abolition of the BMRDA. The Karnataka Municipal Corporation Act was amended by Act No.35 of 1994 to provide for the insertion of three new sections i.e. 503A, 503B and 503C. Section 45 of the Amendment Act further stipulated that on repeal of the BMRDA

Act and the abolition of the BMRDA, all its assets and liabilities, rights, privileges, obligations etc., shall vest in the MPC along with the officers and servants of the BMRDA to be transferred to the MPC. However, the Amendment Act No.35 of 1994 did not provide for the status of a body corporate to the Metropolitan Planning Committee. Be that as it may, it is obvious these Amendments did not indicate an adequate appreciation of the requirements of Article 243ZE of the Constitution and merely continued with the confusing and overlapping institutional situation. As it happened, the Amendment Act of 1994 was not given effect to. Both the Bangalore Development Authority and the Bangalore Metropolitan Region Development Authority have continued to exist. The Metropolitan Planning Committee itself has not been brought into existence. In the meantime, the status of the Bangalore Development Authority itself in the context of the 74th Amendment became an issue in a large batch of writ petitions nos. 26601 and numerous others commonly known as the *Arkavathi Layout case. (2005 (4) KLJ481B).*

The material facts of the case are summarised below:

In this case a large-scale acquisition and development scheme known as the Arkavathi Layout prepared by the Bangalore Development Authority covering nearly 3000 acres became the subject of litigation. Apart from various questions raised about the manner in which the scheme was prepared and acquisition of land was undertaken, some important questions as below about the decision of the Bangalore Development Authority in undertaking this scheme in the context of the provisions of chapter IXA of the Constitution were also raised.

(i) Since Article 243P in Part 1A defines a 'metropolitan area' as the area specified by a public notification, whether the definition of Section 2 (c) of the Bangalore Development Authority Act defining the Bangalore Metropolitan Area is valid.

(ii) In the absence of a Metropolitan Planning Committee which is required to be set up for the Bangalore Metropolitan Area as mandated by Article 243ZE, whether the BDA can undertake such a large scale scheme.

(iii) Whether in the context of the constitutional provisions the BDA continued to have any *locus standi* as a local planning authority or a development authority.

By its decision dated 15th April 2005, the learned single judge of the High Court (Gopala Gowda, J) held as follows:

In Paragraph 13. "The combined reading of clause (c) of Article 243P of the Constitution and explanation to Section 503-B of KMC Act makes it crystal clear that metropolitan area should be the area specified by the Governor by public notification and therefore the definition of Section 2 (c) of the BDA Act has lost its significance and it has become redundant.

Paragraph 13 "In view of the above Article of the Constitution, the definition 'Bangalore Metropolitan Area' in Section 2(c) of the BDA Act being inconsistent with the provision of part IXA of the Constitution, it was in force for a period of one year only from the commencement of constitution (Seventy-fourth Amendment) Act, 1992 and thereafter it is no more in the statute. The reason is, the definition in the BDA Act was neither amended nor repealed. Thus, the definition of 'Bangalore Metropolitan Area' in Section 2(c) of the BDA Act, by operation of law, automatically stood repealed after the expiry of one year from the commencement of the Constitution 74th Amendment. (emphasis supplied)

Paragraph 18. "It is no doubt that the BDA Act empowers the BDA to undertake schemes for development of the Bangalore Metropolitan Area. But, under Section 303-A of the KMC Act the Metropolitan Planning Committee has to undertake such developmental schemes. This is in consonance with Article 243ZE of the Constitution. In other words, in order to undertake the development schemes in Bangalore Metropolitan Area, both the BDA Act and the KMC Act empowers different constituents. But, in respect of the power conferred under Section 15 of the BDA Act there is no support of the Constitution. On the other hand, the power conferred under Section 503-B of the KMC Act is in accordance with Article 243ZE of the Constitution. Therefore, the provisions relating to development schemes in the metropolitan areas contained in the KMC Act shall prevail over the provisions of the BDA Act. In this view of the matter, it has to be held that the BDA has no jurisdiction to take up developmental schemes in the Bangalore Metropolitan Area.

Paragraph "23. For the reasons stated above, Point No.1 is answered against the BDA. *It is held that the BDA has no authority or jurisdiction to take up developmental schemes in the Bangalore Metropolitan Area. On the other hand, the Metropolitan Planning Committee, which is yet to be constituted, has authority and jurisdiction to undertake the developmental schemes in the Bangalore Metropolitan Area* (emphasis supplied)

The decision then went on appeal to a Division Bench (Writ Appeal No.2624 of 2005). The numerous writ petitions, more than 200, raising in the large part similar issues were also taken note of by the Division Bench. The Division Bench (N.K. Sodhi, C.J. and N. Kumar, J) in its decision dated 25.11.2005 held as follows:

"(i) The Karnataka Legislature has enacted the KM Act and KMC Act which pertain to Municipal Corporation, within the meaning of entry 5 of List II. The Karnataka Legislature has also passed laws such as the Karnataka Town and Country Planning Act, 1961, for short 'KTCP Act' and 'BDA Act' which falls under the category of Improvement Trusts. All these legislations are operating in separate and distinct fields. Even if there is any overlapping, there is no inconsistency between any of the provisions.

"(ii) A reading of part IXA of the Constitution would make it clear that it deals with 'municipalities' and that the State legislatures were required to amend their laws relating to Municipalities so as to bring them in conformity with this part. It necessarily follows that this part would not apply to any body or authority which is not a municipality and that the laws pertaining to fields other than the municipalities need not be brought in conformity with this part.

"(iii) Therefore, the legislative intent was to give additional powers to *panchayats* and municipalities. This is achieved by enacting Part IX and IXA and Schedule XI and XII. Then power is conferred on the State Legislature under Articles 243G and 243W to make laws in respect of matters listed in Schedule XI and XII. The provisions contained in Part IX and IXA may be in conflict with the existing laws in respect of *panchayats* and municipalities or the existing law may not be sufficient to achieve the object of the amendment. Therefore, in Articles 243-N and 243ZF 'non obstante clause' namely "notwithstanding anything in the part" is employed to give overriding effect to the provisions contained in Part IX and IXA, over any provision of any law relating to *panchayats* and municipalities in force in a state immediately before the commencement of the Seventy Third and Seventy Fourth Amendment respectively.

"(iv) As is clear from the words used, there was no intention to denude the power of the state legislature to pass laws in respect of entry 5 of List II of Schedule VII, and in particular Improvement Trusts. No obligation was cast upon the state legislature to bring any provision in any other law, which has been validly enacted in respect of entry 5 in List II, in conformity with Part IX and IXA of the Constitution. Therefore, when once the state legislature makes a law in respect of matters listed in the XI and XII Schedules in the law relating to *panchayats* and municipalities or brings the said laws in conformity with Part IX and IXA of the Constitution, the obligation cast on the state legislature is fulfilled.

"(v) *By applying the doctrine of implied repeal it is not proper for the court to hold other laws which do not fall within the category of laws relating to municipalities even if they are inconsistent with Part IXA of the Constitution area repealed by implication* (emphasis supplied). In fact, it is not a case of implied repeal. It would be a case of Municipal Law contrary to the provisions of the Constitution to the extent of repugnancy being void (emphasis supplied). Therefore, there was no intention to override the power of the state legislature in making laws conferred under Articles 245 and 246, and also in respect of entry 5 of List II of the VII Schedule, more so in respect of matters covered under the heading Improvement Trust and mining settlement authorities. Therefore, the state legislature was not denuded of the power to make laws in respect of entry 5, and the laws made continued to be valid.

"(vi) It is competent for the state legislature even after the introduction of Part IX and IXA to pass laws in respect of entries in List II in respect of matters which do not pertain to the *panchayat* or a municipality. It is only in respect of laws either already passed or to be passed in future they must take care to see that the provisions of such law relating to municipalities or *panchayats* are in conformity with Part IX and IXA of the Constitution. The entries in the 11th and 12th Schedules only denotes the area over which the state legislature can pass laws in respect of matters connected with municipalities. In this context the opening words of both Articles 243G and 243W assumes importance. The said law making power is "subject to the provisions of the Constitution" and not "notwithstanding the provisions of the Constitution." *Non obstante* is not employed.

"(vii) "BDA" is constituted for the specific purpose of the Development of Bangalore according to plan." Planned development of towns is a governmental function which is traditionally entrusted to the various municipal bodies. With growing specialisation, along with the growth of titanic metropolitan cities, legislatures have felt the need for the creation of separate town planning or development authorities or improvement trusts for individual cities (emphasis supplied). The BDA is one such authority. It is thus an authority to which is entrusted by statute, a governmental function, ordinarily entrusted to municipal bodies. The BDA is constituted for performing one of the several functions which a local authority may perform. It is a local authority but not a local self-government.

"(viii) Therefore, Part IXA of the Constitution has no application to the BDA Act. None of the provisions of the BDA Act could be said to be inconsistent with any of the provisions contained in Part IXA of the Constitution and therefore none of the provisions of the BDA Act cease to be in force after the expiry of one year from the date of the Seventy-fourth Amendment Act. The orders of the Single Judge ware reversed accordingly. The matter than went on appeal to the Supreme Court preferred by several petitioners affected by the land acquisition. The SLPs presented important constitutional points regarding the *locus standi* of the BDA and adherence to the provisions of Articles 243ZD, 243 ZE, 243 N, 243 G etc. regarding the planning domain of municipalities, metropolitan planning committees etc. The matter was heard extensively during 2007. In March 2007, one of the petitioners first named in the list of SLPs sought to withdraw and his petition was disposed off accordingly. However on other matters the judgement was reserved. As of June 2008, judgement is awaited.

Like the Maharashtra Mills Land related case, the Arkavathi Layout case has also raised very important issues about the planning domain of the *panchayats* and municipalities. Before we identify and discuss the unresolved issues we may refer to two other cases, which are also of some relevance.

The Hyderabad Case

In *Forum for a better Hyderabad versus Government of AP and others (2002) (2) ALD84/2002 (2) ALT 501 decided on 23.1.2002* the issue was raised whether some orders of the AP Government are violative of Article 243ZE and whether by virtue of Articles 243ZE and 243ZF of the Constitution, it is only a Metropolitan Planning Committee which shall be entitled to prepare draft development plans for the metropolitan area as a whole or modify, revise or alter any existing master plan. The AP High Court held as follows:

> The argument that by virtue of Articles 243ZE and 243ZF of the Constitution, the making or amending of development plans for the metropolitan area is confined to the Metropolitan Planning Committee and the provisions of the Urban Areas Development Act, 3975 are not available, is misconceived. The provisions of the Constitution relied on by the petitioner form part of Part IX-A of the Constitution are in the nature of guidelines to be followed by the state legislatures as and when the legislatures frame laws relating to municipalities. No Law has been yet made providing for the Constitution of a Metropolitan Planning Committee and such a body does not exist. It is not the petitioner's case that the A.P. Urban Areas (Development) Act has ceased to exist after the 74th Amendment to the Constitution. The Articles relied on are not self-contained or self operative and

they became effective only when the state legislature makes a law dealing with the subject matter of the said provisions. The contentions raised in this regard by the petitioner in the writ petition would be therefore not valid. The safeguards to be introduced for purposes of subordinate legislation are within the discretion of the State Legislature. Neither Rule 13 nor 13-A offend Article 14. The characterisation of these rules as arbitrary is misconceived. The pattern of these provisions is not different from the innumerable provisions contained in a variety of statutes, which confer the power of subordinate legislation. The dangers in the rule to which the petitioners, refer, are mere figments of imagination.

Bihar High Court Strikes a Different Note

In another important case *Bihar Rajya Panchayat Parishad versus Union of India and others AIR, 2003 Pat 32 decided on 11.9.2003*, the failure of the Bihar government to set up the District Planning Committee under Article 243ZD was agitated. In directing the Bihar government to take all steps necessary to bring the District Planning Committee into operation, the Bench of the High Court (R.S. Dhavan, C.J., and P.N. Prasad, J), the court made several observations pertinent to the planning domain of local bodies.

(Paragraph 3). "When the Constitution of India was amended by the 73rd and 74th Amendments by insertion of chapters on *panchayats* and municipalities a new concept of national planning was being spelt out. This is something which had not been seen before as most municipal enactments are provincial and of the pre-independence era. The basic feature of planning at all levels, village to cities, is now so intended that there has to be an integrated infrastructure for development in all spheres of planning. The Constitution of India now puts an obligation on the state that it will co-ordinate planning in reference to items mentioned in the Eleventh and the Twelfth Schedules. *Institutions of self-government, thus, are to join together as a grid to carry out planning on the items which are mentioned in these schedules.* In the Eleventh Schedule, in the context of *panchayats,* there are 29 items. In the Twelfth Schedule, in the context of municipalities, there are 18 items. The court is not repeating the items which are mentioned in the two schedules."

(Paragraph 6). "Whether it is ill-planned villages, badly planned municipalities or metropolitan areas, further planning, resurrection and restoration of unplanned areas is an effort now identified as a constitutional obligation. Bad planning, affects environment and ecology. Concern for the environment and ecology, and efforts to protect both, is also a constitutional obligation. This is emphasised sufficiently in Article 51A of the Constitution. Whether it is depleting water resources, polluted air, unhygienic villages or municipalities, all put together take a toll of nature. *It is, thus, that the Constitution calls upon the panchayats, nagar panchayats, municipalities (and the DPC/MPC) to join together and plan together with a concept on spatial planning, share the waters equitably amongst all so as to preserve it along with its natural resources, create an integrated development infrastructure and give due regard to environment and ecology*" (emphasis supplied).

(Paragraph 8). "For more than one year, the court has been inquiring from the state government as to when it will position the District Planning Committees so that the planning of subjects entered in the Eleventh and the Twelfth Schedules goes forward as a constitutional obligation. The court has not received any serious answer nor any confidence has been given to the court that there is any serious attempt to place these committees into positions so that work on planning makes a headway without any further delay. Already Bihar has received an answer from the Federal government, its Planning Commission and the Finance Commission that it will not have federal funds until institutions of self-government are working. Elections have taken place, but are these institutions, effectively working to execute the plans referred to in the Schedules to the Constitution? The answer is no. How will the plans be chalked out and executed without the District Planning Committee? In this void a violation of the Constitution is taking place."

(Paragraph 10). "In the circumstances, now that the self-government institutions have been restored and are being run by elected representatives, and the latter are entitled to participate in the planning of their areas as required by the Constitution, while the government may take its own time to frame its legislation in whichever style it may, as an interim measure this court will ensure that the District Planning Committees are put into position without any further delay. The law, in context, did refer, to placing the District Planning Committee in position, for instance, in the Bihar and Orissa Municipal Act, 1992, an amendment was made in 1995 by insertion of Section 51B to provide for a committee for district planning. Likewise, in the Patna Municipal Corporation Act, 1951, Section 41B was inserted also I 1955 to provide for such a committee. Both these amendments to the two enactments took place as a consequence of the 73rd and 74th Amendments to the Constitution."

(Paragraph 11). "It would have been appropriate to have clearly spelt out in each enactment, the details on how to constitute the District Planning Committee instead of making cross references to another enactment. Leaving grey and doubtful areas and reserving power to be specified subsequently by the state government, on how to place and structure these committees is an antithesis to the requirement of the Constitution that the "Legislature of a State may, by law, make provision with respect to (a) the composition of the District Planning Committees; (b) the manner in which the seats in such Committees shall be filled." Instituting the District Planning Committees was conveniently avoided as the Act avoided providing details and referred to yet another enactment. This avoidance to a constitutional obligation for nine years is disrespect to the Constitution of India."

(Paragraph 23). "The District Planning Committees should be in full operation before the preset month is out. Any suggestion which has been given by the High Court in this order is only for the purpose that the Constitution of India should not see embarrassment in being bypassed which has been done for the last nine years and the intention of the High Court is to put the District Planning Committees in position. The suggestions made by the High Court are an ad hoc arrangement. Now it will be entirely upon the state government to replace the suggestions of the High Court by an appropriate legislation whenever it desires to do so."

The Bihar High Court judgement which pre-dates the Bombay Textile Mills Land case, Shanti Patel case and the Hyderabad Forum case does not appear to have been cited in the course of their adjudication. While the Bihar judgement may be regarded by some as only an exhortation or at the most a direction to the Bihar government to set up the District Planning Committee, the judgement does highlight a major purpose of the Constitutional Amendment in regard to planning in general and spatial planning in particular. The constitutional intent that *panchayats, nagar panchayats* and municipalities as institutions of self-government, should join together and through the District Planning Committee or the Metropolitan Planning Committee as the case may be, create an integrated plan for development has been highlighted. The Language of Articles 243ZD and 243ZE are probably the best terms of reference available for undertaking this exercise. The fulfillment of the requirements of these two Articles is not contingent or dependent on what the other provisions of Parts IX and IXA require, in regard to the composition of the *panchayats* and municipalities or in what specific manner the subjects listed in the 11th and 12th Schedules are translated into tasks and responsibilities and how they are devolved on the *panchayats* and municipalities.

The Persisting Issues

The cases from Bombay, Bangalore, Hyderabad and Bihar have certainly helped to identify the major issues of contestation but clarity is yet to emerge on the following points.

(a) Whether in the context of Articles 243G and 243W as well as Schedules 11th and 12th, planning in general, and land use planning or town planning, in particular, are *prima facie* to be assigned to *panchayats* and municipalities.

(b) Whether a state government can claim an inherent or superior power in determining the extent of the planning domain and even so whether the assignment of any functions, preparatory or regulatory, can be so minimal or subordinate as to virtually deny the exercise of the domain itself in regard to that function.

(c) Whether there is any discretion at all to state governments to regard the DPC and the MPC as committees to be set up or not. This point applies to the setting up of wards

Committees as well under Article 243S. *Prima facie,* failure to set up these committees appears to be a violation of the Constitution.

(d) Whether other pre-existing bodies like development authorities can exercise planning jurisdiction on par with the *panchayats,* municipalities, the DPC and the MPC or in exclusion of them.

(e) Whether development authorities and parallel bodies can be regarded at all as bodies 'not related' to municipalities and therefore whether laws pertaining to these bodies can co-exist even though not in conformity with the provisions of Part IXA on the ground that they operate in a different field.

(f) If they are not related to municipalities can powers and responsibilities be conferred on these other bodies by taking recourse to the provisions of Part IX and IXA of the Constitution claiming such conferment is indeed in conformity to the Constitution.

Answers to the above questions can be determined only if the nature of the 73rd and 74th Amendments is fully understood. If these Amendments are interpreted as only an extension of Article 40 in the Directive Principles of State Policy and that their provisions are only an enabling stipulation and not mandatory, then the thrust of the Amendments is lost. A conscious and deliberate exercise on the part of the Parliament in passing these Amendments, their ratification by the required number of states and their subsequent coming into effect in 1992 then gets reduced to an exercise in superfluity.

The Apex Court as well as the High Courts in this country have generally followed the principle that for the purpose of judicial review, the courts should confine themselves to the written text of the Constitution rather than take recourse to the spirit. In regard to the 73rd and the 74th Amendments, one is not pursuing any abstract concept of decentralisation but relying on the text of the constitutional provisions and then determine to what extent state laws are in conformity or an infraction. Granted that the plenary powers of the state to legislate on matters in regard to entry 5 of

List II are not denuded by the provisions of Part IX and IXA. But the fact remains that the exercise of these powers by the state has to be compatible with the provisions. It is a contradiction to hold that state laws should conform strictly to Parts IX and IXA only in so far as elections to the *panchayats* and municipalities and their composition are concerned, but have wide latitude in legislating on the functional domain. This would mean that only portions in Part IX and IXA are a constitutional imperative but others are only provisions of guidance. Taking such a stand would also mean that what these elaborate set of amendments have provided are only for creating a structure for the *panchayats* and municipalities, but it is permissible to a state not to assign functions and powers which would render the structure merely as shells without substance.

These questions have been raised in both the Ranga Reddy *Sarpanches* Association case and the Arkavathi layout case. A reference has been made earlier about the majority decision in the Ranga Reddy *Sarpanches* case as well as the dissenting judgement per Goda Raghuraman J, which forcefully raised the impermissibility of holding constitutional provisions as superfluous if infractions of the same are ignored. Extracts from the majority as well as the dissenting judgements are contained in the Annexure A-8.1.

The focus of the planning domain and the responsibilities continue to be unclear and defused. Recent initiatives like the Special Economic Zones and the conferment of the planning and regulatory powers on the SEZ Authorities have aggravated the already fragmented situation. These are discussed in the next chapter.

Annexure A-8.1

Ranga Reddy District Sarpanches Association versus Government of Andhra Pradesh and Others (2004(1) ALT 659 (LB)

Devinder Gupta C.J., Motilal Naik, Sudarshan Reddy, P.S. Narayana, J. and Goda Raghuram J.)—Extracts from the Judgement

"The Ranga Reddy District Sarpanches Association, represented by its President and Convener, Shri Girish Sanghi and others had invoked the jurisdiction of this court under Article 226 of the Constitution of India questioning certain provisions of the A.P. Panchayati Raj Act, 1994 and certain Government orders and rules by filing W.P. No. 12348/2002. Federation for Empowerment of Local Government by its Presidium Member, Lok Satta by its General Secretary and Dr. Jayaprakash Narayana filed W.P.M.P No.22300/2003 in W.P. No.12348/2002 to implead them as respondents 3 to 5 and in view of the averments made in the affidavit filed in support of the application the said W.P.M.P No.22300/2003 is allowed and proposed parties are impleaded as respondents 3 to 5. The contesting parties had put in lengthy pleadings and also placed ample material before the court in support of their respective contentions. Likewise, Prasanna, Chairperson, District Level Committee, Zilla Parishad, Nalgonda District filed W.P. No.13256/2002 questioning Memo No.32254/Mdl.II/2002-1, dated 18.7.2002.

The writ petitions were heard at length. The factual matrix as reflected in the respective pleadings of the parties, needs no repetition. Elaborate submissions were made by Senior Counsel representing the petitioners and the respondent. The Learned Attorney General of India, the Learned Additional Solicitor General, representing the Union of India and the Learned Additional Advocate General, representing the state of Andhra Pradesh also assisted the court.

Held: "It is for the state legislature to decide by expressing its will through legislation or subordinate legislation as to what extent the Panchayati Raj institutions should be conferred with power and authority. The power of the court in such like matters cannot be stretched too far while exercising the jurisdiction under Article 226 of the Constitution so as to question the political wisdom unless it is established that there is clear infraction and breach of the imperative constitutional provisions. *Adequacy or inadequacy of the powers cannot be gone into unless it is shown that the same offends any provisions contained in any part of the Constitutional scheme. The court is of the view that in pronouncing on the constitutional validity of a statue, the court is not concerned with the wisdom, or unwisdom, the justness or otherwise of the law* (emphasis supplied). If that which is passed into law is within the scope of the power conferred on a legislature and violates no restrictions on that power, the law, must be upheld whatever a court may think of it. The court is also of the view that the words "endow them with such powers and authority as may be necessary to enable them" used in Article 40 of the Constitution and the similar words used in *Article 243G also cannot be so interpreted to mean that the extent of the powers and authority endowed by the state legislature should be limitless or be to the fullest extent* (emphasis supplied). Both the provisions have left it to the wisdom of the state legislature even as regards the extent of the powers and authority to be endowed on the Panchayati Raj institutions.

Held "Argument that in the light of Article 40, Article 243G must be held mandatory cannot be accepted. Provisions of the Constitution have to be read as it stands. *Power to legislate relating to entries in XI Schedule cannot be put on par with power of the state legislature to legislate in relation to entries in the VII Schedule* (emphasis supplied) as the former would not fall under the basic structure concept. The state government is not either an intruder or an encroacher. Minimal checks of control aimed at streamlining the local body administration cannot be styled as excessive. Rules cannot be held to be unconstitutional or *ultra vires*. The court cannot give any form of declaration or a writ of *mandamus* relating to challenged provisions of the statute in view of the clear language of Article 243G of the Constitution.

"Different provisions of the Constitution are to be harmoniously construed and hence it cannot be said that Chapter IX will have the overriding effect over the other general powers to legislate conferred on the Parliament and state legislature as well.

"Where the directive power itself flows from an enabling provision the resultant subordinate legislation cannot be found fault with when the principal power itself is derived from the exercise of only a discretionary power and not from an imperative Constitutional mandate. The Constitutional guidance under Act 243G relating to implementation of schemes for economic development and social justice cannot be equated with an imperative constitutional mandate (emphasis supplied).

"It is pertinent to note that the provisions of the Act are challenged on the ground that they are in contravention of Part IX of the Constitution only and not Part III of the Constitution. A careful reading of different provisions of Part IX would go to show that except the constitution of *gram panchayats* and reservations and elections thereof, all other aspects appear to be not imperative or mandatory and they are only enabling provisions.

"The arms of the High Court cannot be stretched too far while exercising the powers under Article 228 of the Constitution so as to touch such political questions unless it is established that such questions involve clear Constitutional infraction and breach of the imperative provisions thereof. If not, in view of the limitations and parameters in exercising powers under

Article 226 of the Constitution, this court cannot stretch its hands too long so as to engulf such questions on the pretext of judicial activism. This view may be conservative, but this is in consonance with the division of legislative, executive and judicial functions.

"The excessive official control and minimum participation of elected representatives is made a serious ground of attack. The total non-participation of any of the elected representatives in certain Rules had been specifically pointed out. The *panchayat* as institution may have elected representatives and officials as well. It is true that in the policy making, to keep up the democratic spirit, the elected representatives must have the major sway and in the working of the system, the implementation may be left to the officials. It is also true that in the administration of Panchayati Raj institutions, necessary control also may be essential and it is for the legislature to decide by expressing its will through legislation or subordinate legislation to what extent such control should be. What had been pointed out are several inadequacies in this regard. When the object and spirit of a Constitutional Amendment are not contravened, a statutory provision or a G.O. cannot be held to be unconstitutional on the ground of inadequacy. In the working of the system, the state government may have to take necessary steps to improve the system and in doing so if it is felt that the excessive control due to official powers or participation *vis-à-vis* elected representatives are to be rectified, it is within the domain and discretion of the legislature and this court cannot enter upon that sphere while exercising powers under Article 226 of the Constitution. *Writ of mandamus cannot be issued either to make rules in pursuance of a statutory provision nor the court can usurp the legislative function therein if any* (emphasis supplied). It is settled law that the writ of *mandamus* cannot be issued to direct the legislature to enact law on a particular subject.

"The concept of basic structure and federalism cannot be stretched too far so as to include these Panchayat Raj institutions also as part of federal concept in distribution of powers or allocation of powers. A directive in the form envisaged by Article 243G cannot be equated with an enforceable legal right flowing from a constitutional mandate. Autonomy to these institutions is only limited autonomy be it fiscal or otherwise, and the constitutional directive envisaged under Article 243G has to be interpreted as only a discretionary directive and nothing more.

"Article 40 of the Constitution no doubt contemplates the state taking steps to organise village *panchayats* and endow them with such powers and authority as may be necessary to enable them to function as units of self-government. An argument was advanced that in the light of Article 40, if Article 243G is not mandatory, there is no necessity of introducing this Article in Part IX in as much as, if it is to be interpreted as directory or discretionary, the position would have been the same even prior to the introduction of Part IX. This contention cannot be accepted for the reason that a provision of the Constitution normally may have to be read as it stands and cannot be interpreted, as it ought to have been worded. This is neither the province of the court nor the power of judicial review can be stretched that far so as to engulf a situation of this kind.

"The excessive interference by bureaucrats and the non-participation or minimum participation by elected representatives of the local bodies is made the main ground of attack by the petitioners. The state government cannot be said to be either an intruder or encroacher in this regard. The minimal checks of government control is aimed at streamlining the local body administration. This cannot be styled as excessive bureaucratism in the context of limited autonomy which these local bodies enjoy in the light of the constitutional scheme.

"It is undoubtedly for the Parliament to further amend the provision if the Parliament intends to do so to make the provision mandatory. The Rules are not beyond the Rule making power conferred by the statute and hence they cannot be held to be unconstitutional or *ultra vires*. Equally so relating to the challenged provisions of the statute and definitely this court cannot give any form of declaration nor a writ of *mandamus* can be granted in view of the clear language of Article 243G of the Constitution. Definitely the remedy is elsewhere and not before this court by invoking Article 226 of the Constitution (emphasis supplied).

Dissenting Judgement (per Goda Raghuraman J) Extracts

Held: "It is impermissible to treat any constitutional provision as a surplussage. Article 40 is an existing exhortation (unenforceable though), directing the state to take steps to organise village *panchayats* and endow them with such powers and authority as may be necessary to enable them to function as units of self-government. *The Parliament, as a constitutional body, while enacting the 73rd Amendment, must be presumed to have been aware of the existence of Article 40 and its unenforceability in view of Article 37. The consecration to the State Legislatures the field of legislation enumerated in Entry-5 or List-II of the VII Schedule of the Constitution must also be presumed to have been within the knowledge of the constituent body. These are compelling presumptions.* (emphasis supplied). Despite such knowledge if by the 73rd Amendment, Article 243G and H were enacted, is it legitimate or logical to assume that the purpose of the Amendment is merely to reiterate, emphasise and reinforce the availability of legislative power in the state legislature (to make a law to endow such power, authority and responsibility on the *panchayats*) as the Legislature thinks fit. Rarely, if at all, would an enabling grant of power, require such repetitive verbal emphasis and by an amendatory exercise requiring special procedure.

"The expression 'may' taken together with the text, philosophy and object of the 73rd Amendment, court is of the considered view that the expression 'may' occurring in Article 243G approximates more to a constitutional command couched in a deferential verbal choice, in recognition of the fact that the command is addressed to a high authority – the legislature.

"The constitutional command to the legislature of the state is to endow *panchayats* with power and authority that are necessary to enable them to function as institutions of self-government. The subjects and governance areas in respect of which powers and authority should be endowed on the *panchayats* are within the constitutional discretion of the state legislature. The discretion is however not immunised from the scrutiny of the judicial branch. The clause (Article 243G) " as may be necessary to enable them to function as institutions of self-government" is the constitutional instruction to the state legislature, to ensure that the powers and authority endowed on the *panchayats* empower the *panchayats* to function as institutions of self-government.

"It would be impermissible to conclude that the state legislature has the discretion whether or not to endow the panchayats with any powers and authority or to devolve upon them any powers and responsibilities (emphasis supplied). The overall peace, order and good government in the state is the responsibility of the state and, therefore, the discretion of the State Legislature to incorporate in the legislation dealing with the Panchayati Raj institutions, such measures as are necessary to effectuate these purposes of the state is un-exceptionable. A balanced theory of interpretation of the Constitution's decentralisation of power values, warrants the conclusion that while incorporating provisions for control of the Panchayati Raj institutions to achieve the overall and legitimate purposes of the state, such controls ought not to entail total stultification, emasculation or negation of the democratic choice of the local population expressed in the election to local bodies. Governance, power and autonomy in some discernable manner should be of necessity inherent in the elected representatives of the *panchayats* to enable characterisation of these institutions as self-government institutions. *A state legislation that divests or withholds effective power of local governance from the elected representatives of the panchayats would tantamount to a legislation that subverts the constitutional purposes of Part-IX* (emphasis supplied).

"Denial by the state legislation of any financial resources to the *panchayats* whether by way of empowering them to levy, collect appropriate taxes, duties etc., and/or assigning to them such taxes, duties etc., collected by the state government, as would invalidate the functionality of these institutions, would negate the constitutional purpose.

"The corridors, imposed on the *panchayats* by the provisions of the Act and the complementary statutory rules (even to the extent of the financial powers facially endowed), are intrusive and destructive of even a modicum of autonomy.

"If the limits and obligations on the states powers are to have no harmony with the Constitution's purpose, the states must necessarily be prevented not only from formally destroying the local bodies but also from acting in ways that would leave a local body formally intact, but functionally incompetent.

"Even if *panchayats* are not a part of the federal structure, they nevertheless constitute an integral component of some measure of vertical division of the governance power from the hitherto two level model to the post 73rd Amendment – three level model.

"The state is a component of the federal structure under our Constitution and the *panchayats* are not. However, consequent on the 73rd Amendment, the *panchayats* are guaranteed a role in governance, at the sub-state level. Their governance structure is democratic and republican. This characteristic of the *panchayats* is a constitutional grant and must be accorded a meaning, which needs to be effectuated. *The panchayats are legal inhabitants of the constitutional space and have a legitimate share in the governance process though at the sub-state level. They are more than mere dependencies of the state. They are also self-government(s)* (emphasis supplied).

State control directed at destruction and emasculation of the *panchayats'* essential character of being institutions of self-government without redeeming constitutional justification and legitimacy. The control exercised by the state over the functional and fiscal domains of the *panchayats* and over the personnel working threat, disturbs, this delicate but clear balance – the constitutional equilibrium. The replication in the 1994 Act of the provisions of the repealed 1964 Act and the 1986 Act, discloses that the state was not sufficiently sensitive to the constitutional dynamics resulting from the 73rd Amendment.

"The provisions of the 1994 Act and the complementary statutory rules and the administrative instructions transgress the constitutional limitations on the states' role, the permissible limits or participation and control with respect to the *panchayats*; the states' legislative and statutory instructions enable impermissible intrusions into the functional and financial domains of the *panchayats* and usurp total control over the personnel from the *panchayats* and vest such control in the state and state agents; such intrusions and controls by the state stultify the 'self-government' characteristics of the *panchayats* as constitutionally defined. *The transgressions, intrusions and controls, substantially overstep the participatory and oversight functions that the state may legitimately perform in regulating the affairs of the panchayats in the interests of vitality of their functioning and in effectuation of the state's obligation to harmonise the functioning of the panchayats with the larger state interests and concerns* (emphasis supplied).

"The offending statutory provisions are closely interwoven with the other provisions of the Act and cannot be considered or treated as stand-alone provisions. The invalid rigour of a few clauses of these provisions could be softened and harmonised by reading down the strictly textual trajectory. Severance between the clearly invalid and valid parts of the provisions is however not possible and excision of the invalid provisions destroys the integrity of the Act in its entirety. Such invalidation would result in a vacuum in critical operations areas.

"As the excision of the unconstitutional statutory provisions would destroy the ratio of the 1994 Act and render inoperable the entirety of the 1994 Act, the Court declares the Andhra Pradesh Panchayat Raj Act, 1994 unconstitutional (emphasis supplied).

9

Postscript

The background to the 73rd and 74th Amendments to the Constitution has been discussed elsewhere in this book. In the pre-Independence period municipalities enjoyed a fair measure of autonomy as well as some political visibility and clout because several municipal leaders were in the vanguard of the Independence movement. After independence, conscious efforts were made in a few states, to help the *panchayats* become institutions of self-government rather than mere agents of the Government executing some schemes. In states like Karnataka, Tamil Nadu, West Bengal, Maharashtra and Rajasthan, these measures did achieve limited success. The decade of 1960s could indeed be considered as a period of *panchayat* ascendancy. Unfortunately the very fact of this modest success proved to be their undoing because successful *panchayats* especially at the *taluk* and district levels were considered a potential political threat by the State level leaders. Efforts then began to scale down the powers and responsibilities and eventually bypass the *panchayats* and municipalities altogether. In initiating the exercise for amending the Constitution and accord a constitutionally sanctioned space for the *panchayats* and municipalities, it was hoped that what was hitherto derailed by executive action could be secured and safeguarded by a Constitutional Amendment. However, the present analysis of the Case Law indicates that this hope is yet to be fulfilled.

Decentralisation is not merely a legal exercise. Nor is India the only country which has embarked on such an initiative. International experience shows that decentralisation varies from simple modifications to existing administrative arrangements to assigning specific subjects and activities to local bodies with full autonomy. The political implications of decentralisation need to be fully appreciated. Every act of devolution is viewed with some apprehension by the so-called higher levels of government about the loss of power and control. Changes in law have to be viewed therefore, in the socio political context.

The National Commission to Review the Working of the Constitution under the chairmanship of Justice Shri M N Venkatachaliah devoted in its report a separate chapter on decentralisation and devolution. The Commission in para 177 of its recommendations has proposed that the language of Articles 243G and 243W should be amended so that *panchayats* and municipalities are categorically declared to be institutions of self-government and executive functions be assigned to them. In para 178, the Commission has also recommended that the 11th and 12th Schedules of the Constitution be restructured in a manner that creates a separate physical domain for the *panchayats* and municipalities and for this purpose Articles 243H and 243X should be amended making it mandatory for the Legislature of the States to make laws devolving powers to *panchayats* and municipalities. To ensure that financial needs of *panchayats* and municipalities receive adequate consideration, the Commission has also recommended in para 179 that Article 280 should be amended requiring the Finance Commission to take into consideration the recommendations of the State Finance Commissions.

Yet another Commission i.e. the Second Administrative Reforms Commission, chaired by Shri Veerappa Moily, former Chief Minister of Karnataka, set up in August 2005 has recently given its 6th Report (October 2007) titled "Local Governance: An Inspiring Journey into the Future". Some of the recommendations are worth noting.

- One is that there should be three-tiers of administration in urban local governments with the Municipal Council or

Corporation at the city level, Ward Committees at the ward level and Area Committees or Area Sabhas at the neighbourhood level.

- Full functional and financial autonomy should be available in respect of all functions assigned to City Governments.
- Urban planning should be the responsibility principally of the Municipality or the Corporation as the case may be.
- Regional and metropolitan level planning should be dealt with by District Planning Committees and Metropolitan Planning Committees.
- The Commission has recommended the abolition of parastatals and development authorities within urban areas vesting their functions and control in the urban local bodies concerned.
- A further recommendation of the Commission is that there should be a local body Ombudsman to examine the grievances and complaints against urban local bodies. State governments should not take any peremptory action against a local body without reference to the Ombudsman.

A New Threat to the Municipal Domain

Cogent and well considered as these recommendations are, as of date, there is little evidence to show that they are being acted upon. It is clear that the 73rd and the 74th Constitutional Amendments, despite their elaborate prescriptions, are only a necessary but not a sufficient condition, for ensuring democratic decentralisation. The laws and regulations required at the state level to implement the Constitutional provisions have been, to say the least, less than adequate. Unfortunately, every opportunity to dilute, diminish or denigrate the municipal domain is seized upon and utilised with alacrity. The latest is the country wide initiative to set up Special Economic Zones. While the basic objective of the programme to increase manufacturing and employment cannot be questioned, this is sought to be done by setting up several self contained enclaves ranging from a few hundred to a few thousand hectares with so-called high class infrastructure facilities and a host of fiscal concessions. At the time of writing, more than 450 proposals have been approved out of which 222 have been notified where work has commenced. During the past two, three years, several states have enacted laws or notified policy statements seeking to declare the SEZ areas as 'industrial townships' within the ambit of the Proviso to Article 243Q of the Constitution.

As mentioned in the earlier chapter on Elections, the setting up of municipal bodies in existing industrial townships and the legality of applying the Proviso to Article 243Q is the subject of Tata Steel Vs. State of Jharkhand case in regard to Jamshedpur. Currently the matter is on appeal before the Supreme Court. In another case *Saij Gram Panchayat versus State of Gujarat (1999.2 SCC 366)* some of the issues in regard to the creation of an industrial township in a *panchayat* which had been declared as a Notified Area earlier under the provisions of the Gujarat Industrial Development Act, 1962 were considered by the Apex Court. However, the issues regarding the application of the Proviso are far from settled. The spate of recently enacted laws and policy notifications in different states appear to indicate that the setting up of an industrial township under the Proviso to Article 243Q is entirely a matter of administrative discretion and convenience. Several questions, such as the following, still remain to be answered

1. The proviso to Article 243Q appears to relate mainly to situations where an industrial establishment 'per se' is providing municipal services. Can this be extended to entirely new areas where no industry has come up at all?
2. Can the term 'industrial establishment' apply to any parastatal organisation like a development authority or an industrial development corporation which may be only acting as promoters of an industrial area?
3. Can the term also apply to any private real estate company which is setting up an SEZ only as a land developer for eventual disposal to industry, housing projects, commercial establishments etc.?

4. Where a municipality has been in existence for long in the area, can any part of that municipal area be taken out and carved into a separate industrial establishment? What is the criteria and what is the application of mind required to exclude the jurisdiction of an existing municipality from a part of its area as has been done in Gujarat or West Bengal?
5. Can the rights of representation available to citizens of the *panchayats* and municipalities elsewhere in the country be denied to residents of industrial townships? Even though the right to vote is only a statutory right, will this not amount to a patent discrimination offending Article 14 of the Constitution?
6. Is the Proviso to Article 243Q, inconsistent with the basic structure of Parts IX and IXA of the Constitution whose principal objective is to establish democratically elected *panchayats* and municipalities as institutions of self-government?
7. Furthermore, can the provision of municipal services by an existing or proposed industrial township be the only consideration for setting up an industrial township? What about the other responsibilities of the *panchayats* and municipalities in regard to socio economic planning and the numerous development, regulatory and fiscal tasks entailed in the 11th and 12th Schedules of the Constitution.

These matters hopefully will be considered as and when a comprehensive challenge to the relevant state laws and policies is mounted.

The JNNURM

Perhaps money may help when logic is not enough. In 2006 the Government of India launched a large programme of urban assistance under the title Jawaharlal Nehru National Urban Renewal Mission. The Mission covers all the State capitals and several other cities totaling 63. Financial assistance under the Mission is available to cities on a matching basis for a variety of projects of urban infrastructure. The assistance is conditional upon the fulfillment of several reforms, covering legal, financial, regulatory and administrative matters as well as measures to promote transparency and accountability in city governance. The legal reforms include implementation of the provisions of the 74th Amendment and full devolution of the functions relating to the subjects listed in Schedule 12. Tripartite agreements between the Government of India, the State Government and the City concerned with commitment to an agreed time schedule for implementing the reforms have been entered into.

However, the experience over the past two years shows that the reform package has made little progress. Interestingly in many states, urban planning is one function which the governments are unwilling to assign to local bodies or committees like the DPC and MPC though this is required under the Constitution. Whatever the claims of the State Government to superior knowledge or greater understanding of public interest, as stated in the Bombay Mills land case or the Arkavathi layout case in Bangalore, the obvious conclusion is, what is a stake is control over urban land. In keeping with the trends in some other countries, real estate has become one of the most rewarding financial opportunities in India. Until a few years ago urban development departments were dismissed as dealing only with municipal matters and therefore unworthy of any serious political attention. Today it has become a coveted position. When a situation of political crisis developed in Karnataka recently about the forming of a coalition government, one of the issues which could not be resolved was which party's minister should be in-charge of the Bangalore Development Authority or the urban development portfolio!

In regard to rural local bodies a separate Ministry of Panchayats has been in existence for the past few years with a declared mandate of securing the implementation of the 73rd Amendment. An extensive series of Round Table discussions were organised by the Ministry with all the State governments and a set of recommendations were formulated and agreed upon by all the State Ministers who attended these conferences. While some progress has been made in the functional domain of the *panchayats*, it has not been possible to stop the incursions of the State or its Legislators into the sphere of the *panchayats*. Similarly in urban areas the long arm of the State government continues to reach and restrict several parts of the municipal domain. The JNNURM has so far been only a partial and hesitant response to the problem.

Jurisprudence relating to local governance is no doubt a crucial aspect of decentralisation. But there are limits to which adjudication in the Courts of Law can help the process. Besides, Courts prefer to dwell upon the letter of the law, rather than the spirit however relevant it may be for a proper understanding and interpretation of the law. As observed by the presiding Judge in the Ranga Reddy District case of Andhra Pradesh, the remedy may not lie in the court room, but elsewhere.

Bibliography

All India Institute of Local Self Government (1998). *Elections to Urban Local Bodies: Nagarpalika Network*. New Delhi. August.

Chainani, Shyam (2007). *Heritage and Environment: An Indian Diary*. Urban Design Research Institute.

Chatterjee, Manideep (1998). "Calcutta: The Planning Agencies", in R.P. (ed.), *Million Cities of India*. Delhi: Sustainable Development Foundation.

Chaudhary, R.C. and S.P. Jain (1999). *Patterns of Decentralised Governance in Rural India*. Vol. I and II. Hyderabad: National Institute of Rural Development.

Devi, V S Rama *et al.* (2006). *Report of the Task Force on Jurisprudence of Panchayati Raj*. Indian Law Institute. *(Mimeo)*.

Ghosh, Archana (1996). "Municipal Governance in West Bengal: People's Perception and Participation", *Panchayati Raj Update*, February.

Government of India (2002). *Report of the National Commission to Review the Working of the Constitution*. Delhi: Government of India Press.

———. (1991). "Speech of Rajiv Gandhi introducing 64th Amendment Bill, Lok Sabha Debate, 15 May 1989", *Rajiv Gandhi's Selected Speeches and Writings*, Vol. V. New Delhi: Publication Division.

———. (1989). "Inaugural address to Collectors in the workshop on Responsive Administration at Coimbatore, June 1988", *Rajiv Gandhi's Selected Speeches and Writings*, Vol. 4. New Delhi: Publication Division.

Institute of Social Sciences (2005). *Analysis of Case Law*. July. Report submitted to the Ministry of Panchayati Raj. (*Mimeo*).

———. (n.d.). *Status of Panchayati Raj*. Concept Publishing Company.

———. (n.d.). *Review of State Subject Laws and Some Central Laws*. Report submitted to the Ministry of Panchayati Raj. (*Mimeo*).

———. (n.d.). *Review of State Panchayati Raj Acts*. Report submitted to the Ministry of Panchayati Raj. (*Mimeo*).

Jain, L.C. (ed.) (2005). *Decentralisation and Local Governance*. Orient Longman.

Janata Dal (1989). "The Basics of Democratic Decentralisation", *Report on Panchayats and Self Government*. Bommai Committee Report. Committee appointed by V.P. Singh, President, Janata Dal. Delhi. July.

Kashyap, Subhash (2004). *Framing of India's Constitution: A Study*. 2nd Ed. New Delhi: IIPA, Universal.

———. (2004). *Constitution Making Since 1950: An Overview (1950-2004).* New Delhi: Universal.

Kaushik, Susheela *(2001). Sustainable Politics, Women in Panchayati Raj.* Centre for Development Studies and Action.

Lok Sabha Secretariat (2004). *Standing Committing of Parliament on Rural and Urban Development.* 13th Lok Sabha: 56th Report.

———. (2002). *Standing Committing of Parliament on Rural and Urban Development.* 13th Lok Sabha: 37th Report.

———. (1992). *Report of the Joint Parliament Committee on the Constitution 74th Amendment Bill.* July.

Meenakshisundaram (1994). *Decentralisation in Developing Countries.* Delhi: Concept Publishing.

Ministry of Panchayati Raj (2006). *The State of the Panchayats: A Mid Term Review.* November.

Ministry of Urban Development (1989). *Report of the National Commission on Urbanisation.* Vol.1: Recommendations. New Delhi. August.

Narayan Menon, S. and Soumya Kanti Mitra (2008). *Special Economic Zones.* Unpublished. CPR. April. *(Mimeos).*

National Institute of Urban Affairs (1988). *State of India's Urbanisation.* New Delhi.

Panandiker, V.A. Pai (ed.) (2000). *Problems of Governance in South Asia.* Delhi: Konark Publishers.

———. (ed.) (1997). *The Politics of Backwardness.* Delhi: CPR and Konark Publishers.

Rao, Sudhakar (2005). *Guidelines for Good Governance.* Dhaka: CIRDAP, Commonwealth Secretariat. March.

Second Administrative Reforms Commission (2007). *Local Governance; An Inspiring Journey into the Future.* Sixth Report. October.

Singh, S.S. *et al.* (ed.) (1997). *Legislative Status of Panchayati Raj on India.* New Delhi: Indian Institute of Public Administration.

Sivaramakrishnan, K.C. (2006). *Growth in Urban India: Issues of Governance.* New Delhi: Centre for Policy Research.

———. (2000). *Power to the People: The Politics and Progress of Decentralisation.* New Delhi: CPR and Konark Publishers Pvt. Ltd.

———. (1978). *The Indian Urban Scene.* Shimla: Indian Institute of Advanced Study.

Sivaramakrishnan, K.C. and Green Leslie (1988). *Metropolitan Management: Asian Experience.* Washington DC: Oxford University Press for World Bank.

Tinker, Hugh (1967). *Foundation of Local Self Government in India, Pakistan and Burma.* Bombay: Lalwani Publishing.

Venkatarangaiah, M. and M. Pattabhiram (ed.) (1969). *Local Government in India.* Delhi: Allied Publishers.

Others:

Constitution 64th Amendment Bill 1989 (Bill No. 50 of 1989) as introduced in Lok Sabha.

Constitution 72nd Amendment Bill 1991 (Bill No. 158 of 1991) introduced in the Lok Sabha by Shri Venkataswamy, Minister for Rural Development and the Constitution 73rd Amendment Bill (Bill No.159 of 1991) introduced in the Lok Sabha by Smt. Sheila Kaul, Minister for Urban Development on 11 September 1991.

Constitution 73rd Amendment Bill (Bill No. 159 of 1991) introduced in the Lok Sabha by Smt. Sheila Kaul, Minister for Urban Development on 11 September 1991.

"Seventy Fourth Constitutional Amendment Act, Institutional Reforms and Functional Devolution", An issue paper presented at the Regional Meet on *Devolution of Functional and Financial powers to Urban Local Bodies*. Hyderabad: Regional Centre for Urban and Environmental Studies, Osmania University. January 1999.

Speech of Rajiv Gandhi introducing 65th Amendment Bill on 7 August 1989.

Chapter-wise Index of Cases

contd. ...

...contd. ...

Sl. No.	State	Citation	Page No.
9	Karnataka	Basanagowda & Another *versus* State of Karnataka & Ors. (2000(6) Kar.L.J.526)	39
10	Kerala	State Election Commission *versus* Krishnan, WA 2067 of 2000	39
11	Punjab	Bagichi Singh *versus* Punjab State Election Commission, CWP No.7324 of 1999	40
12	Tripura	Ratanlal Nath & Ors. *versus* State of Tripura, 1997 (III) GLT SC 8	40
13	Supreme Court	Bodula Krishnaiah *versus* SEC, 1996(3) SCC 416	40
14	Supreme Court	Lakshmi Chan Singh, 1985-4 SCC 689	41
Cases on Delimitation			
15	Supreme Court	Pradhan Sangh Kshettra Samiti & Ors., 1995 Supp (2) SCC 305	42
16	Andhra Pradesh	Raghunath Rao *versus* Govt. of AP, 1999(1) ALT 39	44
	Andhra Pradesh	Maineni Prabhakar Rao, 2002(3) ALT 114	44
	Andhra Pradesh	D. Suryanarayan & Ors *versus* Govt of AP, 2000(2) ALT 787	45
17	Kerala	Kunhadullah, 2000 (3) KLT 45	37, 45
18	Kerala	K.P. Raveendran & Ors., *versus* State of Kerala, AIR, 2005 KER 319	47
Public Consultation in Matter of Delimitation			
19	Maharashtra	Ganpatrao Bhosale *versus* State of Maharashtra, 1997 (3) MLJ	48
20	Maharashtra	Gram Sudhar Samiti, Mahadulla, 2004(4) MLJ 309	49
21	Maharashtra	Ashok Ganpath Jadhav *versus* State Election Commission, 2004(4) MLJ 150	49
22	Maharashtra	Kamaljeet Singh *versus* State of Punjab, CWP No.337 of 2002	49
23	Andhra Pradesh	P.V.V. Prasad & Ors. *versus* Govt. of AP, 2006(2) ALD 797 WP Nos. 25147, 25771 and 25772 of 2005	51
Some Recent Cases on Delimitation			
24	Uttar Pradesh	Kamlesh Singh & Anr. *versus* Shiv Sewak Singh, CMWP No.59093 of 2005	53
25	Karnataka	Bharamraj S. Parmaj *versus* State of Karnataka, WP No.8003 of 2006	55, 149
26	Karnataka	B.K. Chandrasekhar *versus* State of Karnataka, WP No.3679 of 1999	55, 129

contd. ...

...contd. ...

contd. ...

...contd. ...

Sl. No.	*State*	*Citation*	*Page No.*
48	Supreme Court	Pradyut Bordolai *versus* Swapan Roy, 2001(2)SCC19	87
49	Maharashtra	Anil Tatya Rao Solanki, 2001 (1) MLJ 457	87
50	Uttar Pradesh	Meghraj Singh *versus* State of UP & Ors. CWP no. 15482 of 2001	87
51	Supreme Court	Rabindra Nayak *versus* Collector, Mayurbanj, AIR, 1999 SC 1120	79
52	Supreme Court	Shiv Murthy Swamy Inamdar, 1971 (3) SCC 870	90
Criminal Convictions			
53	Bihar	Lal Rai *versus* State of Bihar, 2003(3) BLJR 1731	91
54	Rajasthan	Hanuman Prasad *versus* District Judge Mirtha & Ors. AIR, 2001 RAJ 398	92
55	Rajasthan	Shiv Ram *versus* State of Rajasthan, AIR, 2002 Raj 416	93
Disclosure by Candidates			
56	Supreme Court	PUCL *versus* Civil Liberties *versus* Union of India	34, 96
Chapter 4: Post Election Cases			
57	Andhra Pradesh	S.K. Khasim B *versus* State Election Commissioner, AP, WP 24001 of 1995	110
58	Andhra Pradesh	Y. Venkat Reddy *versus* District Munsif, 1998 (4) ALT 495	111
59	Andhra Pradesh	Bathina Baby Jyotsna *versus* Govt. of AP, 2002 (2) ALT 158	112
60	Bihar	Bambhola Rai *versus* State Election Commissioner & Ors., 2004(1) CWJC No.2012	112
61	Bihar	Sarachandra Mandal *versus* Phai Bhushan Singh & Ors., AIR, 1974 Patna 40	113
62	Himachal Pradesh	Vimla Devi *versus* State of HP, CWP No.753 of 1998	113
63	Madhya Pradesh	Lakhan Lal *versus* State of MP, LPA No.46 of 2002	114
64	Madhya Pradesh	Chander Bhan Singh *versus* State of MP, WP No.2349/2000	115
65	Punjab & Haryana	Gurdev Kaur & Ors. *versus* Dy. Commissioner, Patiala & Ors., CWP No.2941 of 1993	115
66	Uttar Pradesh	Badan Singh *versus* Election Commissioner, 2003(4) AWC 2898	117
67	Supreme Court	Lalit Mohan Pandey *versus* Pooran Singh & Ors. AIR, 2004(6) SCC 2303	118
Chapter 5: Regularity of Elections			
Cases in the High Court			
68	Karnataka	B.K. Chandrashekhar & Anr. *versus* State of Karnataka, WP No.3679 of 1999	55, 130

contd. ...

...contd. ...

contd. ...

...contd. ...

Sl. No.	*State*	*Citation*	*Page No.*
90	Karnataka	Soubhagya *versus* Returning Officer, Horalavadi Grama panchayat & Ors., 2001(5) KAR LJ 216	191
91	Karnataka	B. Geetamma *versus* Gulfom & Ors., 2003(4) KLJ 401	193
92	Kerala	C.R. Suresh *versus* State of Kerala, 2000 (3) KLT 159	194
93	Maharashtra	Kashi Nath Kodambarao Katake, 1995 (2) MLJ 714	195
94	Maharashtra	Shobha Ashok Patil *versus* Mahananda Rajaram Nikam, 1997 (3) MLJ 353	196
95	Maharashtra	Manjuli V. Civil Judge, Senior Division Wardha, 1969 MLJ 435	197
96	Maharashtra	Pushpa Prakash Kalpande *versus* Collector Amravati & Ors., 1998(1) MLJ 325	198
97	Maharashtra	Mahesh Mujlibhai Mistre *versus* State of Maharashtra, 1999(3) MLJ 84	199
98	Maharashtra	Kasambhai Case, 1998(1) MLJ.1 SC	198
99	Maharashtra	Suresh Balakrishna Pogale *versus* State of Maharashtra, 2003(3) MLJ 782	200
100	Uttar Pradesh	Ejaz Ahmad *versus* Assistant District Election Officer, Azamgarh & Ors. CMWP No.13726 of 1995	200
101	Supreme Court	Ragho Prasad *versus* Special Judge/Additional District Judge & Ors. CMWP No.13290 of 1999	201
102	Uttar Pradesh	Neeraj Kamboj & Ors. *versus* State of UP, CMWP No.40842 of 2000	201
103	Uttar Pradesh	Shamiuddin *versus* Additional District Judge (I), Mathura, CMWP No.13838 of 1997	201
104	Uttar Pradesh	Baldev Singh *versus* Tahsildar & Ors., CMWP No.30727 of 2000	202
105	West Bengal	Vidhya Charan Sinha *versus* State of WB, WP No.1401 of 2003	202
106	West Bengal	Mala Maji *versus* State of WB, WP No. 8805 of 2003	202
107	West Bengal	Nirmala Gorai *versus* West Bengal, WP No.9274 of 2003	202
108	Supreme Court	Saraswati Devi *versus* Shanti Devi & Ors. 1997 (1) SCC 122	203
109	Supreme Court	Kasambhai F. Ghanchi *versus* Chandubhai D Rajput, 1998(1) SCC 285	205
Chapter 7: Removal of Elected Persons			
Category A: No Confidence Motion			
110	Andhra Pradesh	Tiparti Chandramouli, 1998(1) ALT 574	218
111	Andhra Pradesh	Gayam Iswaramma, 1998(6) ALT 308	212

contd. ...

...contd. ...

Sl. No.	State	Citation	Page No.
112	Andhra Pradesh	Samala Jayaramaiah, AIR (1998) AP 205	222
113	Andhra Pradesh	Gogineni Kotiswara Rao, 1999 (3) ALT 496	213
114	Andhra Pradesh	D. Ramachandraiah, 2000(1) ALT 772	218
115	Andhra Pradesh	Nandan Goud, 2004(2) ALT 336	213
116	Assam	Mybeyaima Devi, 2000(2) GLT 421	219
117	Assam	Kanika Chandra *versus* Assam, 2004(2) GLT 417	219
118	Assam	Jiten Sakya *versus* Assam, 2004(2) GLT 233	213
119	Bihar	Vijay Kumar Manmouji *versus* State of Bihar	224
120	Bihar	Hiralal mandal *versus* State of Bihar, 2005(1) BLJR 763 Patna	224
121	Bihar	Bindu Devi & Anr. *versus* State of Bihar (2005), BLJR, 2004 Patna	224
122	Bihar	Phoolmanti Devi & Ors. *versus* State of Bihar, (2004) 3 BLJR 1829	217
123	Bihar	Anita Kumari & Anr. *versus* State of Bihar & Ors. (2004) 3 BLJR 2268	217
124	Bihar	Rambha Sinha *versus* State of Bihar, (2004) 2 BLJR 1408	217
125	Bihar	Chinta Devi *versus* State of Bihar, (2004) 3 BLJR 1456	217
126	Bihar	Sitaram Singh & Anr. *versus* State of Bihar & Ors. (2004) 2 BLJR 1587	217
127	Bihar	Mithelesh Pati Tiwari *versus* State of Bihar & Ors. (2004) 1 BLJR 1032)	217
128	Bihar	Gajendra Narayan Singh *versus* State of Bihar & Ors. (2004) 3 BLJR 2127	217
129	Bihar	Uday Shankar Singh *versus* State of Bihar & Ors., 2003 AIHC 1348	222
130	Gujarat	Rambhai Joitaram Patel *versus* State of Gujarat, 1997 AIHC 2762	213
131	Gujarat	Manubhai F. Patel *versus* State of Gujarat, AIR, 2000 GUJ 170	214
132	Karnataka	C. Kuttaswamy *versus* Prema, WA No.2332/1991	217
133	Karnataka	V. Manjunath *versus* Assistant Commissioner Bangalore, North, 1997(2) KLJ 456	219
134	Karnataka	Muniappa & Anr. *versus* State of Karnataka & Ors., 1999(4) KLJ 42	218

contd. ...

...contd. ...

Sl. No.	*State*	*Citation*	*Page No.*
135	Karnataka	Lakshmappa Balaganur & Anr. *versus* State of Karnataka & Ors., 1994 (4) Kar. LJ 603	224
136	Karnataka	M.V. Shantha Kumari *versus* Jagalur Taluk Panchayat, 2001(4) Kar. LJ 541)	224
137	Kerala	G. Narendran *versus* State of Kerala, OP 4113 of 1992	219
138	Kerala	K. Ambili *versus* Deputy Director, 1996(2) KLT 486	214
139	Kerala	Jacob Abraham *versus* State, 1999 (1) KLT 25	215
140	Kerala	Valsalam *versus* State of Kerala, 2003(1) KLT 858	226
141	Madhya Pradesh	Jagdish Prasad *versus* State of MP, AIR, 1997 MP 184	226
142	Maharashtra	Nimba Rajaram *versus* The Collector, Jalgaon, AIR, 1999 Bom.335	222
143	Maharashtra	Bandopant Mallewar, 1997-10 MLJ 52	223
144	Orissa	Nimai Charan Mohanty *versus* State of Orissa, 79 (1995) CLT 123	219
145	Orissa	Kishore Chandra Sahoo *versus* State of Orissa, 90(2000) CLT 279	225
146	Punjab	Natha Singh *versus* State of Punjab & Ors., 1997(2) PLR 791	223
147	Punjab	Roop Kaur *versus* State of Punjab, 1998(2) PLR 179	215
148	Tamil Nadu	Rasaiyya *versus* State of Tamil Nadu, 2004 (3) MLJ 230	215
149	Uttar Pradesh	Ramashraya and etc. *versus* District Panchayat Raj Officer, Gorakhpur & Anr., AIR, 1998 Allahabad 87	220
150	Uttar Pradesh	Banshoo *versus* District Panchayat Raj Officer, Jaunpur, 1986 UPLBEC 429	221
151	Uttar Pradesh	Smt. Meera Devi. *versus* State of Uttar Pradesh & Ors. AIR, 1998 Allahabad 157.	216
152	Uttar Pradesh	Smt Brij Rani Singh *versus* State of UP & Ors., 2000 AIHC 4083)	223
153	West Bengal	Dilip Bhattacharya *versus* State of West Bengal, 1996 (II) CHN 142	221
154	West Bengal	Menaka Haldar *versus* State, 99 CWN 427	218
155	West Bengal	Ram Chandra Oraon *versus* State of West Bengal & Ors., 2001(2) CHN 83	221
156	West Bengal	Muktasin Hossain *versus* State of West Bengal, 1998(2) CLR 28	221
157	West Bengal	Dalbir Mondal *versus* State of West Bengal, 2000(2) CHN 696	218

contd. ...

...contd. ...

contd. ...

...contd. ...

Sl. No.	*State*	*Citation*	*Page No.*
179	Madhya Pradesh	Kailash Kumar *versus* State of MP, 1999 (2) JCJ 280	238
180	Madhya Pradesh	Kamal Kishore *versus* Janpad Panchayat, 1999 (2) JLJ 370	239
181	Orissa	Subhash Chandra Jaina *versus* State, 1994 LCT 662	239
182	Orissa	Baikunthannath Mohanty *versus* State of Orissa, AIR, 1998 Orissa 150	239
183	Orissa	Sukanta Bhoi *versus* State, OJC 6959	240
184	Orissa	Kanakalata Mallik *versus* Collector, Kendrapada, AIR, 2001 Orissa 161	240
185	Punjab	Dev Singh *versus* State of Punjab, 1996 AIHC 4368	240
186	Punjab	Chand *versus* Special Secretary, Govt. of Punjab, 2004 AIHC 4557	241
187	Punjab	Mange Ram Sarpanch, Gram Panchayat V. Financial Commissioner, 1997(1) AIR, 1997 P&H 252	241
188	Punjab	Kashmiri Lal *versus* Deputy Commissioner, Sonepat, AIR, 1980 OP&H 209	241
189	Rajasthan	Anant Ram Sharma *versus* State of Rajasthan, 1998 AIHC 2809	241
190	Rajasthan	Chaganlal Solanki *versus* State of Rajasthan, 2003 AIHC 984	242
191	Rajasthan	Jagdish Chandra *versus* State of Rajasthan, 2004 AIHC 3081	242
192	Uttar Pradesh	Chunmun *versus* District Magistrate, Sonbhadra, AIR, 1999 ALL 88	242
193	Uttar Pradesh	Chandrajit Rai Bihar *versus* District Magistrate, Pilibhit, 2002 AIHC 1290	243
194	Supreme Court	Tarlochan Dev Sharma *versus* State of Punjab, AIR, 2001 SC 25	244
195	Supreme Court	State of Punjab *versus* Bhajan Singh, 2001 (3) SCC 179	245
196	Bihar	Bihar Mayor Council *versus* Union of India, 2003 (3) BLJR 2012	246
197	Supreme Court	Ramesh Mehta *versus* Sanwalchand Singhvi, 2004 (5) SCC 409	225
Chapter 8: Functional Domain of Panchayats and Municipalities			
Case Law			
198	Andhra Pradesh	Velpur Gram Panchayat *versus* Asst. Collector Marketing, AIR, 98 AP 142	258

contd. ...

...contd. ...